By Popular Demand

By Popular Demand

Revitalizing Representative Democracy through Deliberative Elections

John Gastil

UNIVERSITY OF CALIFORNIA PRESS
Berkeley · Los Angeles · London

University of California Press
Berkeley and Los Angeles, California

University of California Press, Ltd .
London, England

© 2000 by the Regents of the University of California

Library of Congress Cataloging-in-Publication Data

Gastil, John.
By popular demand : revitalizing representative democracy
through deliberative elections / John Gastil.

    p.   cm.
Includes bibliographical references (p.   ) and index.
ISBN 0-520-22364-0 (cloth : alk. paper)
1. Political participation—United States.   2. Elections—United States.
3. Representative government and representation—United States.   4. Forums
(Discussion and debate).   I. Title.
JK1764.G37   2000
324.6'3'0973—dc21

99-086065
CIP

Manufactured in the United States of America
9 8 7 6 5 4 3 2 1 0

10 9 8 7 6 5 4 3 2 1

The paper used in this publication meets the minimum 'requirements of ANSI / NISO
Z39 0.48-1992(R 1997) (Permanence of 'Paper) . ∞

Contents

Acknowledgments

In the course of writing this book, friends and acquaintances provided vivid illustrations of the key concepts in Albert Hirschman's theory of exit, voice, and loyalty. Some grew weary of my endless ranting about elections and found tactful ways of leaving me to chatter by myself. Others hesitated to flee before voicing their concerns about details both minor and major in my manuscript, and the true loyalists continued to listen and offer critiques even after making unheeded but credible threats of eventual exit.

The most influential of the voices in this group was that of Ned Crosby, who developed the idea of a "citizen jury" just one year after Hirschman's *Exit, Voice, and Loyalty* went to press. In the thirty years since, Ned has conducted invaluable experiments in public deliberation and has seen his ideas influence both academics and civic reformers. I thank him for cajoling, challenging, and encouraging me as I wrote this book. For similar reasons, I am grateful to David Mathews at the Kettering Foundation and James Fishkin at the University of Texas at Austin. The innovative programs in public deliberation they created have stimulated my imagination for many years.

Unbeknownst to me, this book has been developing in my mind since 1993, and many people have shaped my thinking during that time. Pat Baca, Michael Briand, John Daniels, John Dedrick, Jim Dillard, Dede Feldman, Mary Feldbloom, Murray Fischel, Cisco McSorley, Gilbert St. Clair, Todd Wynward, and my ever-campaigning parents have changed how I understand political philosophy and American government. I used to joke that by managing political campaigns and studying democracy, I had the advantage of two unrelated specializations, but these friends and family have led me to a bridge that joins those disciplines more securely than I had thought possible.

I also extend thanks to the many friends and colleagues who have helped me develop the ideas in this book. Enjoying the luxuries of a critic, Perry Deess kept me sober yet injected some of the most radical ideas in this book, although he will deny association with my most grievous errors. Cindy Simmons made certain that my use of abstract theory was useful and not self-indulgent. Phil Weiser and Mark Smith helped me anticipate many counterarguments by being the first to make (and refute) them. Bob Kraig has sharpened my understanding of the limits of many proposed campaign reforms. Jim Dillard and Hank Jenkins-Smith helped me bridge political philosophy with empirical research. For offering helpful comments, I also wish to thank Lance Bennett, Haig Bosmajian, Stephanie Burkhalter, Michael Delli Carpini, James Fishkin, Tricia Gardinier, Gordon Gastil, Raymond Gastil, Kevin Sager, Todd Kelshaw, Valerie Manusov, David Messerschmidt, Gerry Philipsen, Sean Rockhold, David Ryfe, Kanan Sawyer, John Stewart, Barbara Warnick, and anonymous reviewers. I also thank Peter Dreyer, Cindy Fulton, and Reed Malcolm at the University of California Press for transforming a manuscript into this book.

Without the encouragement of colleagues at the University of Washington and the opportunity to finish writing during two months in residence at the Kettering Foundation, I would not have completed this book. Kettering offered quiet shelter, and its staff and program officers provided invaluable assistance and a lively atmosphere conducive to thinking and writing. Special thanks go to Edwin Baiye, John Dedrick, Julie Fisher, Randy Nielsen, Rita Shanesy, Hal Schillreff, Estus Smith, Debi Witte, and the summer research assistants for making my visit both pleasant and productive.

As a matter of custom, the final note in such a list of acknowledgments goes to spouse, children, and occasionally pets for trying to pull the author away from the desk to enjoy the outdoors and such. Fortunately, years of reading those apologies have led me to seek the pleasures of an active life without further prompting.

CHAPTER 1

Introduction

There are two fundamental problems in American politics. The first is that most Americans do not believe that elected officials represent their interests. The second is that they are correct.

Public confidence in government is alarmingly low. One of the most reliable ongoing academic studies—the General Social Survey—has asked Americans a similar question about confidence in the U.S. Congress for over twenty years. In 1974, 17 percent of respondents had "a great deal of confidence" in Congress, but that figure dropped to 13 percent in 1984 and to 8 percent in 1994. Meanwhile, the percentage expressing "hardly any" confidence in Congress went up from 21 percent in 1974 and 1984 to 39 percent in 1994. The same survey found that more and more Americans believe that "most public officials are not really interested in the problems of the average man [sic]." In 1974, 64 percent of respondents agreed with that statement, and that number rose to 68 percent in 1984 and 74 percent in 1994.[1]

Not only do Americans have a particularly dim view of Congress, they place little trust in other elected officials. Public confidence in the executive branch of the federal government has declined in tandem with the drop in the public's estimation of Congress. Roughly 10 percent of Americans have "a great deal" of confidence in Congress and the executive branch. When forced to choose, most survey respondents say that state governments "do a better job running things" than the federal government, yet only one-third trust state officials to "do the right thing" most of the time.[2]

More precisely, a majority of Americans have come to believe that elected officials do not represent average citizens. Most Americans think representatives are insincere and unresponsive to the public's real concerns. Eighty-eight percent agree with the statement: "Government leaders tell us what they think will get them elected, not what they are really thinking." Seventy-nine percent agree that "government leaders say and do anything to get elected, then do whatever they want." Seventy percent agree that "the government is run for the benefit of special interests, not to benefit most Americans."[3]

Whether these perceptions are accurate is difficult to judge. One might make this judgment by comparing surveys of elected officials with similar surveys of the general public. For example, a 1987 study found that members of the U.S. House of Representatives had similar views to those of the public on defense spending and foreign policy toward Central America, but representatives' views were out of sync with the public's on aid to minorities, minimum standards of living, government services, abortion, and foreign policy toward Russia.[4]

Another approach is to measure the fit between actual public policies and the public's stated policy preferences. A team of investigators took this approach in a 1993 study of state governments.[5] To permit a simple analysis of all fifty state governments and their citizens, the authors reduced public opinion and public policy to a single liberal–conservative scale. They found a strong correlation between their ideological ratings of actual state policies and the average ideology of the state's electorate.

One can quibble over the mixed results and methodological details of such studies, but the fundamental problem with both of these approaches is their reliance on conventional measures of public opinion. Democratic theorists stress the difference between surface opinion and an "enlightened understanding" of one's interests in light of all available information.[6] There is a profound difference between an unreflective preference based on unreliable information and a more deliberative judgment grounded in accurate data, careful reasoning, and the consideration of alternative viewpoints. To judge the correspondence between the policy priorities of the government and its constituents accurately, it would be necessary to have a more reliable indicator of the public's enlightened or deliberative policy views.[7]

Because few data exist on the public's enlightened policy priorities, it is impossible to demonstrate directly that elected officials often fail to represent the interests of the larger public. Nonetheless, there is still a compelling reason to suspect such misrepresentation. Paradoxical though it may seem, officials interested in reelection should not, in fact, strive to represent the broader public interest. This is because in most campaigns for public office, fund-raising is a primary consideration, and candidates receive contributions from a relatively small number of sources. Wealthy donors, party activists, and myriad special interests give money to candidates who support their own views, and particular views are overrepresented on candidates' contributor lists. Regardless of where candidates get their money, mass-mediated and even door-to-door elections are not exercises in public deliberation. Images, non-issues, and distorted policy debates decide close races far more often than genuine substantive differences in candidates' policy stances. Politicians certainly do scrutinize public opinion surveys, but polls are counterproductive in two respects: rational candidates concern themselves only with the views of likely voters, who make up a small percentage of the general public; and, as explained earlier, conventional polls fail to measure the public's more reflective concerns.[8]

When looked at from this perspective, the apparent "electoral connection" between voters and elected officials in Congress is actually part of the problem. When congressional scholars find similarities between the views of representatives and voters, they sometimes shrug in disbelief. As Robert Erikson and Gerald Wright muse, "It is as though all our individual ignorance and misinformed judgments cancel out, so that average perceptions and judgments are responsive to what the candidates say and do." In these scholars' view, "The result is a more representative Congress than the electorate sometimes seems to deserve."[9] Questions of merit aside, the views that Congress represents are not necessarily those that best serve individual representatives' constituents, let alone the nation as a whole. Inattention and ignorance cause voters to notice (and oppose) only those policies that would impose large, direct short-term costs. Unfortunately, such policies (e.g., new taxes or the elimination of entitlements) may benefit the general public in the long term, and an officeholder's responsiveness to these narrow concerns serves the official's reelection imperative more than the public's interests. In a sense, the material self-interest of a constituency is simply one more narrow interest directing a representative away from any broader public good.[10]

To the limited extent that voters weigh issues during an election, they "override any broad concerns they may have with collective issues and vote in accord with ensuring immediate benefits. . . . Likewise, the legislators may share a growing concern with collective societal and economic reversals," but their "electoral security" is best served by promoting "particularized programs" of concern to specific groups.[11] More than simply compelling Congress to enact self-serving laws, shoddy public oversight frequently causes Congress to avoid "acting on problems or considering specific policy options because legislators fear retribution by ordinary citizens."[12] The result is that "the emerging collective problems of the new era thus go unacknowledged and tear away at the fabric of society."[13] In sum, elected officials may wish to act in the public's enlightened interest for altruistic reasons, but the structure of federal, state, and local electoral systems instructs them to do otherwise.

The importance of this problem is self-evident to any sincere democrat. In theory, representative government should discern and act upon the public's will, whether that means fairly considering the myriad concerns of divided subgroups or discovering the shared aspirations of the public as a whole. If, instead, elected officials represent only the concerns of powerful, vocal individuals and interest groups with unrepresentative agendas, the fundamental goal of democracy is not achieved. When the political system itself reinforces this problem, the system itself must undergo change.

Unrepresentative government is a serious failing, and low public confidence in that same government can prove even more dangerous. Healthy public skepticism toward authority has deep roots in American political history, and this attitude can hold up a democracy when extreme nationalism or hero worship threaten to topple it. Too much distrust, however, can prove just as disastrous as blind faith.

Despite claims to the contrary, few politicians are mind-readers. Consequently, it is difficult for political leaders to discern the aspirations of a public that doubts their sincerity. An honest dialogue between the public and public officials can only take place when there is mutual respect between citizens and officeholders. Deep public mistrust of government makes it that much harder for government to get beyond conventional, but unreliable, manifestations of public sentiment, such as opinion polls, town meetings, and interest groups.

Even when a government glimpses the public will, it has difficulty implementing and maintaining coherent policies without a broad public understanding and appreciation of them over a long period of time. A public that doubts the integrity of sincere school boards, mayors, and governors is unlikely to endorse the policies they adopt, however public-spirited. As a consequence, a governor's welfare reform system or a mayor's economic development program may never come to pass, because the refined policy preferences of special interests offer clear direction compared to the stubborn skepticism of a public unwilling to take government seriously.

In addition, many public programs require active citizen participation to succeed. Community policing depends on active neighborhood watch programs, public schools need parental involvement, drug abuse prevention campaigns require awareness and use of government services, and anti-poverty programs benefit from partnerships with local businesses. When anything governmental is immediately suspect, public cynicism becomes a self-fulfilling prophecy.[14] Without a broad base of reasoned public trust in government and electoral systems, even successfully elected leaders discover that the public will not trust their actions. Without any leeway or public patience, leaders lack the flexibility to act.[15]

At the extreme, public distrust of politicians and elected officials can ultimately erode support for democratic institutions themselves. Such rebellion is unimaginable to most Americans, but history has not been kind to governments that have lost public support. It is not a leap from cynicism to outright rejection. If citizens believe that their government is not only inept but altogether illegitimate, and if they believe elections provide no recourse, they will eventually call into question the entire political system. Even when the government is, in fact, striving to serve the public's best interests, if the public fails to recognize that fact, the government is in danger. For example, extreme anger toward government has played a role in the militia movement and the Oklahoma City bombing.[16] For all of these reasons, growing political cynicism remains a serious problem, whether or not one shares that sentiment.

Many modern reformers believe they have discovered the solution to these problems. The simplest solution is "more of the same." *The Reasoning Voter,* Samuel Popkin's defense of the low-information voter, concludes by arguing that American democracy only needs noisier, more exciting, and more aggressive campaigns. Rejecting calls for more "positive" or deliberative campaigns, Popkin argues that "there is no electoral problem in America that would be solved by restricting television news to the MacNeil-Lehrer format and requiring all the

candidates to model their speeches on the Lincoln-Douglas debates."
Like Popkin, many public opinion and media scholars agree that the
public's ignorance and alienation is no bother so long as there are periodic elections and disagreements among the communication specialists
who shape public opinion. In this view, citizens' voting choices seem
reasonable because they followed the cues given by competing liberal
and conservative elites.[17]

As I explain in chapter 3, citizens' reliance on simple "information
shortcuts," such as choosing candidates based on party membership, results in superficial elections and flawed voting choices. Most voters
have difficulty constructing and articulating clear policy preferences
through conventional elections, and voter ignorance and misjudgment
do have a real cost. Amplifying existing communication channels will
not fundamentally change the nature of American elections, improve
public representation, or rebuild public trust.

A more widespread view holds that the United States needs to implement one of several possible electoral reforms. These include new
voting systems (e.g., proportional representation), term limits, public financing or strict regulation of campaign fund-raising, voluntary rules
of campaign conduct, and the widespread distribution of voting guides.
Each of these reforms has merits, which I discuss in chapter 4. If designed properly, some of the most popular electoral reforms can make
elections more competitive, and others can improve the representation
of minority viewpoints in legislative bodies. Some reforms can improve
voter decision making by reducing the frequency of deceptive campaign
messages or by delivering useful information to attentive voters. Nevertheless, even when taken as a whole, these reforms fall short: they
provide no means of recording the public's deliberative voice, and they
make electoral outcomes unpredictable but no more reliable as a means
of ensuring public-spirited representation. Moreover, public trust in
government has continued to decline, even as states have adopted
sweeping term limits and other campaign reforms.

Many civic-minded reformers turn away from the blood and gore of
electoral politics. Instead, they seek to restore public trust and representative government through renewed community life and citizen dialogue. In *The Promise of Democracy,* a companion to a PBS series on
democracy, James Crimmins argues that "a good representative on a
city council or in the state legislature can bring resources to a city, but
she or he cannot make it a good city. . . . Change comes slowly in our
capitols, and then only reluctantly."[18] In this view, which has become

popular in democratic theory, electoral or governmental politics is separate from "citizen politics" or "civil society." The greatest virtue of this approach is its ability to supplant conventional forms of public voice, which I describe in chapter 5, with innovative forms of civic self-education and community deliberation, such as those I review in chapter 6.

At the extreme, this perspective holds that "civil society is in fact *the* domain of citizens."[19] Citizens can deliberate and take action in their communities without worrying about elections. When turned militantly inward, extra-governmental action by a local community can even lead to disconnection from public life, as when residential community associations use residence fees to replace public infrastructure with private goods and services (e.g., build their own roads, maintain private swimming pools).[20] Interactions with public officials are nonexistent and unnecessary.[21]

There is no doubt that citizens can achieve much outside the official sphere of government decision making. Social bonds, community identity, civic traditions, and a degree of local independence create a wealth of "social capital" that helps local communities thrive both politically and economically. Studies of community politics are replete with examples of local citizen groups taking action on their own behalf, with or without any assistance from public officials and institutions.[22]

Even active communities with abundant social capital can remain disconnected from the electoral process, and they may do so at their peril. Representative institutions in the United States are powerful at the local, state, and federal levels, and a comprehensive theory of public deliberation must ultimately connect the community to its government. Some political philosophers, such as Michael Walzer, have tried to counter the "antipolitical tendencies that commonly accompany the celebration of civil society," but the gap between community politics and formal representative institutions remains wide.[23]

Some reformers, however, have begun to connect face-to-face deliberation with elections. For the past three decades, public policy pioneers have experimented with different methods for developing and recording a deliberative public voice. Programs such as citizen juries and "deliberative polls" bring together representative samples of the public for face-to-face discussions with one another and with expert panels. After a few days of deliberation, these citizen bodies answer survey questions or draft recommendations to tell public officials what policies the larger public might endorse if it had the chance to deliberate. The judgments that citizens reach after participating in these brief deliberative forums often differ considerably from their previous opinions, and those changes suggest that traditional public opinion measures do not always match the public's more reflective policy views.[24] When these random sample forums are conducted in an electoral context, they give insight into how a deliberative public might judge specific candidates and campaign issues.

Unless taken farther, even these deliberation programs will fail to build public trust and improve representation. As I argue in chapter 6, the participants in quasi-juries and large deliberative polls, such as the 1996 National Issues Convention, may experience profound attitudinal and behavioral changes, but their numbers are too small to have a noticeable impact on larger public attitudes and electoral outcomes. Many citizens vicariously participate in these exercises through newspaper accounts and broadcast coverage, but the impact on those people is relatively small.[25]

In some views, the solution to this problem is simply one of scale. Past efforts may have had a limited impact, but future efforts will succeed by invigorating the public and drawing it into an ever-widening network of public forums and deliberative practices. Unfortunately, this approach requires the development of a powerful sense of civic responsibility and a nationwide commitment to active, ongoing participation in public life. As David Ryfe points out, "Asking citizens to do better is a perfectly reasonable goal for deliberative reformers," but "asking them to contradict their basic sensibility toward politics will probably be unsuccessful. Care must be taken to craft principles of deliberation which speak to people as they are rather than imagine them as they will never be."[26]

Thus, for random sample forums to create a powerful public voice with significant electoral impact, it is necessary to use the existing capacities of the public to connect face-to-face deliberation in small groups with the voting choices of the mass public on election day. In chapter 7, I propose such a link. My basic recommendation is that voters should have access to the results of representative citizen deliberation on the candidates and issues that appear on their ballots. Using small random samples of the general public, government institutions could sponsor deliberative panels on past legislative actions, individual candidates, and ballot measures. Panel participants could summarize the results of their deliberations, and federal election officials, secretaries of state, and county clerks could communicate those results to the larger voting public through various means.

For these citizen panels to achieve their intended purpose, they would have to produce high-quality judgments, and citizens would need to be willing and able to consider panel results when voting. If subject to self-deception, "groupthink," and other decision-making illnesses, the panels could falter by reaching unwarranted conclusions and promoting the election of unqualified and unrepresentative candidates. If voters find the panel results to be irrelevant, elitist, or confusing, the panels would also fail to have their intended impact. Chapter 8 addresses these dangers and explains why the panels would generally reach sound and influential judgments. Finally, chapter 9 suggests an experimental approach to implementing citizen panels. By gradually testing some of the main claims underlying the citizen panel reform, it will be possible to gauge both its necessity and electoral impact before institutionalizing panels nationwide.

The citizen panel proposal, however, is the end of this story. The virtues of the panels relative to other reforms are most apparent once one firmly grasps the problems at hand. Those problems, in turn, are best understood when framed within a simple model of political behavior. To that end, I draw upon the work of the economist Albert Hirschman, who bridged the intellectual chasm between economics and political science in his 1970 book *Exit, Voice, and Loyalty*. Hirschman sought to explain the performance of large firms and complex organizations, and I have modified his model to describe the behavior of public officials and voters.

This abstract model is valuable because it provides a simple framework for examining the democratic ideal (chapter 2), existing political practices (chapters 3 and 5), suggested reforms (chapters 4 and 6), and a new proposal for citizen panels (chapters 7–9). Framed within the theoretical model, the American political system's twin problems of public trust and representation, noted at the outset of this chapter, will become more apparent. When carried through the subsequent chapters, the model will also explain why past attempts to solve those problems have failed and why citizen panels might succeed.

CHAPTER 2

Exit and Public Voice in Representative Democracy

Under any economic, social, or political system, individuals,
business firms, and organizations in general are subject to
lapses from efficient, rational, law-abiding, virtuous, or otherwise functional behavior.

Albert O. Hirschman, Exit, Voice, and Loyalty

Democracy doesn't exist. It never has and never will. The distance between the democratic ideal and any actual government, past or present, is so vast that some theorists don't even use the term *democracy*
to describe real political systems.[1] Given this gulf, one might question
the value of examining alternative models of how democracy is supposed to work and, instead, ask to move directly to the practical matter of improving existing political systems. If the reader shares this
skepticism, I beg indulgence, because it is difficult to assess and over-
haul a system without first understanding how it is supposed to function in theory.

Examining different models of democracy is also worthwhile because this brief review reveals that every model of democracy gives at
least some emphasis to electoral accountability and public expression.
Competitive elections and the expression of political dissent are two
ideas central to this book—the real threat of "exit" (in this case, rejecting an unresponsive public official) and the use of a public's "voice."
Later in this chapter, I present a novel application of exit and voice to
elections for public office. The present task is simply to demonstrate
their general relevance to democratic theory. Readers may disagree
about which democratic model America should or does, in fact, follow.
If the central concepts examined in this book fit into diverse conceptions of the democratic ideal, then the insights in subsequent chapters
should prove useful to a wide range of readers.

ELECTIONS AND PUBLIC VOICE
IN IDEAL MODELS OF DEMOCRACY

David Held provides a taxonomy of democratic models that range from classical Athenian democracy to modern capitalist democracy.[2] I shall examine many of these models to illustrate the roles of public voice and elections in each conception of the democratic process. Despite the dramatic differences in the designs of various democratic models, each is structured to ensure a strong public voice and elected representatives who are either accountable for their actions or relatively powerless.

Though quasi-democratic systems of local rule have existed at various times throughout ancient history, the Athenian model has left behind the most powerful legacy. This is partly because of the elaborate design of the Athenian political system and partly because written records of Athenian democratic political philosophy have survived. Athens's government mixed direct election of public officials with selection by lot and the regular rotation of public offices. Even those who were duly elected had short terms in office and, in most cases, were not eligible to run for reelection. This system did not ensure accountability, but it removed the problem of entrenched incumbency by imposing what are now called term limits. At least in its ideal conception, the Athenian system gave members of the public many opportunities to share their concerns with officials. Short terms, the wide distribution of public offices, and frequent meetings of powerful public assemblies were designed to prevent single individuals from having undue influence on policy decisions.[3]

The modern socialist model of democracy (not to be confused with actual systems such as the former Soviet Union) draws upon the Athenian tradition of face-to-face democracy. This ideal model uses many of the same institutions, but for large-scale systems, it replaces the direct assembly with a pyramidal council structure whereby the top-level planning body is connected through individual representatives back to thousands of lower-level, grassroots assemblies. In addition, this system places more emphasis on maintaining socioeconomic equality among citizens to ensure equal influence on policy. Public voice is the engine of this system, and the near-complete removal of representation by large-scale elections makes the system dependent upon the quality of public ideas and their expression.[4]

Modern participatory democracy maintains direct avenues for public involvement in policymaking through referenda and initiatives. The hallmark of participatory democratic models is the challenging and powerful role of the citizen. Citizens may not have much direct authority, but they are expected to be active in their local communities, political parties, and national policy debates. By eagerly and regularly engaging in public discussion, citizens may develop strong opinions and become skilled at the forceful expression of their values. Civic skills and habits will ensure that citizens have a clear voice and that they make their views known both directly and through reasoned candidate choices during regular elections of public officials.[5] Deliberative variants of the participatory model go a step further and encourage regular dialogue among citizens to bring their many views and voices together in search of an elusive moral consensus.[6] But even deliberative democrats recognize that the public's voice must be coupled with an effective electoral process to ensure that public officials remain accountable for the actions they take as authorities.[7]

Historically, relatively few large-scale political systems have modeled themselves on these three democratic ideals, partly because the models depend upon a highly motivated, skilled, and educated public. Many democratic theorists have held a more pessimistic view of the capabilities of the citizenry, and they have recommended a government that guards "the people" from themselves. In the *Federalist Papers,* James Madison advocated this "protective" model of democracy when he argued that "you must first enable the government to control the governed." In Madison's view, the public often forms self-destructive factions, so individual citizens should have only the power to vote for their representatives. Separate branches of government further insulate the political process from factionalism. Even though this model views the general public's voice as bothersome, Madisonian democracy still relies upon periodic elections to provide some measure of accountability.[8]

Madison's vision had a powerful influence on the design of the American political system, but modern American political theorists more commonly describe the U.S. system as resembling a pluralist model of democracy. The basic difference is that pluralists view factions not as dangerous but as "a structural source of stability and the central expression of democracy."[9] America's most influential student of democracy, Robert Dahl, developed the pluralist model in an attempt to describe the actual practice of American politics. Dahl argued that regular elections and political competition among diverse minorities and coalitions ensure a representative process. He later came to recognize important differences between the pluralist ideal and the American political system, but his pluralist model remains largely unchanged. Like the Madisonian model, it relies on elections to ensure the accountability of public officials, but it also stresses the importance of public expression. If the people do not speak, pluralist government cannot craft policies that provide what the average citizen desires. By contrast, the Madisonian model views general public expression as white noise, and the more participatory models look for a "general will" among the public's many voices.

A final, capitalist model of democracy takes Madisonian and pluralist ideas to the logical extreme. The capitalist model of democracy assumes that individuals act in a way consistent with their own self-interest in both economic and political life. Public officials are no exception to the rationality assumption, and they make political decisions that serve their interest in reelection. As a result, individuals and groups have political influence in proportion to their base of economic and political power. If these assumptions hold, then the political system should reach equilibrium so long as there are competitive elections to ensure proper political market performance. Even in this model, public voice still exists, albeit in the form of "market corrections" when officials misjudge the balance of power among competing interests. Regular, competitive elections are also pivotal, for without them public officials would begin to behave like unresponsive monopolies. The capitalist model of democracy is loathsome to many because of its unkind assumptions about human behavior and its reduction of public life to economic competition. Despite its alien form, however, even this purely economic model of democracy still has a place for minimalistic conceptions of voice and electoral action.[10]

Modern democratic theorists disagree about which of these models best describes the American political ideal and existing political institutions.[11] In practice, the American system is a hybrid of different models, with no one of them fully realized. Referenda and other ballot measures give citizens a chance to govern themselves directly, but the U.S. president is elected only indirectly through the Electoral College. Some egalitarian policies—from public education to campaign contribution limits—aim to equalize citizens' potential political influence, yet the most powerful economic interests wield considerable power in the political marketplace. Despite these complexities, it is possible to summarize both American political practices and ideals within a single abstract model, which the remainder of this chapter will develop.

THE EXIT, VOICE, AND LOYALTY MODEL

When Albert Hirschman wrote *Exit, Voice, and Loyalty,* his primary goal was to help readers understand how both competition and the expression of dissatisfaction could improve the performance of failing companies, nonprofit organizations, and nations. Hirschman observed that firms and organizations often experience "repairable lapses" in performance, and if these go unnoticed, they can result in "permanent pockets of inefficiency and neglect."[12] A profit-seeking manager or well-intentioned president may not recognize the decline unless one of two things happens:

> 1. Some customers stop buying the firm's products or some members leave the organization: this is the *exit option.* As a result, revenues drop, membership declines, and management is impelled to search for ways and means to correct whatever faults have led to exit.
> 2. The firm's customers or the organization's members express their dissatisfaction directly to management or to some other authority to which management is subordinate or through general protest addressed to anyone who cares to listen: this is the *voice option.* As a result, management once again engages in a search for the causes and possible cures of customers' and members' dissatisfaction.[13]

Historically, people have used both exit and voice as response mechanisms. Many a firm has lost its customer base because it could not continue to provide the highest-quality product, and innumerable customers have tried to induce change through direct complaint. Many organizations have disappeared after their members found a better place to work, live, or play, but many members have worked for change from within an organization before giving up all hope and abandoning it.

Hirschman argues that whether people use the exit or voice option depends on their attitudes and circumstances. His model assumes that exit is the dominant reaction mode when better alternatives exist and switching products or organizations entails little cost. In a perfectly competitive market, consumers will always favor superior products and quickly exit any commercial relationship with firms that cease to produce the best goods available. Alternative products and organizations are not always present, however, and voice's role increases "as the opportunities for exit decline, up to the point where, with exit wholly unavailable, voice must carry the entire burden of alerting management to its failings." Exit is also more costly when it concerns "standardized durable consumer goods requiring large outlays" or, in organizational terms, when individuals have made a considerable investment in the organization.[14] In these cases, exit loses its appeal, because desertion might require learning a new computer operating system or starting on the bottom rung in a new organization.

Before exercising their voices, however, people take into account a similar cost associated with expression. There are both the opportunity cost of forgoing the exit option and the "direct cost of voice which is incurred as buyers of a product or members of an organization spend time and money in the attempt to achieve changes in the policies and practices of the firm from which they buy or of the organization to which they belong."[15] Using an economic example, the cost of driving to a new grocery store with lower prices is lower than taking the time to compose and effectively deliver a complaint to one's previous store, not to mention the savings that are lost while waiting for the old store to respond by lowering its prices or improving the quality of its goods and services.

Because of these costs, the regular exercise of voice often depends upon a modicum of loyalty to a firm or organization. "As a rule," Hirschman argues, "loyalty holds exit at bay and activates voice." In the absence of loyalty, consumers will quickly switch from an inferior merchant, but if they like a particular store's produce, they may first complain to the grocer before shopping elsewhere for their leafy green vegetables. Such loyalty is not simply a matter of "faith." In comparison with acts of pure faith, Hirschman explains, "the most loyalist behavior retains an enormous dose of reasoned calculation." People will be more likely to exercise their voice and develop loyalty if they perceive that such actions have an impact over time. If loyal customers' voices go unheeded when they complain to the grocer about inferior produce, their loyalty will decline, leading to their eventual exit. Although not necessarily one, the loyalist "looks like, or turns out to be, a sucker" when his or her attempts to salvage a declining firm or organization fail.[16]

Even loyal customers or members may lean toward the exit option if they do not recognize a clear means of exercising their voice. "The propensity to resort to the voice option," Hirschman explains, "depends also on the general readiness of a population to complain and on the *invention* of such institutions and mechanisms as can communicate complaints cheaply and effectively."[17] In other words, an organization or firm will only receive feedback via voice if it has in place a straightforward complaint mechanism that its member-customers are accustomed to using. Exit is a relatively automatic process in this model, whereas voice requires social systems to elicit and properly channel internal dissent.

In sum, Hirschman's model demonstrates that people can respond to declines in product or organizational quality through exit and voice. Dissatisfied people will use the exit option when there are clearly superior and available alternatives and they lose little investment by switching products or affiliations. Exit will also be the favored response when exercising voice involves high opportunity costs and direct costs. People will make their voices heard, though, if they have developed loyalty to the offending organization based upon its perceived responsiveness. Resort to voice will also be more likely if efficient complaint mechanisms are available and familiar.[18]

Hirschman uses this model to derive some surprising insights about both economic and political behavior. In the thirty years since the model was introduced, Hirschman and other scholars have found even more ways in which the model applies to local and national politics. Only some of these observations have relevance to my own use of the model in this book, but it is useful to review those insights to better understand the original purpose and power of the model.[19]

When one considers the interplay of exit, voice, and loyalty, it becomes apparent that some of the fundamental assumptions of neoclassical microeconomic theory are false. Just as democratic theorists have their ideals, so do economists. The difference is that political philosophers (normally) have the modesty to recognize their ideals as just that—ideal types that one dare not dream will take solid form. Many economists, by contrast, begin with the ideal model of a perfectly competitive economy and then presume that the mythical "invisible hand" sweeps markets free of inefficiencies. If consumers and entrepreneurs behave rationally in pursuit of their self-interest, competition will ensure the maximization of their interests, and the dysfunctional firms that fascinate Hirschman will cease to exist.

Economists and many other social scientists accept the general tenets of this idyllic model.[20] Hirschman's writings, however, explain why this theory often fails to explain complex economic realities. First, actual competitive economies can, paradoxically, prove less satisfying to consumers than those with only a handful of firms. As Hirschman explains,

> A competitively produced new product might reveal only through use some of its faults and noxious side-effects. . . . Competition in this situation is a considerable convenience to the manufacturers because it keeps consumers from complaining; it diverts their energy to hunting for the inexistent im-

proved products. . . . The manufacturers have a common interest in the maintenance rather than in the abridgment of competition—and may conceivably resort to collusive behavior to that end.[21]

Simply put, a multiplicity of equally unsatisfactory options is better for a producer than a monopoly. Producers will still scratch and claw the competition to lure more temporary customers to buy their products, but they understand that so long as no one produces a superior product, none of them need change their manufacturing processes.

A dash of competition may also be welcomed by a monopoly that knowingly produces a substandard good or service. Hirschman argues that inefficient monopolies actually invite some degree of competition "as a release from effort and criticism" when their power "rests on location and when mobility differs strongly from one group of local customers to another. If . . . the mobile customers are those who are most sensitive to quality," their exit permits the monopolist "to persist in his comfortable mediocrity." The "lazy monopolist may actually have an interest in *creating* some limited opportunities for exit" because the most quality-conscious customers are also "likely to be most demanding and querulous, in case of any lowering of standards." By showing them an open door, the monopolist encourages their exit and thereby reduces the chance that they will voice harsh criticism that could diminish the confidence and satisfaction of other consumers.[22]

Just as the absence of exit makes a lazy monopolist nervous, healthy competitive firms should dread the silence of a market where consumers speak only with their checkbooks. If consumers quickly switch products in response to even minute shifts in quality or price, a declining firm will be "wiped out before it will have had time to find out what hit it, much less to do something about it." Among other factors, Hirschman argues, it is primarily loyalty that causes influential customers and organization members to "stay on longer than they would ordinarily, in the hope or, rather, reasoned expectation that improvement or reform can be achieved 'from within.' " This measure of "irrational" loyalty conflicts with the ideal of perfect competition, but it actually results in a superior outcome because it gives firms the opportunity to correct themselves before collapsing. The ultimate threat of exit ensures long-term efficiency, but the willingness to use voice prevents the waste of invested resources that results when an otherwise rational firm briefly missteps.[23]

These three insights into illusory competition, lazy monopolies, and the value of loyalty apply to the political realm as well as to the marketplace. Regarding his description of false competition among equally inefficient firms, Hirschman notes that "competitive political systems have frequently been portrayed in just these terms. Radical critics of societies with stable party systems have often denounced the competition of the dominant parties as offering 'no real choice.' " Though Hirschman recognizes that noncompetitive political systems are hardly agents of rapid social change, he acknowledges that "the radical critique is correct in pointing out that competitive political systems have a considerable capacity to divert what might otherwise be a revolutionary ground swell into tame discontent with the governing party."[24]

Public agencies and institutions also sometimes have the same incentives to promote modest competition as do lazy monopolists in the private sector. Hirschman offers the example of public schools:

> Suppose at some point, for whatever reason, the public schools deteriorate. Thereupon, increasing numbers of quality-education-conscious parents will send their children to private schools. This "exit" may occasion some impulse toward an improvement of the public schools; but here again this impulse is far less significant than the loss to the public schools of those member-customers who would be most motivated and determined to put up a fight against the deterioration if they did not have the alternative of the private schools.[25]

For political processes, as for markets, the optimal balance then is a healthy mix of competition and dissent. Just as a perfectly competitive economy is too quick to destroy firms that err, so can highly competitive multiparty politics promote underdeveloped political parties. With an abundance of parties to choose from, "members will usually find it tempting to go over to some other party in case of disagreement. Thus, they will not fight for 'change from within.' "[26]

These few observations are only some of the insights into political life that one can glean from *Exit, Voice, and Loyalty*. Hirschman's work provided other observations about the dynamics of two-party systems, ideological bias, and overreliance on exit and voice. Subsequent essays by Hirschman and other scholars have applied the theory fruitfully to urban neglect, party competition in Israel, Japanese party politics, and the 1989 revolution in the German Democratic Republic. In addition, one scholar has applied Hirschman's ideas to political reforms aimed at democratic empowerment to criticize reforms that fail to balance exit and voice.[27] The same concern is central to this book, but before I use Hirschman's model, I wish to make substantial changes in its details and level of analysis. The remainder of this chapter introduces these modifications.

APPLYING THE MODEL TO ELECTIONS

Few scholars have extended the exit, voice, and loyalty model to the political process, beyond its role in shaping individual political organizations. An exception is Eva Sorensen, who recognizes the potential value of redefining "exit" in relation to a representative government:

> If we take a closer look at political life, exit is limited by the obvious fact that it is difficult to exit from the nation-state. A "genuine exit" calls for a change of nationality. Nevertheless, exit plays a central role in political life in liberal democracies in which the primary means of empowering the citizens is voting. Through voting the individual is granted the power to exit one party to the advantage of another. . . . Voice channels . . . are available through membership of a political party and through participation in the public debate in the media.[28]

I go beyond the traditional exit, voice, and loyalty model in another sense. With only minor exceptions, the remainder of this book examines how citizens influence individual elected officials, as opposed to political parties, public agencies, or governments.[29] This shift from organizational behavior to the actions of public officials is substantial, because exit and voice are now understood to influence the behavior of individual representatives, rather than complex organizations. In practice, many elected officials operate as the heads of small organizations that include paid staff and informal advisers. In the interest of simple prose, however, I shall refer to these officials as individual actors who respond (or fail to respond) to the voice of the electorate.

If the main actors in this new model are elected officials, the central question is what causes representatives to experience what Hirschman might call "lapses from virtuous behavior." The democratic models reviewed earlier all agree that the first task of political representatives is to serve the public. Even the Madisonian model of democracy recognizes that the lay public should be the ultimate judge of whether its representatives are acting in the public's best interest. The variance in democratic theorists' confidence in the quality of public judgment is somewhat moot, as every democratic system uses elections of one kind or another to prevent representatives from becoming entrenched and unresponsive. In every democratic ideal, public officials must be held accountable for their actions as representatives of the citizenry. Whether one believes in a general will of the people or simply in an average interest among conflicting visions of the public good, it is important to understand the circumstances under which elected officials represent the public's interests.

To influence the actions of their elected officials, voters can use exit, voice, or both response mechanisms. In this context, the terms *exit* and *voice* take on a different meaning, and in place of the former I shall speak of "electoral rejection." As I use the term throughout this book, *attempted electoral rejection* is voting for an alternative candidate when a public official seeks reelection. By backing an opponent, a voter seeks to discard the current official and replace him or her with a candidate perceived to better represent personal or collective interests. Just as a consumer switching products has no assurance that such a change will prove beneficial, the voter takes a chance on a new official. Unlike the consumer changing shampoo brands, though, the voter cannot change officials autonomously; instead, the success of the individual's vote depends upon the votes of others. Only when the electorate is thought of as a body does electoral rejection carry with it the certainty of successful exit: thus, *collective rejection* is the successful election of an opponent who challenges an incumbent. I move from the individual to the collective level when I refer to electoral rejection, and I stress the uncertainty of the individual voter's attempt to reject an incumbent official or administration.

In part because of the limited influence of a single voter's electoral choices, the public's capacity for dissent is at least as important as its attempts at electoral rejection. As I use the term, *voice* is an attempt to influence the public decisions made by elected representatives. Hirschman's more narrow use of the term would equate voice only with the expression of dissent against actions that a citizen finds distasteful. I wish to use the term more broadly to include praise, neutral input on a specific issue, and requests for specific votes that are not sparked by the belief that the official will act otherwise. Any citizen's message to a public official may influence that official's actions in the future, whether or not the citizen intended to change the official's decisions.

Whether a given voter chooses to rely upon this voice or backs an opposing candidate in an election depends upon the same considerations presented in the earlier discussion of firms and organizations. Some of these factors become more complicated, but at a high level of abstraction, Hirschman's economic model and the voting model I present are quite similar. Whether a dissatisfied constituent voices dissent or attempts electoral rejection depends primarily upon past experience using voice with an incumbent and the estimation of an opposing candidate's potential for superior representation. Simply put, if a voter perceives that the incumbent has responded well to dissent and the opponent is not much better, it is likely that the voter will remain loyal to the incumbent and rely upon voice to express any dissent. By contrast, if the incumbent is unresponsive and the opponent would better represent the voter's interests, it is more likely that the voter will attempt electoral rejection by voting for an opposing candidate.

Without taking any other variables into account, one can see clearly the costs and benefits of loyalty in this model. If voters in a given city council district have very little loyalty toward their incumbent councilor, they will reject the incumbent in the next election so long as an opponent seems to have greater potential to represent their interests. A sitting councilor from this district may rarely hear constituents' voices, because of their unwillingness to voice concerns, and this lack of communication may decrease the councilor's chances for reelection even further. Over time, because of its readiness to reject imperfect officials, this district would also forgo the benefits of long-term incumbency. By contrast, a district with extremely high constituent loyalty would suffer the opposite fate. This second district would reelect councilors to many terms in office, but overreliance on voice would undermine the electorate's credibility and permit the incumbent to act with impunity. The sitting councilor might hear many complaints, but if the district's loyalty was blind, dissent would manifest itself only as voice and never as a real electoral challenge. Between these extremes, a healthy public develops a modicum of loyalty toward responsive elected officials but conditions that loyalty on actual performance.[30]

THE ROLE OF DELIBERATION

Though it may not be obvious, this simple model relies upon two critical assumptions. This model assumes that voters know what government actions are in their own best interest, and it assumes that voters know a great deal about the intentions and actions of incumbents and challengers. In reality, voter self-awareness and political knowledge vary tremendously over time and across different social groups, so it is preferable to change these underlying assumptions into model variables. This makes the model more complex, but it also highlights the importance of two forms of public deliberation. For citizens to exercise their voice and vote effectively, it is necessary that they have sound insight into both their own interests and the virtues of competing candidates.

Because they depend upon clarification of interests and the articulation of policy judgments, the expression of an authentic public voice and well-informed attempts at electoral rejection are only likely to occur when they follow a period of sustained deliberation. I define *public deliberation* as discussion that involves judicious argument, critical listening, and earnest decision making. Following the writings of John Dewey, full deliberation includes a careful examination of a problem or issue, the identification of possible solutions, the establishment or reaffirmation of evaluative criteria, and the use of these criteria in identifying an optimal solution. Within a specific policy debate or in the context of an election, deliberation sometimes starts with a given set of solutions, but it always involves problem analysis, criteria specification, and evaluation.[31]

Lest this process sound too tepid, I should stress that the deliberative discussion of problems and solutions can include emotional appeals. As Jane Mansbridge insists, "We must avoid the traditional, frequently male, mandate to 'keep emotions out of it.' . . . Appeals for the common good require an emotional and cognitive probing of one's own feelings of empathy, admiration, revulsion, or horror." Mansbridge recognizes that "appeals to emotion *can* be dangerous," and she suggests that "emotional appeals must therefore stand up to reflection in tranquillity."[32] The point is simply that the expression of strong feelings has its place in deliberation.

Having defined *public deliberation,* I now wish to clarify the meaning of *democratic deliberation,* a term that further specifies the ideal relations among the people taking part in a discussion within a democratic political system.[33] To be democratic, deliberation must include diverse participants from the larger public, and it should use an egalitarian decision rule (e.g., consensus or majority rule) to resolve conflicts among participants. Some deliberative theorists, such as Joshua Cohen, argue that "ideal deliberation aims to arrive at a rationally motivated *consensus,*" but striving toward consensus does not require the use of a strict consensus procedure, which gives each participant veto power over any collective decisions.[34]

In addition, participants in democratic deliberation must have equal and adequate opportunities to speak, and they must be able to comprehend what other participants say. Participants in democratic deliberation also have a responsibility to avoid manipulative discourse, provide other participants with any relevant knowledge they possess, and consider carefully what others say. Using Jürgen Habermas's terms,

participants in an "ideal speech situation" must have adequate opportunities to examine the meaning of one another's statements and challenge one another's "validity claims."[35] If all of these conditions are met,
a discussion can be called both deliberative and democratic.

The basic purpose of deliberation is to make sound decisions.
Though the philosopher John Rawls used the term sparingly in his 1971
treatise *A Theory of Justice,* deliberation is the central mechanism in his
method of evaluating public policy. Rawls's influential moral theory argues that people can judge a policy by imagining that they are unaware
of their actual social position. Behind this hypothetical "veil of ignorance," people can objectively evaluate the degree to which a policy pro-
tects the public's basic freedoms and ensures a decent quality of life for
the least well-off.[36] Rawls argues that such a philosophical exercise is
most fruitful when conducted in a deliberative process:

> We normally assume that an ideally conducted discussion among many per-
> sons is more likely to arrive at the correct conclusion (by a vote if necessary)
> than the deliberations of any one of them by himself. . . . Discussion is a way
> of combining information and enlarging the range of arguments. At least in
> the course of time, the effects of common deliberation seem bound to im-
> prove matters.[37]

Rawls adheres to the commonsense notion that many minds are better than one at finding an optimal solution to a problem. Though public skepticism about the value of committee decisions persists, Rawls's
faith in group discussion appears to be well founded. Research in social
psychology and small group communication has found that, on balance, group discussion generally results in higher-quality decisions than
do methods that rely upon single individuals. Moreover, past research
has shown that group discussion leads to better decisions than nonin-
teractive methods of collective decision making. In sum, groups produce
better average decisions than individuals, and groups that engage in deliberation outperform nominal groups that simply pool individual opinions without open-ended discussion.[38]

Deliberation is even more important for complex social and political
problems. Unlike technical or scientific puzzles, public policy problems
are inextricably interconnected, difficult to define and study, and impossible to remove completely. The evaluation of alternative solutions
to public policy problems requires value judgments, as well as technical
analysis.[39] The latter feature is most important: political deliberation
is not only valuable as a means of grappling with complexity, it also
serves democracy by helping citizens clarify the implications of their

basic values for public policy choices. The more enlightened a public's understanding of its own interests, the more likely it is to govern itself effectively.[40] Disentangling the beliefs and motivations underlying surface-level policy preferences is difficult, and deliberation can transform disagreement by reducing initial opinions to sets of contestable "presumptions," only some of which will stand up under scrutiny.[41]

Amy Gutmann and Dennis Thompson make a slightly different argument for deliberation. Though these authors recognize the virtue of discussion as a means of pooling information and developing citizens' interests, they emphasize its value as a legitimate method of addressing moral conflicts. "Deliberation," they argue, "is the most appropriate way for citizens collectively to resolve their moral disagreements not only about policies but also about the process by which policies should be adopted." Gutmann and Thompson criticize those who would leave moral issues for the courts to resolve or bar their entrance into the political realm altogether. In their view, political deliberation is the only fair and effective means of handling moral conflict. Deliberation requires both citizens and representatives to present reasons and justifications for their views and to consider alternative views. When successful, deliberation can confer legitimacy upon even majoritarian policy decisions, so long as those decisions take conflicting views into account. Even if it does not produce a solution acceptable to all, it may at least preserve mutual respect among the parties to an unresolved debate.[42]

Relating these advantages to the exit, voice, and loyalty model, deliberation can strengthen the public's voice, ease its ability to collectively reject unrepresentative officeholders, and inspire a modest loyalty to responsive elected officials. A strong public voice requires that citizens develop their interests in relation to policy and articulate those interests clearly. Public deliberation has precisely those qualities when it takes place in an open setting and is inclusive of a diverse sample of the larger public. At least those directly participating in deliberation are likely to sharpen their own understandings of public policy problems and the solutions that best reflect their basic values. If public officials learn the results of the deliberation, the process can also serve as a means of clearly expressing the participants' judgments to elected representatives.

Having developed their interests more fully, participants in a deliberative discussion are better able to evaluate candidates effectively. Once voters know how they view an issue, they are more likely to examine candidates' positions and actions on that same issue. Unrepresentative public officials stand out under such scrutiny. Moreover, to the extent that open deliberation orients discussion toward the common good, such discussion increases the likelihood that voters will support policies that they believe will serve the general public's interests. If those beliefs develop simultaneously during collective deliberation, voters will be more likely to reach shared judgments, and that may, in turn, lead to similar candidate evaluations. If more evaluations are in sync, then voters should more often act in concert and collectively reject unrepresentative elected officials. Simply put, deliberation might lead voters not just to collective policy judgments but also to collective electoral action opposing (or supporting) incumbent officials, depending on the correspondence of those officials' actions to the voters' shared interests.

At the same time, an electorate that engages in deliberation with its public officials might develop a stronger loyalty toward those officials who demonstrate not only responsiveness but also respect for the deliberative process. Democratic citizens perceive deliberation as a legitimate means for arriving at public decisions, and officials who conflict with majority opinion but explain their views and consider voters' positions might withstand opposition during elections because of their willingness to deliberate. As suggested earlier, a measure of reasoned loyalty benefits the representative system by keeping in officials who might misstep from time to time yet remain genuinely responsive to voters' concerns.

THE PSYCHOLOGY OF CITIZENS

Deliberation's value extends beyond the reasoned judgment it permits, but to understand this additional virtue, it is necessary to make one final addition to the revised exit, voice, and loyalty model. The effective use of a citizen's voice and vote also depends upon a set of psychological variables necessary to sustain democratic political action. In chapter 1, I argued that healthy governments require public trust and that meaningful deliberation can bolster the citizenry's confidence in its political institutions. In addition, deliberation can change how citizens view themselves, their abilities, and their responsibilities. To this point, the revised model has assumed that citizens recognize the value of participation and have confidence in their abilities to speak and vote wisely. As with deliberation, it is worthwhile to remove this assumption and consider these psychological characteristics as variables in the model.

The effective use of political voice and vote depends upon the maintenance of democratic institutions that reinforce important public attitudes and beliefs. When authors write about the importance of a strong "civil society," some of what concerns them is the public's willingness and ability to use its opportunities for political expression and electoral action.[43] Hirschman calls this the "readiness" to exercise voice; citizens are ready to voice dissent or attempt electoral rejection when they have both the necessary skills and confidence in those abilities. In the case of public voice, citizens cannot express their concerns effectively without basic literacy and a modest public-speaking ability. In addition, citizens must know how to reach public officials, whether they seek a face-to-face audience or simply want to send a letter. Anyone reading this book surely has those modest skills, but it is important to remember that over 20 percent of adult U.S. citizens have only rudimentary literacy skills, and only a quarter of the citizenry know the names of their U.S. senators.[44]

Also, people often develop skills without gaining confidence. This phenomenon is so widespread among people of all backgrounds that psychologists have given it a prominent place in the literature on human behavior. *Self-efficacy* is the belief that one can competently perform an action, such as brushing one's teeth, defending oneself against an attacker, or writing a letter to the editor.[45]

Despite its general significance, self-efficacy is not always an important influence on people's behavioral choices, and its relevance to political life can not be taken for granted. Research in political science, however, has found a clear and consistent impact for this variable. These studies have demonstrated a strong connection between a person's political self-efficacy and his or her willingness to vote and express dissent through both conventional means, such as letter-writing and demonstration, as well as more radical means, such as civil disobedience.[46] The readiness to use one's voice, then, depends not only upon objective skills but also upon one's subjective assessment of those same skills.

Complicating matters further is the difference between one's own perceived abilities and the skills one attributes to fellow citizens. Obviously, a person's confidence in his or her ability to express dissent is unshaken by any doubts as to other people's communication skills. But one's sense of *group efficacy* is important when one considers expressing dissent through a group or organization.[47] A good deal of political expression comes through collective entities, and if citizens have doubts about the competence of groups they have joined (or are considering joining), they are less likely to try channeling dissent through those bod-ies. Why try making oneself heard through a citizen action group if one suspects that the group is incapable of drafting a coherent press release, let alone of reaching agreement on what its members wish to say? A modicum of group efficacy is necessary to maintain active participation in community associations, public forums, and interest groups designed to channel public voices to policymakers. In addition, without a related sense of group efficacy (i.e., confidence in the competence of the general electorate's ability to conduct an equally thorough candidate screening), a talented and self-assured voter might decide that an attempt at elec-toral rejection is not worth the bother.

Even with a strong sense of self- and group efficacy, citizens may still not exercise voice, believing that their actions, although competently performed, will have no impact. Cognitive psychologists refer to this be-lief as "outcome expectancy"—the expectation that one's actions will result in a desired outcome. Hirschman underscores the importance of this expectation by arguing that loyalty ultimately depends upon the ex-pectation that one's voice will have influence.[48] Past research has shown that in politics, as well as other spheres of action, a person's outcome expectancy is a powerful predictor of whether he or she will take ac-tions that require effort.[49] Only if citizens believe that public officials will act upon their advice will they go to the trouble of writing, calling, e-mailing, or directly addressing elected representatives.[50]

Political scientists call this belief "perceived system responsiveness." It bears some correspondence to the political trust discussed in chapter 1. With regard to voting, one may or may not trust that casting a bal-lot for a candidate is likely to influence the outcome of an election. As for voice, citizens vary in the degree to which they trust elected officials to give a meaningful response to one's expressed concerns. In these ways, low public trust is one of the important beliefs underlying sus-tained political action.[51]

If public expression and electoral rejection are so difficult, why do people take political action at all? To answer this question, I focus on the relatively simple act of voting. Voters unsure of the impact of their vote might still do so. Some voters might make a pessimistic assessment of their ability to make an accurate and influential voting decision yet vote nonetheless because they place such a high value on the influence that they might achieve. This consideration, which psychologists call "outcome valuation," is regularly paired with self-efficacy and outcome expectancy in research on behavioral choice. With regard to voting, however, this belief hinges on the unspoken hope that one's single vote will be the one that "makes the difference," and save in the smallest local elections, that is closer to an act of faith than a rational calculation. Research on voting in the United States suggests that the more common motivator to vote despite one's sense of helplessness is the lingering sense of civic duty that many citizens feel. Whether one thinks of duty as a behavioral habit, a cultural reflex, or a heartfelt conviction, it appears that many people continue to vote "because that is what citizens do."[52]

Once again, this set of political beliefs and orientations is important because it undergirds sustained citizen participation in public affairs. Democratic political institutions must "shape the psychology of citizens," because the system depends upon the involvement of those citizens. Deliberation, the expression of a strong public voice, and effective electoral action all require a citizenry with self-confidence, some confidence in system responsiveness, and genuine concern for the outcomes of political actions.[53]

CIVIC NEGLECT

And what of those who neither place a high value on their political influence nor glow with civic pride? If exit is daunting to this group of citizens, do they then turn to voice? Perhaps some idle cranks fall into that category, but many more citizens use neither exit nor voice. A subset of these know that their interests are not well represented, and another subset have not even made that initial calculation. It may come as a surprise, but Hirschman's original model had nothing to say about this residual group of individuals who have opportunities for exit and voice but do not use them. One group of scholars using the model to study urban politics quickly discovered this group of citizens. In their view, failure to respond when perceiving political problems amounts to *system neglect*. This term underscores the fact that the use of neither exit nor voice is still a behavioral choice—the choice to neglect the system through nonresponse.[54]

Civic neglect is easy to recognize. When neglect becomes a prevalent response mode, one can expect large percentages of a public to stop voting altogether. These nonvoters are unlikely to follow politics closely. They skip political sections of the newspaper, avoid political television programming, and even eschew policy- or campaign-oriented political conversation. When asked about their views, citizens neglect-

Exit and Public Voice

civil neglect

29

ing the system will demonstrate limited political knowledge and undeveloped opinions, but they will demonstrate strong distrust of government and elected officials.

When open and egalitarian political institutions are in place, civic neglect can still become widespread if citizens lack the sense of efficacy and motivation necessary to use those institutions effectively. Even when the public is brimming with confidence and civic responsibility, neglect might still result from a sober assessment of the difficulty of making the sound judgments that underlie effective voice and voting choices. In a typical political system, such "rational neglect" is likely, given the difficulty of arriving at deliberative judgments. The rational utility-maximizing denizens of economic models are not only presumed to doggedly pursue their self-interest, they are also assumed to know their interests. By contrast, in the model of representative democracy presented herein, a fundamental problem is the discernment and articulation of citizens' policy judgments. Chapters 3 and 5 demonstrate the rarity of adequate deliberative judgments, but here I wish to stress the profound difficulty of this problem even in theory.

Before a citizen can recognize the failure of an elected official to represent his or her interests, a citizen must first determine what those interests are.[55] When one looks beyond self-interested policy judgments to a citizen's estimation of what policies best serve the public interest, citizens must also make the effort to understand the needs and concerns of their fellow citizens—a challenge far greater than coming to know one's own interests. Once interests are developed, they must become more than tacit if they are to be of use in evaluating the performance of elected officials and the merits of political challengers. Much of what we come to know about ourselves and our social world is understood only unconsciously, and although we can generally use that knowledge in practice, it is difficult to apply it systematically unless it becomes conscious.[56]

Both exit and voice are also equally dependent on a related accomplishment—the successful evaluation of the incumbent's performance with regard to a citizen's interests or those of the general public. Now, the competent citizen must not only formulate interests but determine whether or not those have been (and will continue to be) served. Has the representative in question voted "properly" on relevant legislation? Has the representative made the voter's key issues top priorities while in office? Unless the voter can connect interests to performance, the voter will not know whether to reject an incumbent representative, let alone whether to exercise voice as a means of protest.

If the voter does decide that a public official has done a poor job as representative, yet another task lies ahead. As discussed more thoroughly in chapter 3, a voter must seek out alternative candidates as a means of electoral rejection and make similar judgments about the future performance of those candidates. This task is difficult because challengers usually have incommensurate political track records, if any at all. A voter must often make judgments based on hunches, analogies, and the misleading claims of the candidates themselves to gauge the likelihood that the opponent both shares the voter's views and will prove capable of pursuing those interests with the same vigor, skill, and resources as the incumbent.

Requiring interest formation and articulation, as well as incumbent and challenger evaluation, political exit is not the same as switching long-distance phone companies. The physical act of voting is not daunting to most citizens, but calculated acts of public expression and attempted electoral rejection are time-consuming and difficult. Only with the cognitive and emotional underpinnings described earlier can one expect citizens to avail themselves of opportunities for effective public expression and electoral action.[57]

DELIBERATIVE POLICYMAKING

As presented thus far, this model highlights what can go wrong in a representative system. In this final summary of the model, I demonstrate what happens when such a system operates properly. This description reveals a final, implicit element of the model. The point of government—even democratic government—is good public decision making. Just as citizens can only make sound judgments after deliberating, so public officials can only govern wisely after careful research and reflection.[58] Deliberative citizens might reach some clear judgments on particular issues and treat their representatives as sworn delegates, expected to do exactly as they have been instructed, but more often representatives must conduct their own deliberations and act as trustees of the public's best interest.[59]

From one perspective, the model of representative democracy that I have described is designed to promote just such deliberation by public officials. As shown in figure 1, citizens' choices about how to use voice and votes indirectly depend upon official deliberation. If officials reach a sound deliberative judgment about the public interest and then act

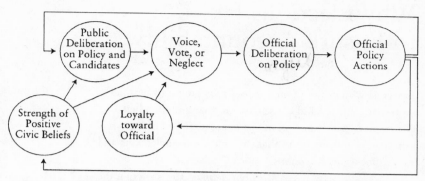

Figure 1.   Model of Democratic Deliberation and Representation

upon that judgment, they should fare well on election day *so long as cit-izens reach the same judgment in their own deliberations.*[60] After all, in the ideal model of representative democracy, when citizens evaluate policies and candidates, they take into account the actions of elected officials. This feedback loop ensures accountability for officials' actions, and that, in turn, creates an incentive for officials to deliberate carefully lest their judgments and subsequent actions fail to impress the deliberative electorate.

To summarize, voting and public voice have important roles in the democratic process, no matter how one defines democracy. In addition, a healthy representative political system requires ongoing policy deliberation and intensive candidate evaluation during campaigns. Both of these processes require active citizen deliberation about private and public interests. Without an underlying set of political beliefs (e.g., self-efficacy, public trust, and civic responsibility), deliberation and the twin mechanisms of voice and vote may fall into disuse, resulting in widespread civic neglect.

The model of democracy developed in this chapter demonstrates the necessary features of a healthy representative system. To promote the creation of deliberative public policy decisions by elected officials, a political system must have institutions that sustain ongoing citizen deliberation, nurture a resilient and motivated public, and provide clear opportunities for the influential expression of political voice and the real threat of electoral rejection. The next four chapters will assess the success of U.S. political institutions in maintaining a vigilant citizenry and stimulating productive political responses to lapses in public representation.

CHAPTER 3

Why Elections Fail
to Ensure Accountability

Everyone who grows up in our society is bound to become
aware, at some level of consciousness, that an individual
vote is more nearly a form of self-expression and of legitimation than of influence and that the link between elections and
value allocations is tenuous.

> *Murray Edelman,* Constructing the
> Political Spectacle

In theory, elections in representative democracy ensure accountability
through lively candidate competition and careful voting decisions. In
the ideal election, voters begin with a relatively well-developed sense of
self-interest and some conception of the public good. Though those
views may shift slightly over the course of an election, voters remain
steadfast in their values and never lose sight of their primary concerns.
Meanwhile, a list of qualified but diverse candidates appears for every
public office, and voters have a wide range of choices to consider. Voters examine the candidates by meeting them face-to-face, attending
public forums, listening to speeches, watching debates, and sampling
the offerings of a wide variety of relevant printed and electronic media.
The candidate whom voters judge most suitable is then charged with
pursuing the public's interest as its representative. When the next electoral cycle begins, if the official seeks reelection, his or her voting
record becomes one of the electorate's primary considerations when
comparing the incumbent with the new set of challengers.

Most Americans' experience of elections is far from that ideal. Voting is, as Murray Edelman observes, closer to "a form of self-expression" than an act of political influence. Benjamin Barber aptly describes
the uninspiring experience of most voters: "Our primary electoral act,
voting, is rather like using a public toilet: we wait in line with a crowd
in order to close ourselves up in a small compartment where we can re-

lieve ourselves in solitude and in privacy of our burden, pull a level, and then, yielding to the next in line, go silently home."[1]

This chapter examines why elections fail to provide a strong connection from deep public concerns to real public policy. The problems underlying this failure are underdeveloped public judgments, superficial voter evaluations of candidates, and the shallow pool of contestants for elected office. Together, these problems thwart attempts at electoral rejection of unrepresentative incumbents, thereby making officials less accountable for their actions. In addition, public awareness of these problems leads citizens to neglect the political system, worsening the very problems that spark voter apathy and cynicism in the first place.

INTERESTS AND IDEOLOGY

A fundamental requirement for democratic self-governance is that the public must develop clearly defined interests that it can articulate during and between elections. One of the principles of democracy is that an individual is the best judge of what is in his or her best interest. Democratic political processes presume that it is best to let each individual articulate his or her own wants and needs. Other people may sometimes be in a better position to judge one's interests; however, there is no way to know when that is the case, so it is safer to assume the competence of every individual to decide his or her own interests. This principle, which Robert Dahl calls "the strong principle of equality," does not presume that individuals know their own interests; rather, it just asserts that no individuals "are so definitely better qualified than the others" that they should have the ultimate authority to make decisions on behalf of those others.[2]

Presuming self-awareness does not make it so, however. Does the typical American voter, in fact, know what policies are in his or her best interests? And if voters ultimately seek to discern the interests of the larger public, can they tell what is best for the city, state, or nation as a whole? It is impossible to answer those questions because there is no independent ground from which to judge the accuracy of citizens' perceptions of the public good. Some philosophers make compelling claims that freedom and equality are relatively "neutral" standards for making such a judgment,[3] but I wish to ask a more simple question. Regardless of the substance of their views, do individual citizens have well-informed and coherent policy positions?

By "well-informed and coherent," I mean three things. First, a well-informed view is one that is based upon a modest amount of relevant principle of equality(handwritten margin note)

information—both facts about an issue and awareness of different perspectives on an issue. The more informed the average voter is, the better the result. Second, the public's policy judgments are coherent if they
connect logically to one another and to underlying values. Different
logics can lead from the same basic values to different policy choices,
but the question is whether those connections have been drawn at all.[4]
Third, to be considered coherent, a citizen's views on one issue should
not contradict his or her views on another issue. In sum, an informed
and coherent belief system starts with a set of fundamental values, then
uses the fruits of a rigorous information search to connect those values
to mutually reinforcing policy choices.

Well-informed Americans ought to know a good deal about public
issues and government. Michael Delli Carpini and Scott Keeter studied
this subject in depth in *What Americans Know about Politics and Why
It Matters* (1996). Using survey data from the National Election Studies, they reported discouraging results: "Only 13% of the more than
2,000 political questions examined could be answered correctly by
75% or more of those asked, and only 41% could be answered correctly by more than half the public." On questions regarding political
institutions and processes, the median respondent gave correct answers
49 percent of the time. On foreign affairs, the median was 44 percent,
and on domestic politics, the median was 39 percent. Across the population, knowledge was distributed in a bell-shaped curve, with relatively few respondents having very high or low knowledge scores, except that a relatively large percentage of Americans knew very little
about domestic politics. The poor performance of respondents on these
knowledge questions led the investigators to conclude that the American public's judgments are "hardly the stuff of informed consent, let
alone of a working representative democracy." The authors also found
that despite all the varied changes in public education, journalism, and
politics over the past fifty years, "citizens appear no less informed
about politics today than they were half a century ago." The bad news
is that they also "appear no *more* informed."[5]

Evidence from both public surveys and psychological experiments
shows that most Americans' political views are often not only poorly
informed but also rather incoherent. One of the most comprehensive
and well-supported theories of public opinion paints a humbling portrait of how we think about political issues. The political scientist John
Zaller brought together previously unconnected findings on attitude instability, public opinion shifts, media discourse, reelection campaigns,

and survey method effects to create the "receive-accept-sample" model of public opinion. According to this model, we routinely *receive* media messages on issues, and the less sophisticated among us *accept* these messages uncritically (those more politically savvy simply filter out messages that conflict with their predispositions). When asked to state our opinions (or cast a vote), we *sample* among the messages we have accepted, which have become "considerations" in our heads. The view we state is merely the average of these considerations that come to mind. One of the central implications of this model is that "individuals do not possess 'true attitudes,' in the usual technical sense of the term, on most political issues, but a series of considerations that are typically rather poorly integrated." Most people do not "have 'just one attitude' on issues."[6]

A useful metaphor for understanding Zaller's claim is the "attitude pie." In this view, attitudes don't exist as coherent entities, as popularly imagined. Instead, a typical person holds conflicting views on an issue, plus a measure of neutrality. In two dimensions, one can think of an attitude as a pie sliced into thirds—one piece favoring a policy, one piece opposing it, and one piece representing a neutral attitude. When asked to give an opinion in a survey, a citizen might say she supports welfare reform, yet that support might only represent the largest "slice" of her different views on the issue: 40 percent of her thoughts on the subject might support reform, but another 35 percent might oppose it, with neutrality accounting for the remainder of her attitude.[7]

"Latitude theory" suggests another way of understanding indefinite attitudes. This theory "depicts a preference not as an optimal point on a dimension of opinion, but as a line segment, within which all points may be roughly equivalent in attractiveness."[8] A person's attitude toward free trade is not really a single point on a spectrum (e.g., 5 on a ten-point scale), but rather a *range* of acceptable positions (e.g., 2 to 6 on the same scale). In this view, attitude instability is typically just movement within this range of acceptability, and citizens are not so much indecisive as they are flexible.

An open-minded person always welcomes conflicting considerations, and an ideal judgment weighs different facts, ideas, and perspectives in making a decision. That decision might remain open to reconsideration in light of new information and insight, but it is unlikely to change in the meantime because it was reached through careful deliberation and reflection. Though latitude theory and the attitude pie metaphor suggest ways in which unstable attitudes can still be well formed, the evidence

marshaled by Zaller suggests otherwise. More often than not, ambiva-
lent and undefined attitudes appear to be the result of limited information and inadequate reflection.

For most citizens, Zaller's receive-accept-sample model suggests that
the main determinant of policy views is the balance of opinions expressed in the mainstream media. Thus, the public's reported attitudes
hinge upon the average attitudes communicated through radio, television, newspapers, magazines, the Internet, and other mass media. Careful analysis of such media messages is a task far beyond the scope of
this book, but two observations about the quality and authenticity of
the public attitudes created through this process should give one pause.
First, as the media critics Jay Blumer and Michael Gurevitch note,
"Less and less of the political communication diet serves the citizen
role—due to the predominant presentation of politics as a game; the ir-
relevance of campaign agendas to the post-election tasks of government; and the diminished space and time devoted to policy substance."[9]
Both qualitative studies and systematic content analyses have found
that the political news reaching mass audiences in the United States focuses more on the game of politics than the substance of policy and
elections.[10] Second, there is no doubt as to the fact that paid media
(e.g., political advertising and public relations campaigns) overrepre-
sent the views of wealthy individuals and corporations. Political observers and cultural critics have provided ample evidence of this bias,
but it is nearly inevitable that an uneven distribution of wealth results
in an uneven distribution of paid, mass-mediated political messages.[11]
When this steady stream of unbalanced messages flows into the drying
creek bed of political journalism, the result is a river of public opinion
biased toward particular interests.

The history of American public opinion, however, demonstrates that
public opinion does have some independence from media influence.
The reason is that relatively sophisticated and ideological citizens tend
to choose the messages they sample; even more important, these citizens do not uniformly *accept* the messages they receive. Regardless of
the balance of messages in the media, these citizens can form what *appear* to be informed and coherent policy views by sleight of hand. If a
person can at least form a general ideological bias, he or she can rely
on political elites who share that ideology to reach judgments instead:
"Ideology . . . is a mechanism by which ordinary citizens make contact
with specialists who are knowledgeable on controversial issues and
who share the citizens' predispositions." In other words, so long as at

least some of the mass-mediated voices that citizens hear represent their own orientation, ideological citizens can "learn" stable, consistent attitudes from those elites. In this way, Zaller argues, "Ideology can make a valuable contribution to democratic politics in a society in which people are expected not only to have opinions about a range of impossibly difficult issues, but to use those opinions as the basis for choosing leaders and holding them accountable."[12]

Ideology is not the norm for citizens. As Lance Bennett argues, "Most individuals struggle with internal belief conflicts, making the measurement of stable beliefs and dispositions beside the point, not to mention an unlikely result."[13] Though the pure concept of ideology may be somewhat mythical, it is still useful to estimate how many voters think along such lines. Based on a careful examination of National Election Study data, it appears that roughly half of the American electorate are "nonideological," in that their political attitudes and behaviors show little ideological consistency. Roughly 20 percent of the electorate show unambiguous signs of ideological organization, usually along the lines of the liberal-conservative dichotomy, which remains popular in American politics. Another third of the electorate demonstrate at least some higher-order structuring of their political beliefs.[14] Other researchers have demonstrated that even nonideological thinkers still organize their political beliefs into lower-level schemas,[15] but only those with an ideological orientation that corresponds to ongoing political discourse will have the advantages Zaller describes. One can only "make contact with specialists" and adopt their ideologically consistent policy positions if one recognizes one's ideology in them.

Even for the fifth of the population who think ideologically, Zaller's characterization is far from flattering. Citizens who are politically knowledgeable and ideological obtain large amounts of political information and simply filter out ideologically inconsistent views. The result is far from a well-reasoned set of attitudes. Instead, these citizens develop a crude copy of the views of elites who appear to share a similar ideological orientation. As a result of careful filtering, ideological citizens appear to have developed a coherent set of informed attitudes corresponding to a more basic set of core values. In truth, these citizens have assumed that like-minded elites hold attitudes that the citizens themselves would hold if they thought through the issues. That assumption permits ideological citizens to articulate views on a broad range of policy issues without devoting scarce time and energy on researching those same issues. Sometimes, however, citizens' genuine interests will not correspond to those of their favored ideological elites. Elites and the lay public often diverge upon class lines, such as when liberal and conservative elites fail to recognize the social and economic realities confronted by average citizens.[16] More frequently, the unique circumstances of individual citizens result in a set of particular interests that diverge from generalized ideological positions. A liberal Kansas farmer, for instance, is likely to have many interests that differ from those articulated by Ted Kennedy and other representatives of the liberal elite. The most serious problem, however, is sorting out disagreements among ideologically similar elites. If one identifies oneself as a conservative, it is not enough simply to average the views of Pat Robertson and Steve Forbes. Within every ideological camp, there are deep divisions on important issues that make it difficult for citizens to learn and adopt consistent views.

More generally, elites model attitudes that dismiss alternative points of view, and they pass this extremism down to citizens who might otherwise prefer a more balanced policy position. This problem becomes acute when citizens seek to understand the larger public good. Ideological filtering of elite messages does not help a citizen develop a broad public perspective on current issues. Such a viewpoint would listen to and incorporate diverse viewpoints and seek out common ground upon which all parties can stand. Citizens cannot develop an inclusive public voice if they systematically dismiss ideologically divergent views.[17]

Despite these limitations, there is still value in picking up "cues" from ideological elites. There are simply too many issues for average citizens to study and develop nuanced views on every policy debate. Identifying oneself with a liberal or conservative ideology and adopting the views of corresponding elites has its hazards, but it does permit a busy citizen to take strong positions on complex issues. So long as citizens must make a wide range of political choices, such cue-taking is an attractive alternative to exhausting research or studied indifference.

HOW VOTERS EVALUATE CANDIDATES

Just as citizens have difficulty developing well-informed and coherent policy views, they also face a serious challenge when asked to make voting decisions. The popular science-fiction television program *The X-Files* ends its opening montage with the now-famous phrase, "The truth is out there." For most elections, this is the case. A diligent voter with unlimited resources and cognitive abilities can find out which candidate will best represent his or her interests. Discovering the "truth" about candidates is just a matter of time and effort. But learning enough information about every viable candidate in every competitive race would take a considerable effort and a very large stretch of time. On a typical even-year general election ballot, voters often have over a dozen elections to consider. The high-profile races—president, governor, and Congress—are followed by elections for secretary of state, the state legislature, judgeships, county and city positions, school board seats, and anything and everything else down to the most obscure local offices. In many states, one can add to those offices a list of referenda, initiatives, and other ballot measures.

To undertake the study of each election would require both skill and will. Research skills would be necessary to reach a broad range of information sources about the candidates, and intellectual and political talents would enable a voter to decode and process the information obtained. No voter would put those skills to such hard use, however, if he or she did not also have the conviction that doing so would prove useful. Returning to the psychological concepts introduced in chapter 2, a voter would need enough self-efficacy to believe that he or she can competently perform exhaustive candidate evaluations, an expectation that the research will result in correct evaluations, and the confidence that fellow voters will be able to do the same. Underlying those beliefs, to overcome the voter's awareness of the low probability of his or her vote influencing the election's result, there must also be a driving sense of duty or a powerful concern about its outcome. Few voters have the necessary constellation of abilities, beliefs, and motivation to study the candidates on their ballot tirelessly in this way.

RETROSPECTIVE VOTING

Nonetheless, voters do attempt to make candidate evaluations, and how they reach those imperfect judgments varies considerably from one election to the next. The most widely studied race of them all—the presidential election—appears to trigger a special form of candidate evaluation. In presidential elections, citizens often engage in what Morris Fiorina has called "retrospective voting." Many Americans evaluate presidential incumbents based on the actual condition of the nation. In addition to taking into account candidate issue stands and their promises for the future, voters take a hard look at what they have experienced under the president's administration before deciding whether to reelect.[18] To take an extreme example, an event such as the Great Depression can doom a president's chances of reelection no matter how artful a dodger that politician may be. Though much modern presidential advertising threatens to mislead or even deceive unwary voters, it appears that the electorate selects presidents partly based on the state of the economy, among other "hard data." To paraphrase the famous sign posted in the Clinton campaign headquarters in 1992, it is, indeed, the economy, stupid.

Once again, such voting behavior is the exception. Fiorina argues that the retrospective voting model does not work very well outside of the presidential election. In his view, the model's weakness stems from the decline of political parties in America. He cites the example of the 1978 elections, before which the Democratic Party held power in both the White House and on Capitol Hill. In that year's congressional elections, voters' ratings of Democratic incumbents depended "only weakly and erratically" on perceptions of government's success at addressing "inflation, unemployment, or anything else of a programmatic nature."[19]

More important, crude retrospective voting is usually an ineffective method of candidate evaluation. If a voter looks at the condition of the local or national economy and judges candidates on that basis, the voter is using an objective but not necessarily relevant piece of information. Forces beyond the control of public officials cause most economic shifts, and an incumbent may deserve no credit or blame for one's fortunes. Presidents *can* have a noticeable short-term economic impact, and economists have named such election-year tinkering "the political business cycle." If successful, the president might trigger a brief spurt of economic growth, but voting based on that short-term change would be a mistake.

Even when voters more broadly judge the incumbent's overall performance, few know much about the actual performance of most of their public officials. Some voters may judge presidents based on overall economic trends, but how many voters have solid indicators of the performance of state legislators, judges, school board members, and secretaries of state?[20] A study of the perceptions of city and county services in Kentucky found evidence of considerable error in citizen evaluations of the local government: citizens sometimes associated nongovernmental functions with public institutions, they sometimes attributed functions to the wrong institution, and they often failed to recognize some of the functions that local government performed.[21] A study of gubernatorial elections found similar signs of misjudgment: idiosyncratic voter *perceptions* of the economy significantly influenced vote choices, but there was no relationship between *actual* economic indicators and electoral outcomes.[22]

Nonetheless, there is evidence that voters sometimes make accurate connections between legislators' actions and real short-term policy outcomes. The congressional scholar Douglas Arnold describes these linkages in detail in *The Logic of Congressional Action.* In Arnold's view, a representative's action is "traceable" when "a citizen can plausibly trace an observed effect first back to a governmental action and then back to a representative's individual contribution." Relatively few effects are traceable; most go unnoticed by stakeholders, have multiple interconnected causes, or have little visible impact on individual constituents. With the aid of concerned interest groups, however, citizens do sometimes trace connections between individual representatives and specific outcomes. This potential for citizen oversight prevents career-minded legislators from enacting disastrous policies that would cause unnecessary and immediate harm to their constituents.[23]

Unfortunately, Arnold points out how this same process results in the avoidance of good legislation and the passage of unsound bills. Because citizens only notice short-term negative impacts on their own lives, "legislators' fear of retrospective voting impels them to avoid . . . politically infeasible policies," including some proposals that would produce good long-term outcomes. Instead, legislators look for "politically attractive policies" that appear to have the same benefits (in the short run) but "spread the costs more widely, impose them as later-order effects, or push them further into the future." When casting about for such an alternative, representatives sometimes run into "politically compelling policies" whose "intended effects are popular, irrespective of whether the proposed means will really achieve those ends." Meanwhile, legislators tend to avoid "politically repellent options" because citizens either fail to see how the instruments could bring about the desired effects (e.g., subtle economic incentive mechanisms) or provide benefits only to disliked or marginalized social groups. Overall, "to the extent that citizens are poor policy analysts, they may obtain policy instruments they favor but fail to get the policy outcomes they really want because their chosen instruments are incapable of producing the desired effect."[24]

In sum, retrospective voting does occur in relatively high-profile elections. At first, this approach to electoral decision making appears to fit the ideal model outlined in chapter 2: voters assess the performance of incumbents and reward only those who serve the public's interest. As it is practiced, though, retrospective voting is a flawed and even counterproductive method of candidate evaluation. Those voters who do make cognitive connections from the past (objective macroeconomic indicators, personal economic experiences, and other perceived indicators of incumbent performance) in their voting choices often make faulty and unreliable linkages. Retrospective voters often misjudge short-term impacts, misplace responsibility for those outcomes, and overlook long-term impacts. As a result, these voters routinely misjudge incumbents' ability and willingness to represent their interests in office. Candidate selection errors are even more likely when retrospective voting based on incumbent performance becomes "a choice for or against the incumbent" without regard to the challenger.[25] If a voter knows nothing of the challenger in a race, simply "throwing out the bum" becomes a dangerous gamble.

IDEOLOGY, PARTISANSHIP, AND COGNITIVE SHORTCUTS

To move beyond such simplistic candidate selection methods, some American voters turn to ideology. A small portion of the electorate evaluates candidates through indirect sources of information about their policy views. For example, a sophisticated voter might know that the Center for Tax Responsibility shares his or her views on public spending. The voter can then evaluate an incumbent based upon the rating that the center gives to that representative's voting record. Though the voter still does not know the incumbent's voting record, the voter may infer with confidence that a high rating of the incumbent by the center signals that the representative acted in sync with the voter's own policy preferences. Such inferences are quite logical, and an ideologically self-aware voter familiar with a political organization's rating system has as good a chance as any of making sensible candidate evaluations. When such voters have adequate information and a viable opponent to consider, their behavior comes close to the ideal presented in chapter 2. If a representative's constituents have a clear ideological bent and obtain solid information about all candidates, these voters have the potential for successful electoral rejection of incumbents who stray too far from their ideologically defined interests. That threat, in turn, might win such a constituency sound representation in government.

Such a combination of factors is rare, however. Even when there are alternative candidates to consider, limited political sophistication, low motivation, and citizens' self-doubt about their abilities and influence lead the vast majority of voters to make inadequate candidate evaluations, if any at all. Those who choose to vote use more radical "cognitive shortcuts" to translate small amounts of information (of uncertain accuracy) into final judgments.

Samuel Popkin, a polling consultant and public opinion scholar, has examined these short cuts carefully in relation to presidential campaigns. One of the most commonly used metaphors for such thinking is the Drunkard's Search: when a drunken man stumbles outside of a bar at midnight and drops his keys, he drags himself over to the streetlight to look for them; the keys probably fell elsewhere, but he can only see the pavement that's under the light. Thus, rather than trying to piece together all the information they have obtained, voters make judgments based on the one or two pieces of information in which they have some confidence. Popkin stresses the importance of personal information in a presidential race, but the metaphor works equally well for other salient facts that a voter might glean from an election—or even from the ballot itself.[26]

Many political observers argue that one particular fact—a candidate's party—is enough information to make an informed choice about which candidate will best represent a voter's interests. Though relatively few voters have strong ideological orientations, as many as three-quarters of the electorate identify with either the Democratic or the Republican Party. For example, in the 1998 House elections, 73 percent of voters described themselves as either Democrats or Republicans. Eighty-nine percent of Democratic voters backed Democrats, and 91 percent of Republican voters backed Republicans. Nonaligned voters, by contrast, split their vote almost evenly between the two parties. Statistics for House elections from 1980 to 1996 show a consistent pattern of from 77 to 92 percent of partisans voting for their party's candidate.[27] Numerous other studies have found that political partisanship is the most powerful predictor of voting choices in a wide range of partisan general elections in the United States. For example, voter partisanship predicts roughly 50 percent of all voting in the presidential election.[28] Highly sophisticated partisans sometimes even use party-identification cues in nonpartisan elections by reading party "voting guides" or "candidate slates."

Nonetheless, both the prevalence and value of partisan voting cues are overestimated. After having chosen to vote Republican, for example, voters are more likely to identify themselves as Republican in response to an exit poll. Moreover, some voters' party identities and voting choices match only coincidentally; they may cast their votes and adopt a party identity based on the individual characteristics of the candidate.[29] Even if voters were to choose at random between Democrats and Republicans, half of all partisans would support candidates of their own party anyway. Finally, citizens who do not vote in congressional elections (if in any elections at all) have weaker partisan loyalties. Focusing on the partisanship of likely voters is, therefore, misleading.

In any case, there is considerable evidence that the power of the partisan cue is declining. After studying the past forty years of party politics in the United States, Martin Wattenberg concluded, "Once central and guiding forces in American electoral behavior, the parties are currently perceived with almost complete indifference by a large proportion of the population." Consistent with this view, surveys conducted in 1994, 1996, and 1997 have found that between two-thirds and three-quarters of Americans report that they regularly vote for candidates of parties other than their own in at least one race per election.[30]

Table 1 shows, however, that over the past quarter-century, strong partisans of the two major parties have never made up more than a third of the voting-age population. The table also shows that the percentage of partisans in the general population has changed little during that same period. Some observers have argued that despite the scarcity of self-identified party loyalists, independents are actually far more rare. In this view, "pure independents" make up only 10–15 percent of the electorate, because most independents actually "lean" toward one of the two major parties. Self-reported voting data from 1962 to 1990 show that these "leaners" were no less partisan than "weak" Democrats and Republicans. When viewed from another standpoint, however, it is just as noteworthy that over one-quarter of "weak" partisans vote against their party in U.S. House elections. Whether this makes the weak partisans independent or the leaning independents partisan is a definitional question. The fact remains that only a fraction of the electorate consistently vote for just one party.[31]

One example of the decline of political party identification is the case of Maine, which some political observers view as a bellwether state. In the 1998 election, the Democratic Party campaigned vigorously in the gubernatorial election, but not with an eye toward recapturing the governor's seat. Late polls showed the Democratic candidate, Tom Connolly, with just 6 percent of the vote, well behind the Republican candidate and the independent incumbent, Governor Angus King Jr. As the

TABLE 1

PERCENTAGE OF VOTING-AGE U.S. CITIZENS WITH A
STRONG PARTY IDENTIFICATION, 1972–1994

	Strong Democrat (%)	Strong Republican (%)	Total Strong Partisans (%)
1972	15	10	25
1980	18	9	27
1984	17	12	29
1986	18	11	29
1988	18	14	32
1990	20	10	30
1992	18	11	29
1994	15	16	31

SOURCE: U.S. Bureau of the Census, *Statistical Abstract of the United States, 1997,* table 461, based on surveys conducted by the Center for Political Studies, University of Michigan, Ann Arbor.

New York Times explained prior to election day, "If Mr. Connolly does not pull at least 5 percent of the vote on Nov. 3, under Maine law the party will lose its official recognition," and it "would not be able to hold a primary and officially nominate candidates" in the year 2000.[32] In the end, the Democrats got 12 percent of the vote in the gubernatorial election, while the Republicans managed to win only 19 percent.

Maine's successful independent governor has inspired candidates and voters in other states to abandon the major parties. The most surprising example of this influence was the successful 1998 campaign of the wrestler-turned-governor Jesse "The Body" Ventura in the historically liberal state of Minnesota. In a three-way open-seat race against nondescript Republican and Democratic challengers, Ventura persuaded just over a third of Minnesotans to support his Reform Party candidacy. The Minnesota electorate that supported Ventura did not do so because of his political party per se. Rather, voters largely ignored his Reform Party affiliation and embraced him because his personal history, campaign style, and rhetoric were so different from those of traditional Democrats and Republicans.[33]

Not only is support for the two major parties declining, but partisanship is also most common among those voters who are the most knowledgeable and ideological. Strong Democrats are the most liberal voters, while strong Republicans are the most conservative, and this relationship is even stronger for those voters with the most political knowledge.[34] For example, a national survey found that only 32 percent of partisans successfully distinguished the two major parties' positions on four out of four major policy issues. The 37 percent of partisans who distinguished the parties on only one or none gain less information from a candidate's party membership because they are not entirely sure what such membership implies.[35] Since the most knowledgeable voters are the only ones who often make sophisticated ideological judgments about candidates, partisan voting cues are most readily available for those voters who need them the least.

Making matters worse, those less sophisticated voters who rely upon partisan cues are more likely to have incidental party affiliations. For most Americans, political party membership is not a "fundamental belief . . . but rather an inherited trait."[36] When a person votes for Democrats because his or her parents voted for Democrats, that voting pattern represents the person's actual concerns only to the extent that child and parent share similar values, circumstances, and knowledge. Historical party realignments, such as the African-American shift toward the Democratic Party during the Civil Rights era, show that people can change party membership in response to changing party platforms or shifts in voters' own attitudes. Nonetheless, party identity remains stable for most Americans regardless of changing personal and political circumstances.[37] Party membership influences other attitudes and candidate evaluations far more often than these beliefs influence membership.[38]

Even if a large proportion of the electorate do rely on partisan cues when making voting choices, this dependence is often counterproductive. Recalling the general model of representative democracy in chapter 2, one of the primary purposes of elections is to give an electorate the opportunity to reject an incumbent who has failed to represent its interests. When voters base reelection decisions entirely on the candidates' party membership, they necessarily overlook other information about the incumbent and challenger. Though publicly available, an official's voting record often goes unnoticed. Thus, a congressional district populated by liberal Democrats might consistently reelect a conservative Democrat over a liberal Republican because the former shares the majority's party identity. More generally, voters' reliance on partisan cues permits representatives to act against their constituents' interests. If a single representative consistently deviates from the party line even on roll-call votes, the party may sabotage that particular incumbent's reelection bid, but if the party as a whole violates its membership's interests, such deviation is hard for an individual voter to detect, let alone deter. Aside from egregious violations of voters' concerns, representatives have considerable latitude so long as partisan voting predominates. "Although cases are known where a single wrong vote led to defeat, it is by no means easy to nail members with their voting records," notes Gary Jacobson, one of the most prominent congressional scholars.[39]

The use of "open primaries" worsens the situation by permitting voters to cross party lines in the primary election. In states such as California, primary voters select one candidate from among the entire pool of candidates in each race, and candidates advance to the general election if they win more votes than any other in the same party. Voters can support Democrats in some primary races and Republicans in others, regardless of their own party affiliation. Californians embraced this electoral reform as offering "more choice" in the primaries, but the system can easily be abused to select general election candidates out of sync with their own party. The candidacy of an unopposed Democratic incumbent might, for example, encourage Democratic voters to support the most incompetent or unpopular Republican in the primary. With Republicans divided among a group of candidates, this Democratic voting bloc can thus bring victory in the primary to the worst Republican choice. Alternatively, Democratic activists in a strong Republican district can use this system to support a liberal Republican in the primary, leaving Republican voters with nothing but liberals in the general election.[40] When voters use a candidate's party as a shortcut to evaluation, they risk serious misjudgment, and the open primary makes the risk even greater.

A more serious problem with partisan cueing lies in the limited range of parties Americans can choose from today. In most races in the United States, voters must choose either a Democrat or a Republican. In a satire of this situation, the animated television program *The Simpsons* imagined what would happen if the Democratic and Republican candidates in the 1996 presidential election were actually Kang and Kodos, tentacled space reptiles seeking to conquer Earth. On the eve of election day, Homer Simpson unmasks the aliens before a large crowd assembled on the steps of the nation's capitol. Unperturbed, one of the aliens explains, "It makes no difference which one of us you vote for. Either way, your planet is doomed. Doomed!" In reply to this boast, a bold spectator declares, "Well, I believe I'll vote for a third-party candidate." Kang and Kodos writhe and laugh maniacally. "Go ahead," they retort.

"Throw your vote away!" In the closing scene, legions of human slaves toil to build a giant ray gun, while an alien administrator bellows, "All hail President Kang!"

Though the Democratic and Republican parties often see eye to eye on fundamental economic class issues, they differ in many important respects. Party allegiance is a meaningful choice between the ideological left-to-center and center-to-right, and the party unity displayed in roll-call votes in Congress has increased in recent decades.[41] If party identity is becoming more ideologically grounded, as some election scholars claim, this trend would result in more meaningful partisan voting.[42]

Nonetheless, reliance upon just two parties makes a citizen's choices extremely narrow. Beyond the factions within parties, there are many ideological identities that cross party lines. The Libertarian Party, the Reform Party, and other independent and multifaceted parties provide other choices, but the reality of winner-take-all elections is that those parties have few opportunities to elect their candidates to public office. Voters can register with and vote for a third party to play the role of spoiler, as the Green Party has done in New Mexico, but taken as a whole, third parties play only a marginal role in U.S. politics.[43] In sum, because two choices obscure the real diversity of meaningful viewpoints among which one might otherwise choose, parties only crudely represent Americans' concerns.

The ultimate failing of partisan cue reliance, however, is an inescapable feature of conventional American elections. Simply put, partisan cues are useless in nonpartisan elections and party primaries. When choosing among finalists in a nonpartisan general election, less sophisticated voters usually remain unaware of the candidates' party loyalties, or the candidates may belong to the same party. Innumerable political observers have declared the party voting cue to be the connection between public preferences and political representation, yet no such connection exists in numerous local and statewide nonpartisan races for judgeships, executive offices, councils, and boards. Though nonpartisan systems are often designed to make local government "less political" and avoid graft and corruption, the net result is the removal of the one cue that most voters rely on to distinguish among competing candidates. For this very reason, many political observers oppose the very concept of nonpartisan elections, let alone changing some local elections from partisan to nonpartisan.[44]

For the same reason, it turns out that *every* election suffers from dependence on partisan cues. When two Democrats face off against each other for a chance to challenge a Republican incumbent in the general election, partisanship is of no use in judging their relative merits. In this sense, every winner-take-all system using a partisan general election still requires a choice among candidates of the same party in the primary. In districts and locales where the vast majority of residents belong to a single party, overreliance on the partisan cue is particularly hazardous. The domination of one party in the general election means that the outcome of the election is actually determined in that party's primary election. For that crucial decision, voters must look past party membership for guidance. If most voters have become accustomed to relying on partisan cues to choose candidates, they will lose their bearings in primaries and vote blindly or simply abstain.[45]

One might counter that political parties manage their own primaries and indirectly ensure that the most representative party member goes on to the general election. The problem with this argument is that it is false. That may have been the case at one time, but incumbents are now stronger than the local parties. Renomination and reelection depend upon the decisions of the incumbent, over whom the party has precious little control.[46] "Few congressional candidates find opposition from the local party leaders to be a significant handicap; neither is their support very helpful," Gary Jacobson observes.[47] In other words, party primaries are often critical decisions for voters, yet overreliance on partisan cues makes these choices extremely difficult.

In sum, relatively few voters use their ideology as a guide when making voting decisions. Many more voters use partisan cues as a guide to voting. By doing so, they hope to overcome the limitations of their own underdeveloped interests. If a voter decides that the Democratic or Republican Party adequately represents his or her interests, candidate party membership can then be used to guide otherwise complex voting decisions. The use of these cues may be in decline, but partisan voting has limited value, in any case. Strong partisan loyalty can actually obscure poor representation by diverting attention from the actual views of candidates and the performance of incumbents. The limited two-party system in the United States also makes it difficult to represent diverse public viewpoints in partisan voting. When the diversity of viewpoints on current issues is condensed into a binary choice, many ideas and concerns get lost in the process. Finally, partisan cues are useless in nonpartisan and primary elections. Since election to nearly every office requires winning either a party primary or a nonpartisan election, reliance on party membership as a voting guide is inadequate.

POLITICAL CONVERSATION AS A PERSONAL SHORTCUT

Despite their drawbacks, partisan cues (and ideological cues) are appealing, because they give voters a way to make seemingly sophisticated choices without tremendous effort. What voters need is a more reliable cognitive shortcut to use during campaigns. If voters banded together into small groups, they might be able to pool their limited knowledge into relatively nuanced judgments. Like-minded citizens could compare their candidate preferences, and citizens with divergent views could consider one another's viewpoints. Even relatively passive and uninterested voters could use the summary judgments of these localized reference groups to make voting decisions. Such a system of information distribution, deliberation, and collective decision making could not only improve the quality of individual voting choices but also the likelihood of successful collective rejection of unrepresentative elected officials.

Many voters do, in fact, make "collective" judgments, whether as a couple, a family, or a group of friends.[48] National surveys conducted in 1981 and 1990 found that roughly 70 percent of Americans "often" or at least "sometimes" discuss political matters when they get together with friends.[49] One study of voters in the vicinity of Albany, New York, prior to the 1998 presidential election found that 88 percent had discussed the election in the past week. On average, people reported talking about the campaign with seven or eight people during that week.[50]

The frequency with which spouses, families, and housemates vote together has led many political campaigns to target voters "by household." When a precinct walker or a telephone survey interviewer learns that one adult in a household is favorable toward a particular candidate, the campaign then attributes that preference to all voters in that residence. Campaigns are wise to aggregate voters within households: families do tend to vote together, because there is tremendous political influence within typical American families.[51]

Do these social networks of political influence result in more informed candidate evaluations? Perhaps campaign conversations can make what Zaller calls an "unsophisticated" voter into a sophisticated one. Recall that in Zaller's model of public opinion formation, a sophisticated voter is distinguished by the ability to filter out messages that are contrary to his or her preexisting ideology. Regular political conversations between sophisticated voters and less sophisticated ones permit the latter to substitute a social sieve for a cognitive filter of mass-mediated messages.[52]

Research suggests that this portrait is only half-true. It is certainly the case that much political conversation flows directly from the media: a recent focus-group study found that more than a quarter of all statements in an open-ended discussion had direct or indirect references to both factual news programming and entertainment media. A study of the 1992 Pittsburgh newspaper strike also demonstrates a relationship between mass media coverage of elections and the quantity of political conversation: the strike "limited voters' exposure to media reports concerning the local U.S. House races, and interpersonal discussion of those elections declined in response."[53]

Though conversations do transmit media messages, the interpersonal relay messengers are not necessarily the most sophisticated voters. The most careful modern study of political conversation suggests that the people who most influence their fellow citizens are distinguished, not by their political knowledge and expertise, but rather by their mere *interest* in politics. Even if the most influential political conversants were politically sophisticated, the value of their influence is questionable, because they are noted only for their ability to filter out ideologically dissimilar views. Political deliberation requires the consideration of alternative views, but research suggests that the most influential discussants are those who accurately understand that their conversation partners share views the same as their own.[54]

Despite its limitations as a means of reaching sophisticated candidate evaluations and collective electoral action, campaign conversation has at least one redeeming quality. As a modest form of public deliberation, it motivates people to get more involved in elections and, specifically, to take the time to vote.[55] At the very least, crude candidate evaluations combined with the act of voting come closer to attempted electoral rejection than the passive act of nonvoting.

VOTER SOPHISTICATION AND ELECTION VISIBILITY

The preceding discussions have demonstrated the different ways in which voters can make candidate evaluations. Whether a voter primarily considers a candidate's past record, ideological commitments, party membership, or other characteristics depends upon some of the variables presented above, such as the voter's ideology and party identity, as well as the type of election (nonpartisan, party primary, or partisan). Two more variables play an important role in influencing candidate evaluations. The first consideration is a voter's *political sophistication*.

As defined by Robert Luskin, a person is politically sophisticated "to the extent to which his or her political cognitions are numerous, cut a wide substantive swath, and are highly organized. . . . A political belief system that is particularly large, wide-ranging, and organized is an ideology."[56] The more politically sophisticated a person becomes, the more likely it is that he or she will pay close attention to elections, search out diverse information sources, and critically examine messages received.

A highly sophisticated or "politically aware" voter is more able and inclined to think *and vote* based upon complex information about candidates in an election. Moderately sophisticated voters seek out a modest amount of political information and make some effort to relate it to what they know about political parties and their own interests. The least sophisticated voters only learn about candidates passively, when the candidates reach out to them through television, radio, and other media, and these voters do little to process the information they receive. Using data on political ideology and involvement and the category definitions presented above, roughly a third of voters fall into each of these three categories.[57]

How a voter of low or high political sophistication evaluates candidates also depends upon the nature of the campaign itself. In particular, elections vary in the overall intensity of candidates' campaigns and the media coverage of those campaigns. At the high end of the spectrum is the presidential election, to which there is no comparison. Every day for weeks, if not months, voters are pelted in a hailstorm of information and opinion about the presidential candidates. The intensity of the presidential campaign is so great that it saturates the consciousness of even the most reclusive voter, and only a few high-visibility races for governor or the U.S. Senate compare to it in intensity.

Because of its importance and stature, the presidential election has attracted the most attention from scholars of voting. The most influential works on voting have studied presidential elections, and this narrow focus may have caused past research to overgeneralize from the one anomalous election to others.[58]

Campaigns of moderate intensity, such as typical gubernatorial or U.S. Senate elections, cost far less than a presidential race. Spending only a million dollars or so, a candidate can usually make voters aware that an election is taking place with modest television and radio advertising and a professional campaign organization. In a small town, just a few thousand dollars and a large grassroots effort can create a campaign of sufficient visibility that voters know the candidates by name when they arrive at the polls or fill out their absentee ballots. Political scientists normally call these "low-information" races because relatively few political messages reach voters.[59]

But there is a stratum of elections beneath even the so-called "low-information" races, and here lie most elections for public office. The vast majority of election research has focused on presidential and congressional elections, but those elections are for only one of the over 80,000 governments across the United States. Most races for office in the 50 state governments are very low-profile, as are the vast majority of elections to office in over 3,000 counties, 19,000 municipalities, 16,000 townships, 14,000 school districts, and over 33,000 other special districts across the United States[60] Most voters are hardly aware of these elections and may not even know a single fact about the candidates until they see names and other details on the ballot. In Texas judicial races, for example, roughly four-fifths of voters could not recognize the names of major candidates just minutes after voting. In 1976, because he shared a familiar surname—Yarbrough—with a former senator and gubernatorial candidate, voters unwittingly elected to the Texas Supreme Court a candidate who claimed he "took his instructions from God."[61] The lowest of the low-intensity races even surprise some voters, who proclaim, "I didn't know there was an election" for the state legislature, county council, municipal judgeship, or school board. As Harry S Truman once remarked about a local elected office in Pittsburgh, "What in the hell's a prothonotary?"[62]

Local representatives, as well as the more obscure state elected officials, barely make a blip on the average citizen's radar. As James Fishkin muses, "I know almost nothing about most of the 200 to 350 people [who represent me], and they certainly know almost nothing of me."[63] Public awareness of these elections is sometimes so low that turnout is under 20 percent or even below 10 percent. Capitalizing on this fact, the Christian Coalition began targeting local elections in 1990 because it knew that a small, activist core could prove decisive in them. Victory required few votes, and "stealth candidates" could win support without voters knowing what special interests they actually represented.[64]

Table 2 brings together voter sophistication and campaign visibility to demonstrate how candidate evaluation varies depending on these two variables, plus the partisan nature of voters and elections.[65] The table identifies the primary evaluation method of different combinations of voters and elections. The four evaluation methods can be summarized as decision-making shortcuts used by voters to select candidates:

TABLE 2

HOW A VOTER'S MAIN CANDIDATE EVALUATION METHOD
DEPENDS ON CAMPAIGN AND VOTER CHARACTERISTICS

	Type of voter			
Type of election	Independent, unaware voter	Independent, aware voter	Partisan, unaware voter	Partisan, aware voter
Low-visibility nonpartisan/ primary	Name	Name	Name	Name
Low-visibility partisan	Name	Name	Party	Party
High-visibility nonpartisan/ primary	Media	Ideology	Media	Ideology
High-visibility partisan	Media	Ideology	Party	Ideology

NOTE: The cells in the body of the table correspond to four evaluation methods:

Name	vote for the candidate with the more familiar name and positive personal attributions
Media	average all free/paid media messages and vote for the candidate with the most positive rating
Party	vote for the candidate who shares voter's party identity
Ideology	average all free/paid media messages produced by like-minded ideological elites and vote for the candidate with the most positive rating

1.   Name: If little is known about the candidates, vote for the candidate with the more familiar name. If some positive and negative personal information is known about candidates (e.g., incumbent went to the same school as the voter or dresses poorly), average those considerations and choose the candidate with the best average rating.

2.   Media: Average all media messages (e.g., campaign ads, newspaper/television campaign coverage) received and choose the candidate with the best average rating. All messages are treated as being equally credible and relevant.

3.   Party: Choose the candidate who shares the same party affiliation as the voter.

4.   Ideology: Excluding messages provided by elites with a dissimilar ideology (e.g., ads produced by ideologically dissimilar organizations, endorsements by ideologically dissimilar newspaper editors), average all media messages received and choose the candidate with the best average rating.

For ease of presentation, table 2 includes a few simplifications. The figure substitutes "awareness" for political sophistication, and it collapses awareness into two categories—unaware and aware. Table 2 also collapses ideological and political sophistication into one variable. Voters with high political awareness are presumed to both attend to political messages and to approach them with a clear ideological orientation. In reality, most voters falling into one category also fall into the other, but a minority of ideologues lack political sophistication and vice versa. For the same reason, campaign intensity is collapsed into two categories—low- and high-visibility. The dividing line between those categories is, roughly, a moderate-intensity congressional election.

In a typical low-visibility nonpartisan or primary election, the Name model best describes candidate evaluation. Because they have no party affiliation, independent voters also select candidates using Name in low-visibility partisan elections. If asked to explain why they voted the way they did, these voters might say they "preferred" their candidate of choice, without any deeper explanation, or they might admit that they simply chose the one candidate whose name they recognized or whose hand they had shaken.[66] In a high-visibility election, independent voters with low political awareness use the Media voting method because they receive a significant number of mass media and advertising messages about candidates.[67] Low-awareness partisan voters also use the Media evaluation method in high-visibility party primaries and nonpartisan races. Having received some relevant media messages, many of these voters will be able to recall more substantial arguments for and against candidates; some may even be able to mention key candidate actions and use those as a partial basis for voting.[68] Party is the primary evaluation method for partisan voters in partisan races, with one exception: partisan voters with high political awareness use their ideological sophistication to filter media messages and identify the optimal candidate.[69] Highly aware independent and partisan voters use this Ideology method in every high-visibility election, although true independents have considerable difficulty identifying like-minded ideological elites in highly polarized media environments.

Table 2 is a crude summary portrait of candidate evaluation, but it makes clear two of the central points in this chapter. First, only partisan voters with high political awareness use party or ideology to evaluate candidates in three of the four types of elections. If only 20 percent of the public is ideological, and 20 percent of those are independent, roughly 15 percent of the electorate votes using partisan or ideological cues for most types of elections. Second, only high-visibility partisan elections trigger ideological or partisan voting for three of the four types of voters. Not only are these elections the exception, but they are nearly all coupled with party primaries in which only a fraction of the electorate makes ideological candidate evaluations. In sum, most voters in most elections are making simplistic candidate evaluations.

POWERFUL INCUMBENTS AND SCARCE OPPONENTS

The difficulty of successful electoral rejection stems not just from ill-defined interests and crude candidate evaluations, but also from the limited pool of candidates requiring evaluation. Imagine that a relatively liberal Republican voter learns from liberal ideological elites that people with liberal values should support Medicare, cuts in defense spending, and a progressive tax system. Having clarified some of her basic policy concerns, this earnest citizen might exercise her voice and ask for these policies from a conservative incumbent who represents her in Congress. Rebuffed by the incumbent, the citizen then prepares to become a voter exercising her right to attempt electoral rejection by studying the candidates opposing her Republican incumbent. This story might end any number of ways, but it is likely that this citizen-voter will end up frustrated by the range of alternative candidates available. In some stories, she is shocked to discover that there *is* no opponent in the primary or general. Or perhaps the incumbent has only a more conservative opponent in the Republican primary, or the Democratic nominee opposing the incumbent has views resembling those of the incumbent. Or, most likely of all, the Democratic primary election results in an opponent who is neither politically viable nor capable. Even if the voter had, in theory, all of the skills necessary to recognize her (and the larger public's) genuine interests and to evaluate competing candidates, she may find herself with no real choice.

Recall that in chapter 2, a necessary precondition of successful collective rejection of unrepresentative incumbents was the existence of alternatives. In the case of elections, this means that (a) one or more electoral opponents must have a chance of winning the election, (b) opponents' policy positions must differ from those of the incumbent, and (c) opponents must have at least minimal competence to pursue those policies in office. America has a long-standing tradition of debate and conflict, and its democratic political philosophy and institutions are primarily adversarial in nature.[70] Nonetheless, many factors contribute to a relatively shallow pool of candidates willing to run against incumbents at all levels of government.

One reason that potential candidates often decline to oppose an elected official is that they dislike the personal criteria by which candidates are judged. For the highest offices, media coverage of campaigns devotes considerable attention to uncovering the "character" of candidates by scrutinizing their personal lives. Tempting targets, such as Gary Hart and Bill Clinton, have habituated the media to looking for personal weaknesses while covering the candidates in presidential primaries. Both the Democratic and Republican parties have been frustrated by the unwillingness of possible candidates to step into the political arena for this reason. Though the media pay scant attention to the personalities and family lives of lower-level candidates, there remains a widespread perception that campaigning for any political office exposes one to inappropriate scrutiny.

For similar reasons, fierce negative campaigning also has turned away potential candidates. Citizens contemplating a career in public service cannot help but notice the harsh television ads and mudslinging mailers exchanged by candidates in other races. Though a low-intensity campaign against an incumbent might never prompt such an attack on the challenger, prospective candidates must still weigh the odds that they will be unfairly attacked, or that their past missteps will be broadcast for all to see. Whether running for federal, state, or local office, the fear of becoming the target of a negative campaign makes qualified citizens wary of seeking election.[71]

But even angelic candidates and thick-skinned sinners avoid running for office because of the long odds of defeating an incumbent. By virtue of their position, elected officials have numerous advantages over challengers. Members of Congress, for instance, can send mail to constituents without charge. They have travel and communication allowances, constant invitations to public events, regular media exposure, a district office, and paid staff.[72] Even before a campaign begins, the electorate is normally quite familiar with the incumbent's name, while unable to recognize that of the challenger. An aggressive campaign can reduce but not remove that advantage. After the 1990 and 1994 House elections, for instance, an average of 91 percent of voters reported having had some contact (from a piece of mail to a handshake) with incumbents, but only 40 percent reported contact with a challenger. Eighteen percent said they had met the incumbent, compared to only 3 percent who had met the challenger.[73] Given the frequency with which

name recognition, vague favorability, and similar superficial considerations influence elections, the sheer visibility of an incumbent is a high
hurdle for a challenger to jump.

The greatest advantage of incumbency, however, is fund-raising ability. The rising price of seeking the presidency has received considerable
attention, but costs are climbing for other offices, as well. A tremendous amount of money has been spent on House and Senate races nationwide for decades, and the cost of election has continued to grow.
Candidates for the House and Senate spent $740 million dollars in the
1997–98 two-year election cycle. To make matters worse, Gary Jacobson explains, "a vastly disproportionate share of the growing pot of
campaign money has gone to incumbents and candidates for open
seats."[74]

The average cost of contested races is far more than even those figures would suggest. Some unopposed incumbents initially raise funds to
intimidate potential opponents and keep them off the ballot, but once
that task has been accomplished, "safe" incumbents raise relatively
little money. The bulk of fund-raising and spending occurs in the handful of competitive races across the country. To take an extreme example, in the 1996 race for the lone congressional seat for North
Dakota, one of the nation's least-populated states, with a relatively
small economy, the Democratic incumbent, Earl Pomeroy, spent
$971,000 defeating the $434,000 campaign of his Republican opponent (55 percent to 43 percent). High-profile competitive races involve
much greater sums. When Senator Jesse Helms, the long-time incumbent, fought off the challenge of Harvey Gantt in the 1996 North Carolina Senate election, Helms outspent his opponent by nearly two-to-
one, even though Gantt spent $8 million.[75]

The national trend of escalating campaign costs has parallels for
most state and local offices as well. In California, for example, it is now
common for candidates for the state legislature to spend as much, or
even more, than candidates for U.S. Congress in comparable districts.
New candidates for the California legislature now need to raise
$500,000, or possibly more, to compete against an incumbent. These
high stakes for state races led one Los Angeles Times reporter to note
that "even back-bench legislators attract $100,000 or more from single
sources."[76] In New Mexico, one of the poorest states in the United
States, candidates for the state legislature have in the past routinely run
for office on budgets under $15,000. In 1996, however, a highly com-
petitive Democratic primary set an ominous precedent, with three can-

didates spending over $60,000 apiece. Though running for high-profile office usually costs more, the price tag on relatively minor state and local races is getting higher with every election cycle.[77]

Aside from the daunting fund-raising requirements of an effective challenge, Gary Jacobson notes, the personal financial cost of running has escalated: "The investment of time and energy . . . required to run an all-out campaign is daunting. A serious House candidacy is a full-time job—with plenty of overtime. Most non-incumbents have to finance the campaign's start-up costs while forgoing income from their regular work for many months."[78]

The high personal and financial cost of campaigning has contributed to the dearth of candidates for public office. Surveying nine congressional districts in Tennessee in 1998, for example, the Associated Press reporter Rachel Zoll identified only one credible challenger. The 1997–98 Tennessee congressional delegation included five Republicans and four Democrats, reflecting the parity between the two parties statewide, and in the 1996 presidential election, President Clinton defeated Robert Dole in Tennessee by just two percentage points. Nonetheless, no Tennessee incumbent has lost reelection to the House since 1974, and the 1998 elections proved no exception. When Zoll asked local analysts to explain the lack of credible challengers, they gave two explanations: the "intensive and intrusive media attention" candidates receive and "the high cost of running."[79] Tennessee is no exception: the number of experienced challengers choosing to run against congressional incumbents has declined from 1950 to 1990.[80]

What is true for national races is also true in low-profile races. As James MacGregor Burns and his colleagues explain in their survey of state and local elections: "Getting good people to run for office is . . . a challenge. The spiraling cost of campaigns and the advantages enjoyed by incumbents have deterred many good potential candidates. Others are repelled by the nasty and negative tone of recent elections. Unless a democracy produces able citizens who are willing to run for office, it loses its ability to hold incumbents accountable."[81]

For these reasons, the opponents that incumbents face in both high- and low-profile races usually have serious liabilities. Some lack basic intellectual and political skills, and many more are political extremists. There is no way of preventing unqualified candidates from seeking local, state, and federal offices, but it is striking how often such candidates appear as the only opposition on the ballot. This problem of unchallenged incumbency is by no means new. Just one example among many was the candidacy of Tom Metzger as the Democratic nominee in a San Diego County congressional district twenty years ago. Metzger was the Democrats' standard-bearer because no other candidate dared oppose the incumbent. The Democratic Party gave so little attention to the race that it had failed to notice that Metzger was a neo-Nazi (he later became infamous nationally when he unsuccessfully defended himself against the charge of inciting racial violence in Oregon).

Although voters are asked to choose every year between well-qualified and politically distinct candidates, many of these elections turn out to be meaningless, because the challenger cannot compete against the well-funded incumbent. These challengers choose to run against the odds, but precious few ever manage to beat those odds. In partisan races in strong Democratic or Republican districts, challengers cannot overcome the unpopularity of their own party, and in more evenly matched districts, nonpartisan races, and primary elections, the incumbent derives a decisive advantage from name recognition and a larger advertising budget. The dramatic victories of underdog challengers make for good stories because they are the exception, but their occurrence in no way changes the overall pattern of uncompetitive elections.

There are situations in which voters have the luxury of choosing among equally qualified and viable candidates. A few incumbents inhabit volatile districts in which every new election is as stressful as the last: the late George Brown represented his southern California district in the House from 1972 to 1999, but he only managed to do so by fighting off one challenger after another. He won his 1996 reelection campaign with 50.5 percent of the vote, and he won with 51 percent in 1994.[82]

Most competitive races, though, feature no incumbent—either because one lost in the primary or because the incumbent has chosen to retire or run for another office instead. When these "open-seat races" take place in even marginally competitive districts, they often result in aggressive campaigns and even higher levels of candidate spending. For example, after Bill Bradley announced his retirement from the U.S. Senate, two New Jersey congressmen ran against one another in the 1996 general election. The Republican, Dick Zimmer, was pro-choice and moderate on many social issues, but he nonetheless clashed with his Democratic opponent, Robert Torricelli, on many issues. With each of the candidates spending over $8 million, neither had a clear financial edge, and after a hard-fought election, Torricelli won with 53 percent of the vote.[83] The central question, however, is whether voters have a realistic

TABLE 3
REELECTION RATES OF HOUSE AND SENATE CANDIDATES, 1972–1998

	Main Presidential Candidates	Percentage Reelected U.S. House of Representatives (%)	U.S. Senate (%)
1972	Nixon–McGovern	94	74
1974	—	88	85
1976	Ford–Carter	96	64
1978	—	94	60
1980	Carter–Reagan	91	55
1982	—	90	93
1984	Reagan–Mondale	96	90
1986	—	98	75
1988	Bush–Dukakis	98	85
1990	—	96	97
1992	Bush–Clinton–Perot	88	82
1994	—	90	92
1996	Clinton–Dole–Perot	94	91
1998	—	98	90
Average from 1972 to 1998		94	81

SOURCE: U.S. Bureau of the Census, *Statistical Abstract of the United States, 1997*, table 447. 1998 figures are calculated directly from 1998 election results. The percentages represent the number of incumbents who won both primary and general elections divided by the total number who ran for reelection.

chance of voting out of office an incumbent who is unresponsive to their voices. In open-seat races such as the Torricelli-Zimmer election, voters are selecting among new representatives, rather than judging the adequacy of an official's previous term in the same office. In this sense, such races are qualitatively different from the incumbent-challenger elections that I focus on throughout this book.

Together, these factors result in a very secure incumbency for most public officials. Periodically, there is a public cry of "Throw the bums out!" Ross Perot tried to ride such a wave of protest into the White House in 1992. The reality is that even such elections result in little turnover. In the case of Congress, for example, 88 percent of U.S. representatives and 82 percent of senators won reelection despite the cry for reform and new candidates from "outside the Beltway" (see table 3).[84] For the House, reelection rates since 1972 have never been below that mark, though the Senate had a period of turnover following

Watergate and leading up to the Reagan landslide of 1980. Even including this unusual period, reelection rates stand at an average of 94
percent in the House and 81 percent in the Senate. Whereas in the
1970s, voters "hated Congress but loved their own member," now
"voters hate incumbency but at least tolerate their incumbent."[85]

Upon closer inspection, reelection is even more of a certainty than
table 3 suggests. A few highly volatile congressional districts across the
country account for most of the turnover. Most representatives have
even higher probabilities of reelection, with 65–85 percent of House incumbents typically winning with at least 60 percent of the vote—a victory margin of 20 percent or greater. After studying the significance of
incumbency in 150 years of congressional races, John Alford and David
Brady conclude that "personal incumbency advantage now rivals partisan advantage in its contribution to reelection margins."[86] Beyond the
relatively high-profile U.S. House and Senate races, typical state and
local incumbents enjoy at least as powerful an inherent advantage over
their challengers. Since these low-visibility races do not receive significant media exposure and seldom attract well-funded opposition, these
elected officials are often even more secure in their jobs.[87]

NONVOTING, DISTRUST, AND CIVIC NEGLECT

Some might argue that high reelection rates simply reflect the public's
satisfaction with its representatives. Were this the case, one would expect that at least half the population would have very favorable views
of local, state, and federal public officials. As suggested in chapter 1,
however, public confidence in government is low. Taking a closer look
at public trust, table 4 shows that only one in twenty American adults
have "a great deal" of confidence in their public officials and political
institutions, and roughly one-third have "very little" confidence in
them. More qualitative research has also found evidence supporting the
claim that the majority of Americans feel "shut out" of government and
have come to "hate" the political process.[88]

Not only is public confidence in representative institutions low, it is
in decline. As mentioned in chapter 1, 17 percent of respondents in
1974 had "a great deal of confidence" in Congress, but only 8 percent
reported the same view in 1994. Twenty-one percent expressed "hardly
any" confidence in Congress in 1974, and 39 percent held this view in
1994. In 1974, 64 percent of respondents agreed that "public officials

TABLE 4
AMOUNT OF CONFIDENCE IN PUBLIC INSTITUTIONS
AMONG VOTING-AGE U.S. CITIZENS IN 1996

Institution	A great deal (%)	Quite a lot (%)	Some (%)	Very little (%)	No answer (%)
Local government	5	26	43	23	2
Federal government	5	18	44	31	2
Congress	3	12	42	39	4
Political organizations, parties	4	11	39	43	4

SOURCE: U.S. Bureau of the Census, *Statistical Abstract of the United States, 1997*, table 460, based on Gallup survey *Giving and Volunteering in the United States, 1996* (Washington, D.C.: Independent Sector, 1996).

are not really interested" in the average person's problems, and that figure had risen to 74 percent by 1994.[89]

When placed in a broader context, some of this decline in public trust actually may have been healthy. In his history of American public life, Michael Schudson points out that "there can be too much trust as well as too little." High public trust in the 1950s and 1960s partly "reflected a moment of unusual consensus in American life held together by Cold War paranoia, middle-class complacency, postwar affluence, and the continuing denial of a voice in public life to women and minorities." Thus, "Some of the skepticism about major institutions today is amply warranted. . . . Then again, some of it seems to express a deeper alienation and aimlessness."[90]

This alienation manifests itself in the perception that American elected officials do not *represent* the public. Reviewing 1995 data introduced in chapter 1, table 5 shows that depending on the words one uses, 60–88 percent of Americans agree that representatives are insincere and unresponsive to the real concerns of the public. Whereas nearly two-thirds of Americans in 1964 agreed that "elections make the government pay a good deal of attention" to the public, only 42 percent held that view in 1996. Or, in more general terms, in 1964, 32 percent agreed that "the government pays a good deal of attention to what people think," but only 15 percent held that view in 1996.[91]

It is not so much the political institutions themselves that people distrust—it is the people elected to represent them within those govern-

TABLE 5

DISTRUST OF CANDIDATES AND PUBLIC OFFICIALS, 1995

Statement	Strongly Agree (%)	Total Who Agree (%)
Government leaders tell us what they think will get them elected, not what they are really thinking.	61	88
Government leaders say and do anything to get elected, then do whatever they want.	55	79
Politicians work for themselves and their own careers, not the people they represent.	41	73
The government is run for the benefit of special interests, not to benefit most Americans.	37	70
Government leaders are out of touch. They don't know or care about what's going on in the rest of America.	30	60

SOURCE: Alan F. Kay, *Locating Consensus for Democracy* (St. Augustine, Fla.: Americans Talk Issues Foundation, 1998), 2.

mental bodies that bother the average citizen. One national poll making this distinction found that only 24 percent of those surveyed approved of the performance of members of Congress, but 88 percent approved of the institution of Congress, "no matter who is in office"[92] Another survey found that 95 percent of Americans agreed that "the American form of government is still the best for us," and 90 percent disagreed with the statement, "There is not much about our form of government to be proud of."[93]

Along with deep public distrust, the number of eligible American citizens who do not vote concerns many political observers. Though many bemoan the "steady decline" in American electoral participation,[94] voting in major elections has not changed dramatically in recent decades. The more important point is that turnout remains very low. Table 6 shows that voter turnout in presidential general elections has not declined dramatically since 18- to 21-year olds were given the right to vote prior to the 1972 election. Roughly half of the electorate has voted in each presidential general election for the last seven elections. During the forty years prior to 1972, turnout for the eligible electorate ranged from 51 percent (Truman-Dewey in 1948) to 63 percent (Kennedy-

TABLE 6

VOTER TURNOUT IN GENERAL ELECTIONS, 1972–1998

	Main Presidential Candidates	Turnout (%)
1972	Nixon–McGovern	55
1974	—	38
1976	Ford-Carter	54
1978	—	37
1980	Carter-Reagan	53
1982	—	40
1984	Reagan-Mondale	53
1986	—	36
1988	Bush-Dukakis	50
1990	—	37
1992	Bush-Clinton-Perot	55
1994	—	39
1996	Clinton-Dole-Perot	49
1998	—	36

SOURCE: Federal Election Commission. Data available at http://www.fec.gov/pages/electpg.htm.

Nixon in 1960). Turnout during nonpresidential general elections has also remained steady at around 37 percent for the past twenty-five years.[95]

Voting rates for most elections are lower. Even-year general elections usually draw out substantially more voters than do primaries, odd-year general elections, and local and special elections may bring out as little as 10 percent of the electorate. Those who show up on election day also tend to stop voting as they reach the lower-profile races farther down the ballot. This process is called voter "roll-off" or "drop-off." From 1972 to 1996, for example, there was usually a 3–5 percent drop-off from presidential to House elections nationwide. That means that one in twenty citizens counted as voting did not, in fact, do so in the congressional elections. The drop off for lower races is much more substantial. As an illustration, table 7 shows the extent to which voters in Bernalillo County, New Mexico, "dropped off" as they went down their ballots. For example, 8 percent of those who went to the polls or filled out absentee ballots declined to vote for a state corporation commissioner, and when they got to a state Supreme Court retention election, in which they had the choice of retaining or rejecting a sitting justice, 22 percent declined to vote. Drop-off of this magnitude is common, and uneven drop-off among different voting groups can make the voting population even less representative of the larger population.[96]

TABLE 7

VOTER "DROP-OFF" IN THE BERNALILLO COUNTY, NEW
MEXICO, NOVEMBER 1996 GENERAL ELECTION

Public Office	Ballots without a Vote (%)
U.S. President	2
U.S. Senate	3
U.S. House of Representatives	4
State Corporation Commissioner	8
Court of Appeals, Position 1	11
Supreme Court (retention vote)	22

SOURCE: Bernalillo County Clerk. Data available at http://www. bernco.gov/clerk/election.html.
NOTE: Offices are listed in the order they appeared on the ballot. To reduce table size, some offices have been omitted. The Supreme Court retention election gave voters the option of voting "for
or against" a sitting justice.

What is the source of persistent nonvoting and drop-off among those
who do choose to vote? One view is that nonvoting reflects public complacency or approval of government.[97] Low public trust and confidence
in government, however, suggest that nonvoting reflects frustration and
alienation more than complacency and satisfaction. Another view is
that nonvoters are engaging in a meaningful form of public protest. For
example, the radical activist Erwin Knoll argued that his vote would
count the most if he refused to cast it. A willful nonvoter once suggested a more indirect protest to an interviewer: he didn't vote because
he didn't want to "encourage them."[98] Given the ineffectiveness of this
form of protest, it is not surprising that research on nonvoting finds no
support for the protest explanation.

Together, deep public distrust, nonvoting, limited candidate scrutiny,
and even ill-defined public opinion are signs of a growing *civic neglect*.
As explained in chapter 2, when dissatisfied citizens fail to use their
vote (and their voice), their inaction constitutes neglect of the system.
By declining to register their disapproval, citizens permit poor representation to persist. Even in those cases where public officials do face
serious challenges to their incumbency, because of the public's inattention and superficial candidate evaluation, strategically sound challengers would be mistaken to focus their campaigns on a substantive
critique of incumbents' public records. Genuine policy debate on a
complex issue wins few voters during campaigns, which are more commonly characterized by misleading accusations, personal insinuations,
and one-sided attacks.[99] Exchanges between candidates are more vitri-

olic than deliberative. The point here is that such behavior is not irrational, but rather an honest attempt by campaigns to tailor their messages to the reality of the American political environment. Reaching apathetic and withdrawn citizens requires the constant repetition of loud and simple messages. Sober dialogue on current issues is a luxury only safe incumbents and unaspiring opponents can afford.[100]

This pattern of civic neglect, nondeliberative campaigning, and questionable representation has self-reinforcing qualities. As James March and Johan Olsen argue in *Democratic Governance*, "Political actors act on the basis of identities that are themselves shaped by political institutions and governance."[101] Individuals' experience of the political process shapes their understanding of themselves, their civic capabilities, and their understanding or "accounts" of the process itself. The electoral process described in this chapter leads voters to conclude, as Murray Edelman argues, that voting is closer to "self-expression" than powerful political action. Repeated lessons in futility are likely to engender a helpless or cynical self-identity as a voter, cause civic skills to atrophy, and lead to even more skeptical beliefs about the value and impact of elections.[102] Then, in turn, "voters who are left feeling that they are not represented are very likely to feel alienated and detached, and as nonparticipants they are unwilling to shoulder the sacrifices that may be required to promote the common good."[103] When this detachment leads to nonvoting, it further weakens the effectiveness of elections by making the remaining voting population less representative of the general public.[104]

When this process is repeated over time, it reinforces some of the very problems that lead to hasty candidate evaluation, distrust, nonvoting, and misrepresentation. To put it mildly, the American electoral process does not appear to be a self-correcting system. Instead, the extreme difficulty of challenging unresponsive elected officials fosters a civic neglect that further erodes the electoral process.

CHAPTER 4

Appraising Radical and Conventional Electoral Reforms

If voters look for information about candidates under streetlights, then that is where candidates must campaign, and the
only way to improve elections is to add streetlights.
                    Samuel Popkin, The Reasoning Voter

The severity of the problems outlined in chapter 3 has inspired many
attempts at reforming elections in the United States. Some of the most
radical critics of modern American elections suggest discarding the representative system for a more direct form of democracy, whereas others
embrace the principle of representation but find fault with winner-take-
all district elections. In this chapter, I briefly discuss these proposals, but
I devote more attention to the relatively modest changes that political
reformers have already put in place. In the broadest sense, these reforms (and suggested improvements to them) are all in the spirit of
Samuel Popkin's call for adding streetlights to elections so that average
voters can make better choices on their ballots. More precisely, this
metaphor concerns voters' ability to see clearly the real abilities and beliefs of the candidates.

   If political reforms, be they modest or monumental, can help voters
tell a sound candidate from an unrepresentative one, then they might
open wide the door to effective electoral action. And if voters regularly
begin to reject officials who are unresponsive and out of touch with the
general public, it may lead to governance that better corresponds with
the public's best interests. Ultimately, that is the criterion by which all
electoral reforms must be judged.

DIRECT DEMOCRACY

Critics of representative democracy argue that government serves the public's interest only when the two become one. In this view, it is too difficult to make representatives accountable for their actions even with periodic elections, and, in any case, the public is capable of governing itself directly. If a democratic system makes all decisions in this way, vote and voice become unnecessary, because the public has no bad representatives to reject or chastise. Instead, citizens deliberate together, then express their views directly through their own votes. If their votes produce policies that undermine the public's interest, they have no one to blame but themselves. Even when writing in theoretical terms, however, advocates of direct democracy do not go that far.

The most influential writer on direct democracy was Jean-Jacques Rousseau, who argued for direct self-governance in *The Social Contract* over two hundred years ago. Rousseau maintained that government and its laws can only embody the general will if they come directly from the governed. Rousseau envisioned face-to-face assemblies of citizens as the ideal form of democratic deliberation and policymaking, but he reluctantly recognized the limits of this vision. "It is impossible to imagine," he wrote, "that the people should remain in perpetual assembly to attend to public affairs." Thus, even Rousseau recognized that a direct system of democracy would have some measure of representation, although the public might be divided into small electorates that maintained an intimate relationship with their representatives.[1]

One of the most recent proposals for a such a system came from Frank Bryan, a University of Vermont political science professor, and John McClaughry, a Vermont state senator. In *The Vermont Papers: Recreating Democracy on a Human Scale* (1989) these authors outline a system that places the greatest amount of political power in the hands of local shires made up of 10,000 people in five to ten towns. In this vision of democracy, citizens would make most of the important decisions of their lives within these shires. True direct democracy would take place in small town meetings, and these face-to-face assemblies would also elect the most powerful local representatives. State government would have relatively little power, and its primary role would be channeling funds to the shires and providing them with technical assistance on matters of policy. Relatively few decisions would be made at state and federal levels, and shires would even have ways of playing a direct role in the nation's foreign policy.

Get some
Rousseau
quotes

Kevin O'Leary suggests another means by which large-scale institutions can be brought down to the community level. He proposes that every congressional district in the United States should have a legislative assembly, representing fifty subdistricts. The 435 such assemblies across the country "would have the duties of helping to set the legislative agenda and . . . deliberating and voting on bills that have passed the House." In effect, a bill that made it through Congress would then have one more stop before reaching the president. If deemed sufficiently important by the joint executive committee overseeing the network of assemblies, each local body would deliberate and vote on a bill, and their votes would be decisive.[2]

Local legislative assemblies would not be a form of direct democracy per se. They would make federal government more local, however, and because of the small size of the local assemblies, the process appears closer to the ideal of direct democracy than the present system. Because they would constitute yet another layer of representation, the assemblies would nevertheless suffer some from of the problems detailed in chapter 3. In effect, the proposal creates another layer of government but does not fundamentally change the process by which average voters select and influence representatives. No doubt the assemblies would give even greater influence to their most active constituents, but that would further increase the influence of the most influential.

John Burnheim has proposed a different system of direct government. Like the Vermont shire system, Burnheim's "demarchy" shifts considerable power away from federal and state governments to local authorities. Demarchy decentralizes power not only vertically but also horizontally: whereas the shire system would have powerful local governments to manage the business of each town and shire, demarchy splits up those local powers for each major public function. The local transportation bureau and the hospital board, for example, would govern themselves separately. Moreover, the public officials who managed these agencies would not be elected; instead, a random lottery would periodically select representatives from among the citizens who used each public good.[3]

The idea of direct legislation has become popular in many countries, however, and it is, in some ways, practiced in the United States. Many states permit citizen-sponsored referenda and initiatives. Through an initiative, voters can propose a legislative measure or a constitutional amendment by obtaining the required number of signatures on a petition. A referendum gives voters the chance to approve or reject a policy normally referred to the electorate by the state government. In a review of the history of referenda and initiatives in the United States, Thomas Cronin found that "voters have been cautious and have almost always rejected extreme proposals" that have appeared on their ballots. Among other accomplishments, voters have used the initiative process to promote women's suffrage, remove poll taxes, establish presidential primaries, and enact sunshine laws to ensure open public meetings.[4] Over the years, referenda have also become very popular, with 80 percent of Americans even supporting "a national referendum system in which all citizens voted on proposals that deal with major national issues."[5]

Unfortunately, referenda and initiative elections suffer from the same maladies that plague elections for public office. For instance, surveys have found that "as many as one-third to a majority of those voting" report feeling "uncomfortable about voting because they needed more information or more time to discuss the issue or to read the voter pamphlet more carefully, or found that the statement was too hard to read and comprehend."[6] When an initiative on the ballot receives little notice, voters may have nothing to base their vote upon other than the confusing wording of the initiative itself. In relatively high-visibility referendum elections, such as the recent votes on affirmative action and the civil rights of homosexuals in Western states, average voters are likely to have much more information, although much of it may be misleading, deceptive, or simply inaccurate.[7] For these elections to work properly, they would have to be far more deliberative in character, and chapter 7 suggests a way in which states might improve the initiative and referenda processes.

Even when initiative elections work properly, however, they do not provide a substitute for representative government. They can complement indirect democracy with periodic opportunities for direct citizen involvement in policy decision making, but few consider the initiative process a practical method for conducting all of the public's legislative business. This reality brings back into focus the difficulty of ensuring effective electoral relief from bad representation, and the remainder of this chapter examines different proposals for meeting that challenge.

ALTERNATIVE VOTING SYSTEMS

Democratic reformers committed to representative government find fault, not with the notion of representation, but with aspects of particular election systems. The strongest of these criticisms question the basic design of most federal, state, and local elections in the United States. The American system relies upon "winner-take-all" contests in single-member districts. Candidates run in party primaries or multicandidate nonpartisan primaries, and the winners in these primaries compete in the general election, with the top vote-getter winning the contested public office. Minor variations include multiseat contests, such as a school board race with five candidates running for three seats, multiple seats within the same districts or only at-large seats with no districts, and judicial retention elections in which a judge runs against the "No" vote to keep the seat he or she already holds. In all of these elections, the design is basically the same: voters cast one vote for each seat, and individual candidates win if they get the most votes.

CUMULATIVE AND PREFERENTIAL VOTING

Even modest changes in this basic design can sound shocking to Americans, although such variations are usually designed to ensure more political equality. When President Clinton nominated Lani Guinier for the position of assistant attorney general for civil rights in 1993, Republicans (and some Democrats) vilified her for supporting alternative voting systems. Guinier's critics decried her views on civil rights and elections as "anti-democratic" and dubbed her the "Quota Queen." Just a month after naming her, Clinton withdrew her nomination, with the explanation that he had reread her writings and disagreed with her views.

What had Guinier advocated that caused a political battle and cost her the nomination? With regard to representative government, Guinier had endorsed a system called cumulative voting. As she described it, "Under cumulative voting, voters get the same number of votes as there are seats or options to vote for, and they can then distribute their votes in any combination to reflect their preferences. Like-minded voters can vote as a solid bloc or, instead, form strategic. . . . coalitions to gain mutual benefits."[8]

The advantage of such a system is that it ensures significant minorities some representation in government bodies. In a winner-take-all system, a subgroup of the public might cast one-third of the votes yet never win an election. Cumulative voting reduces the likelihood of creating a permanent minority by permitting voters to cast all of their votes for one candidate instead of requiring those votes to be spread across separate races for each seat. Guinier gives the example of

Chilton County, Alabama, which simultaneously elects all of its school board and county commission seats. In that county, Guinier explains, "Any group with the solid support of one-eighth the voting population cannot be denied representation . . . because any self-identified minority can plump or cumulate all its votes for one candidate." A handful of other counties and cities, as well as some corporations, use the cumulative voting method, and political, ideological, and demographic minorities have used the system to ensure themselves vocal representatives on governing bodies.[9]

Other deviations from the winner-take-all model are common outside the United States. Preferential voting is practiced in the Irish Parliament, the Australian Senate, and even on the Cambridge, Massachusetts, city council. This system also has candidates run for several seats at once, but rather than voting multiple times, each voter picks a first-choice candidate, a second choice, and so on. If a candidate receives more first-choice votes than are needed to win a seat, those surplus votes (chosen at random) get transferred to the backers' second choices. Also, the candidate with the fewest votes has his or her backers' ballots all transferred to their second choices. This process is then repeated, looking for any candidates who have enough first- or second-choice votes to win a seat, and so on. In practice, roughly seven in eight voters end up backing a winning candidate.[10] Again, the point of such a system is to ensure that voters are represented.

Cumulative and preferential voting both have the virtue of empowering small blocs of voters. Nevertheless, these systems do not address the basic problem underlying ineffective electoral competition against unrepresentative incumbents. They provide no deliberative process whereby voters formulate their interests more clearly (other than perhaps a vague identity as a minority voting bloc), and they do not aid voters in making systematic candidate evaluations. Moreover, these systems might not even make use of those interests. By making electoral victory possible for candidates supported by less than a full majority, these systems might invite some new candidates into the electoral process, but money and personality would continue to play powerful roles in elections.

UNIVERSAL REPRESENTATION

In their book *Reinventing Congress for the Twenty-First Century,* Sol Erdman and Lawrence Susskind argue that party politics and

geographic districting are the direct causes of political stagnation and
poor policymaking, particularly in the U.S. Congress:

> Since each member of Congress is elected by a majority vote of citizens
> whose political priorities directly conflict, most legislators shy away from
> dealing with real priorities. Instead, they try to represent some simplistic
> common denominators that the majority of local voters might accept—
> whether or not these commonalties have substance or coherence. Thus, one
> legislator defends his district's obsolete arms factory, although it harms the
> economy and security of the world his constituents inhabit. Another advo-
> cates less government and a balanced budget, but without any reduction in
> locally popular programs.[11]

They propose that the U.S. House of Representatives switch to a system of "universal representation." In this system, a large pool of candidates run for the House, and each voter selects a first-choice candidate,
a second choice, and so on. Once all the ballots are collected, the candidate with the fewest first-choice votes is dropped, and the votes are
transferred to those voters' second-choice candidates. This process of
elimination continues until 250 candidates remain. In a follow-up election, each of the 10–15 percent of voters who had none of their choices
elected would get to vote again and select one among the remaining
250 candidates. Finally, each of the 250 representatives receives a "voting strength" proportionate to the number of citizens who voted for
him or her. In a way, this system is proportional representation, except
that voters cast their ballots for specific individuals rather than political parties.

Erdman and Susskind argue that universal representation would give
even greater power to minorities and ensure more public accountability than do other electoral systems. "Since universal voters would have
many choices of candidates," they argue, "representatives would feel
far greater pressure than they do now to address the priorities of their
constituents. . . . Congressmen and women would have voters at their
backs [and] scores of challengers on the sidelines."[12] By creating a like-
minded constituency for each representative, elected officials would
have less difficulty knowing and representing the interests of their constituents.

Erdman and Susskind's system has other important features, such as
streamlined information transmission to help voters learn about candidates and public financing for voter education and some forms of campaigning. They imagine that the most highly motivated voters would
spend several hours, or even days, evaluating the list of congressional

candidates, which could number in the thousands. At the same time, they recognize the existence of some lazy (i.e., less sophisticated) voters and suggest that those could send a standardized issues questionnaire to the election commission clearinghouse "and let its computer select candidates" by matching the voters' policy priorities with candidates' stated agendas.[13]

Would this system result in a better pool of candidates, more self-aware voters, and better candidate evaluations? Would representatives who failed to represent the interests of their backers face quick electoral defeat under it? It is hard to guess exactly how such a system would function and whether it might transform the values, skills, and habits of the electorate. Because it links representatives to substantive voter preferences, rather than parties or geographic districts, it might inspire voters to deliberate upon their own views and to choose a representative carefully. Unless the implementation of the system transforms the political process itself, however, it is likely that like cumulative and preferential voting, universal representation will not serve the interests of most of those citizens who either do not vote or vote based on inadequate candidate evaluations. The systems complicate the act of voting considerably, and that makes informed voting even more difficult.

Moreover, the questionnaire-matching method of voting in Erdman and Susskind's system could make it even harder to defeat incumbents who failed to represent the public's genuine interests. Depending on its structure, the survey questionnaire would probably institutionalize non-deliberative opinions rather than promoting more deliberative policy judgments and voting decisions. Also, so long as lazy voters' questionnaire responses remained stable, the voters would continue to elect candidates who gave matching answers, regardless of their actual actions as elected officials. The computer might try matching voter questionnaires with the actual votes cast by public officials, but who would program it to judge the implications of those policy votes?

PROPORTIONAL REPRESENTATION BY PARTIES

Regardless of the voting system, the less sophisticated voter must have a way to make an intelligent vote, because such voters exist in abundance in all large-scale quasi-democratic political systems. Most countries address this problem by simplifying rather than complicating voters' electoral decisions through the party-list form of proportional representation (PR). In this system, voters simply choose a party, rather than a candidate, and all of the seats for a governing body are filled simultaneously by giving parties seats in proportion to the number of votes they received, as long as the party earned at least a minimum percentage of the total vote. Through internal processes, the parties then assign individuals to the seats they have won.

Relative to the winner-takes-all system, PR has the advantage of electing public officials sympathetic to minority interests. In the United States, even when the supporters of a third political party are numerous, their geographic dispersion is likely to ensure their electoral defeat in every district. Under a PR system, such parties would win seats in proportion to the size of their memberships. If 5 percent of Americans strongly identified with the Libertarian Party and voted accordingly in a congressional election using the PR system, 5 percent of the members of the House of Representatives would be Libertarians. The other voting methods described earlier have this same advantage of minority representation, but the PR system is much simpler.[14]

Does proportional representation ensure effective electoral action? The answer to that question is complicated by the fact that voters do not elect individual representatives in the party-list version of PR. Voters shift allegiances to new parties, not new candidates, so the electorate evaluates entire parties, not candidates. Presumably, voters can better match their interests with a party platform than with individual candidates, and it may even be easier to track and evaluate the performance of a party in parliament than that of an individual representative. If a party is part of a majority coalition in a PR system, for instance, a voter can easily judge whether it has made environmental remediation a top priority. By contrast, because of the limited power of individual representatives in the present U.S. system, voters might mistake legislative failure for a lack of effort or interest on the part of a well-meaning representative.

The PR system also aids collective rejection of unrepresentative incumbents by making a single voter more powerful: for an elected body with 400 members, if only one-quarter of 1 percent of the electorate shifts allegiance away from an unrepresentative party, that party loses a seat. In the United States, a change in representation requires a sufficient number of disenchanted voters to move an incumbent's vote total below that of at least one challenger, and that can require a synchronized shift of 10 or even 30 percent of the vote.

MODEST ELECTORAL REFORMS

All of these systems, however, suffer from a problem of circumstance in addition to any errors in design. As Lani Guinier's experience demonstrated, major departures from the winner-take-all voting system can frighten or even enrage many Americans. Though a dispassionate discussion of these systems might win them more support, Americans have become attached to the notion of district representatives. Over time, the winner-take-all district system has become a tradition, and a wholesale departure from that system is unlikely in the near future. Thus, many electoral reformers have turned their attention to making changes within the basic framework of the existing system. In the remainder of this chapter, I review suggested changes in the number of terms an incumbent can hold office, the way campaigns are financed, how candidates present themselves during elections, and what information citizens obtain before voting.

LIMITING TERMS IN OFFICE

Perhaps the simplest reform proposed in recent decades is term limits. Advocates of term limits have argued that the failures of American government stem from long-term incumbency. As discussed in chapter 3, incumbents have tremendous advantages over challengers both by virtue of their office and because of the fund-raising ability that their office affords them. Elected officials grow dependent on campaign contributions, which ensure reelection, and consciously or not, they begin to represent the interests of contributors rather than those of their constituents. According to term-limits proponents, if elected officials were limited to a finite number of terms in office, they would be out of office before they lost touch with the general public. Whenever an official reached his or her term limit, the next election would be guaranteed to bring into office a new representative.[15]

The simplicity of their design and their indisputable ability to remove incumbents from office has made proposals for term limits popular across the country. Public opinion is quite favorable toward term limits, and more than half of the states in the United States have set limits for the number of terms that their state legislators can remain in office.[16] Under these laws, elected officials can hold seats for only six to twelve years, although many individuals have found that they can successfully leap from one body to the other (in roughly the same geographic district) to double the length of their political careers.[17]

The term-limits approach to reform has various drawbacks. A 1995 U.S. Supreme Court ruling found that congressional term limits would require a constitutional amendment, so this approach will be difficult to extend above the state level. Aside from this barrier, term limits inevitably result in a decline in the average experience and skill of lawmakers. When grappling with the minutiae of complex policy debates, such inexperience may foster dependence on permanent (and unelected) legislative staff, as well as on seasoned lobbyists. Prior experience does not necessarily improve an elected official's moral judgment, but it does prove useful when crafting legislation and navigating the legislative process. In a few years, states will be able to take stock of the impact of term limits and better understand their impact on legislative competence.

The more serious problem with limiting terms is that this reform does not directly address the central problems introduced in the first chapter. In essence, the term-limits approach gives up on the problem of effective electoral rejection of unresponsive incumbents.[18] Instead of making incumbents accountable or even just vulnerable, this reform removes them altogether after just a few years in office. Elected officials are removed from office by time, rather than public protest. Framed in the model presented in chapter 2, a system of severe term limits admits that citizen vote and voice are powerless, and to avoid a downward spiral into civic neglect, the system instead gives citizens periodic competitive elections between new candidates.

When viewed in these terms, it is clear that the term-limits proposal is far from an automatic fix for the problems of low public trust and questionable representation. Term limits only remove long-term incumbency from the list of possible causes. To succeed, term limits would have to do more: they would have to transform the nature of campaigns, such that victors are more representative of the public's deliberative interests and citizens come to recognize and appreciate their improved representation. Even advocates of term limits do not claim such far-reaching effects.[19] Proponents hope that term limits will restore public trust in government, but the successful enactment of term limits in numerous states has done nothing to halt the decline in public confidence.[20]

CHANGING THE ROLE OF MONEY

Other reformers have focused more closely on the role of money in American political campaigns. As illustrated in chapter 3, elections have become increasingly expensive. From 1972 to 1974, contributions to House candidates increased an average of 8 percent in real dollars per two-year election cycle. Contributions to U.S. Senate candidates grew 12 percent every two years.[21] As Larry Makinson of the Center for Responsive Politics writes: "Elections these days are big business. . . . To win a seat in a state legislature, a big city council or the U.S. Congress . . . takes not only an attractive candidate, but a good organization and plenty of advertising. And that takes money."[22] Chapter 3 showed that dependence upon money has a powerful effect upon who can run for office. Candidates without sufficient personal funds or considerable backing by major donors rarely have any chance of victory and—unless idealistic, self-promotional, or delusional—choose not to run for office.

Those serious candidates who do run for office, with the exception of some independently wealthy individuals, also alter their behavior during campaigns because of their dependence on major donors. Candidates spend long hours trying to raise funds, and that fund-raising takes time away from contacting voters. Rather than meeting with citizens and considering their interests, many candidates spend more time meeting with potential contributors and modifying their policy positions or priorities to win contributions. The logic behind this behavior is simple: in one well-scheduled hour, a candidate for U.S. Congress might be able to earn ten or twenty votes through direct contact with undecided voters at a meeting, at their doors, or on the phone. Meeting or talking with donors, however, a candidate might be able to raise enough money to buy advertising that sways hundreds of votes. Since the candidate's opponent generally takes the latter approach, a candidate who relies upon direct contacts rarely wins in such elections. As even the most local races become more media-savvy and cable television facilitates advertising to narrower geographic and demographic target audiences, the incentives for larger budgets (and more fund-raising) increase even in small-scale elections.[23]

To encourage more contact with voters and less fund-raising, some political reformers have argued for public financing for all major elections. The idea of taxpayer money replacing political action committee and individual contributions is not decidedly un-American: presidential campaigns are funded, in part, by citizens who voluntarily check a box on their federal income tax forms. Advocates of public financing argue that virtually all other elections would benefit from full or partial government funding. Survey data suggest that, depending on the design of the system, the electorate might support such an idea. For instance, a 1996 Gallup poll of likely voters found that 64 percent favored a proposal for the federal government to provide "a fixed amount of money for the election campaigns of candidates for Congress, and that all private contributions be prohibited."[24] A 1997 Gallup poll found that support dropped to 43 percent, however, if in conjunction with public financing, "all contributions from individuals and private groups are banned."[25] After the 1998 election, Arizona and Massachusetts joined Maine and Vermont as states where voters have endorsed some form of voluntary public financing for candidates who accept various campaign financing restrictions.

More modest proposals, some of which have become state or local law, recommend that the state provide matching funds and other perks to candidates who conform to strict campaign financing guidelines. In a *Washington Post* opinion piece, Thomas Mann and Norman Ornstein argue for a system that encourages small in-state donations in U.S. House and Senate elections. Under this plan, a federal fund would match any in-state individual contribution of $100 or less by placing a 10 percent tax on all contributions over $500. Candidates who followed these rules and obtained sufficient small in-state donations would then receive free air time, "contingent on the candidates themselves delivering the messages."[26]

Pushing candidates toward small contributions, however, may simply result in different fund-raising strategies by candidates and more independent expenditures by political action committees and other interest groups, which are difficult to regulate effectively and constitutionally. Paradoxically, limited public financing or systems that make it more difficult to amass campaign contributions could have the perverse effect of making campaigns less competitive. A study of U.S. House and Senate campaigns from 1978 to 1994 found that "the critical financial determinant of election outcome is not how much the top spender invests in a campaign, but whether the other serious candidates have sufficient funds to get their message to the voters." In 1994, the average budget of winning House candidates was $738,117, but most proposed spending caps are much lower. In this view, incumbents start with large advantages based on public visibility, constituent service, and campaign experience, so challengers need to be able to raise as much money as possible to reach voters.[27]

One more approach to campaign finance reform tries to reduce fund-raising pressure by providing candidates with the most expensive campaign resource—air time. The League of Women Voters Education Fund, along with groups as diverse as the conservative American Enterprise Institute and the liberal Brookings Institution endorse a proposal for a "broadcast bank" of roughly $500 million (indexed for inflation) in advertising vouchers. In their scheme, every television and radio station in the United States would contribute an equal amount of prime air time to a bank, which would then allocate advertising vouchers to individual candidates and political parties, who could use the vouchers in whichever elections they chose. Advertisers would need to follow just two simple rules: each ad would have to air for a minimum of sixty seconds, and for the duration of the commercial, the candidate would have to appear on screen (or his or her voice would have to be heard on radio). The system would put no constraint on further media buys, while providing candidates and parties with a bank roughly the size of the political air time purchased in 1995–96.[28] The only sizable obstacle standing in the way of this relatively simple and powerful plan is the amount of profit it would take away from commercial broadcasters, which have thus far successfully resisted the proposal.

Even if campaign finance reforms create more competitive races, that would not necessarily change the quality of the decisions that voters make. Just as the term-limits laws enacted in many states create a mandatory but mindless turnover in elected officials, more competitive elections might replace more incumbents, but the reforms do not improve the accuracy with which voters time those replacements. For this reason, a public financing scheme might prove to be nothing more than a rich person's term limit, which removes incumbents from office through costly elections without promising a superior replacement.

IMPROVING CAMPAIGN DISCOURSE

By removing the pressures of fund-raising altogether, full public financing proposals at least have the potential to expand the pool of qualified candidates and increase the percentage of campaign energy devoted to voter contact. Even increases in the quality of candidates and the quantity of voter contacts, though, do not ensure a corresponding increase in voters' ability to recognize and reject unrepresentative elected officials through campaign deliberation. In the view of some reformers, only direct efforts to improve the deliberative quality of campaigns will solve the collective electoral action problem. If voters receive more high-quality information and watch fewer misleading or confusing campaign ads, the electorate will better understand the candidates and make more informed choices on their ballots.

Many critics of contemporary campaign discourse point to the prominent role of negative ads. In the American political vernacular, a negative ad is any written or broadcast campaign advertisement that criticizes an action or quality of an opponent. A negative ad might remind voters that an incumbent voted for a tax increase, or an attack ad could focus on the criminal background of a candidate's family. The purpose of negative ads is to win elections by winning over undecided voters, persuading an opponent's supporters to switch allegiance, or causing undecided or opposing voters not to vote.[29] There has been some debate about the third of these effects, but both experimental and field studies of attack ads show that such advertising often results in a modest (5 percent) drop in voting for a given election.[30]

More refined critiques of campaign discourse distinguish between substantive criticisms and illegitimate attacks. One form of illegitimate attack is the outright falsehood or misleading statement. Some mass media responded to these ads in the 1990 election by reporting on the ads themselves. This "adwatch" approach aimed at scrutinizing campaign ads and revealing any false or exaggerated claims that candidates made to voters. Unfortunately, two studies of the adwatch response suggest that it is not always effective: a study of a 1992 Pat Buchanan attack ad on President George Bush found that viewing an adwatch caused voters to discredit the ad somewhat; however, a study of an attack ad in the 1992 North Carolina gubernatorial campaign found that by rebroadcasting the negative ad, the adwatch format can enhance the intended effect of the ad.[31]

A more extreme response is to ban or prohibit all misleading ads, whether they be on the attack or on the defensive. In the 1998 Ohio gubernatorial race, for example, a county judge granted a request by the Democratic candidate, Lee Fisher, to ban a television ad created by his Republican opponent, Bob Taft. Fisher's request pointed to two statements in Taft's ad. First, Taft's ad used a partial quotation from a Cleveland newspaper article explaining that Taft had campaigned in favor of a proposed tax increase on a public ballot but "didn't raise the taxes himself." Taft's ad responded to a Fisher attack by quoting, "Taft didn't raise the taxes. . . . " Second, Taft counterattacked by claiming that as a state senator, Fisher had cast the "deciding vote" that raised Ohio's income tax in 1983. Fisher argued that any senator's vote for the measure, which passed 17–16, could have been the "deciding" one, which Taft later acknowledged.[32]

Notwithstanding that some judges may make rulings such as the Ohio ban on misleading ads, the First Amendment bars such action as an infringement upon free speech, and the U.S. Supreme Court has consistently ruled against any such restriction. The Court's position is a sound one, because permitting judges to rule on the quality of political discourse invites unwarranted censorship and unduly politicizes the judicial branch. In the Ohio case, the defendant responded to the ruling by attacking the judge's neutrality (the judge had contributed $125 to the plaintiff's campaign). In this way, the main consequence of involving judges in partisan contests may be to undermine the legitimacy of the judiciary.

A more modest approach to unruly and manipulative campaign discourse is to work for voluntary codes of campaign ethics. In 1996, a Maine public library joined with a public policy institute to encourage the state's ten candidates for federal office to agree to a voluntary Code of Election Ethics. By signing the code, candidates agreed to follow four principles: honesty, respect, responsibility, and compassion. Box 1 shows the full text of the agreement, which combines broad guidelines with specific rules.

Box 1

The Maine Code of Election Ethics, 1996

Honesty and Fairness

I shall emphasize my views, beliefs, and experiences. I am committed to an open and public discussion of issues and to presenting my record with sincerity and frankness.

I shall not use or agree to let third parties use subtle deceptions, half-truths, falsifications, or such practices as push polling. If such practices are used by third parties without my approval, I shall repudiate it immediately and publicly upon my knowledge of its occurrence.

Factual claims made by my campaign will be supported by publicly available documents provided by my campaign office.

Respect

I shall avoid demeaning references to my opponent and demeaning visual images of my opponent.

I shall respect my opponent. I shall not use or allow to be used personal attacks, innuendo, or stereotyping.

Responsibility

I shall ensure that my campaign staff and campaign supporters will observe these principles of fair campaign practices. I take full responsibility for all advertising created or used on my behalf by staff and supporters.

I shall conduct my campaign openly and publicly, discussing the issues as I see them, presenting my record and policies with sincerity and frankness, and criticizing without fear and without malice the record and policies of my opponent and his or her political party that merit such criticism.

I will not condone or allow third-party advertising which does not meet the principles contained in this document. If such practices are used by third parties without my approval, I shall repudiate it immediately and publicly upon my knowledge of its occurrence.

Compassion

In the conduct of my candidacy, I shall show compassion at all times for my opponent. I shall remember that the campaign process is fundamental to representative democracy and that my behavior in the campaign affects the integrity of our society.

SOURCE: http://www.campaignconduct.org.

The Maine Code inspired similar efforts, such as the Project on Campaign Conduct, sponsored by the Pew Charitable Trusts. With the project's assistance, the candidates in Washington State's second congressional district reached agreement on a similar code of conduct. In return, the candidates' ads can display a logo that depicts the shaking of hands and says, "Honesty, responsibility, fairness" and "Hold us accountable."[33]

The advantage of such codes is that they are voluntary, pose no threat to the freedom of political expression, and put pressure on holdouts to agree to reasonable standards for campaign conduct. In this way, they might promote substantive debate on relevant issues, and that would help voters accurately evaluate candidates and make better-informed choices. If they make campaigns more deliberative, they might also attract a higher-quality pool of candidates, many of whom had avoided running for public office because of the unduly hostile climate of past campaigns.[34]

The weakness of the voluntary codes is the fact that they come with no enforcement. In Maine, for example, many federal candidates returned to vicious attack ads in the final weeks of the campaign despite having pledged to refrain from such behavior. As the Ohio Project on Campaign Conduct explains, "rather than establish a formal monitoring process or 'ethics police,' we're encouraging the voters to let the candidates know how they feel about nasty campaigns."[35] Unfortunately, this simply puts another burden on the voters, whose difficulty reaching efficient and sound candidate judgments inspired ethics codes in the first place.

GUIDING VOTERS

A different approach is to provide voters with more high-quality information, rather than trying to improve the quality of the messages that the candidates themselves produce. Returning to the epigraph from Samuel Popkin that opens this chapter, "If voters look for information about candidates under streetlights, then . . . the only way to improve elections is to add streetlights." If civic activists find attack ads distasteful, they can offer voters an alternative source of information about the candidates.

In Ohio, for example, voters did not have to rely on the attack ads exchanged by the two leading candidates in the 1998 gubernatorial election. Any voter who visited a public library, the Internet, or any number of coffee shops and public spaces could pick up a copy of the *Ohio Voters Guide* put out by the League of Women Voters. A quick glance at the fourth page showed voters the candidates' educational backgrounds, occupations, and relevant professional and voluntary experiences. The candidates also provided written answers to two questions, "How would you increase economic stability for all Ohioans?" and "Do you support a permanent, stable funding source for the House Trust Fund? Why or why not?"

Many voters find publications like the *Ohio Voters Guide* useful. A study of a similar voting guide in Bernalillo County, New Mexico, found that as many as a third of the registered voters in the county at least glanced at the guide before voting.[36] For many voters, a League of Women Voters guide is the only readily available source of information in low-intensity elections, such as those for state legislature or district judge. Poll workers often see voters walk into the voting booth clutching a printed guide, and those voters may read as they vote or refer back to selections they have already marked in their guides.[37]

Though voting guides can be helpful, they often contain vague or distorted information. The Ohio questions mentioned above illustrate two basic problems. The first question is too vague, permitting both Republican and Democratic candidates to make statements such as, "Every child must graduate with basic reading and writing skills." The second question is specific but noncontroversial; both candidates said they supported affordable housing. Moreover, because the guides rely upon unchallenged candidate statements, they remain subject to misleading or false statements.

For this and other reasons, the state of California prints and distributes an official voting guide with state funds. Once candidates submit their statements to the editors of the *California Voters Guide,* opponents can challenge the statements, and state judges rule on whether those challenges reveal factual inaccuracies. Despite public mistrust of government, the California secretary of state's office has found that the state-sponsored *Guide* has considerable influence on California voters. All of them receive it, and as many as one-third read and use it.[38] Writing from personal experience, I recall walking door-to-door during one election in San Diego and receiving a puzzled response from a voter when I tried to give her information about a congressional candidate. "Why would I need this?" the voter asked. "I'll just read the *Voters Guide.*" (The irony is that congressional races are not, in fact, in the state's *Guide.*)

No matter what the quality of a guide's questions and answers, printing costs create space limitations that prevent detailed portraits of all of the candidates running for public office in a major election. On the Internet, no comparable limits exist. Project Vote Smart, the Democracy Network, and many other organizations have produced elaborate websites with several pages of information (and links to other sources of information) on each election. Some of these on-line voting guides permit interactive candidate evaluation: voters can answer a series of questions and compare their responses to candidate answers, just as Erdman and Susskind describe in their vision of universal representation (presented earlier in this chapter). These on-line guides can even provide up-to-the-minute information, including adwatch-style critiques of candidate claims and daily campaign financing updates to reveal any untoward contributions that happen to arrive just before election day.[39]

Though only a relatively small percentage of voters currently use these on-line guides, as Internet use increases among the general population, they will probably come to play at least as important a role as their paper-and-ink forerunners. These guides will also become more popular as their design improves. For example, the printed guides provide voters with a paper document they can bring to the polls or refer to easily while filling out an absentee ballot. An ideal Internet voting guide would permit users to note candidate preferences and other votes as they navigated the site, then print out a marked sample ballot or a one-page summary of voting choices.

Finally, some newspapers have begun to change the basic framing—or "master narrative"—of their state and local campaign coverage by deemphasizing attacks and counterattacks and focusing on the real concerns of their readership. As the journalism scholar Jay Rosen explains in the case of the 1992 election coverage provided by the *Charlotte Observer,* the newspaper "succeeded in changing the master narrative from the story of how the campaign was won to a new story: the story of citizens voicing their concerns, and listening to what candidates said about them." Stories report on the experiences and aspirations of local communities, then connect local issues to the candidates running for public office. Other papers followed the example of the *Observer,* Rosen explains, because "everyone in journalism is tired of the horse race as a master narrative."[40]

What is different about this form of campaign reform is that it addresses the most fundamental requirement for effective electoral rejection—the development of voters' policy views. Attempts to regulate campaign discourse or provide more information on the candidates take for granted that the voters already know what they want from their elected representatives. Chapter 3 demonstrates that, in fact, most voters do not understand government and politics very well and often fail to link their underlying values to even general policy preferences. By talking with voters and reporting those conversations in their newspapers, journalists simulate the face-to-face deliberation that helps citizens develop and recognize their interests. In this way, a newspaper can help its readers by both arriving at evaluative criteria and applying those criteria systematically to candidates.

Were all voters newspaper readers and all newspapers supportive of this innovative form of public journalism, American elections might produce different results. Unfortunately, neither of those preconditions exists, nor are they likely to. Newspapers are businesses, and if those businesses decide that such coverage boosts advertising revenue through an expanded affluent readership, then papers might change their coverage. There is no strong evidence to that effect, but it is not an inconceivable evolution.

The more fundamental problem is that newspaper readers are already and will always be the most informed and sophisticated voters.[41] Other voting guides, whether printed or on the Internet, have the same drawback. A study of the California voting guide, for instance, found that 92 percent of users were regular voters even in primary elections. The majority of users had a bachelor's degree, with 28 percent of all users having obtained a graduate degree. This is not to say that such a guide has no benefit: over two-thirds of the users surveyed found the voting guide "very helpful."[42] The problem is that conventional voting guides and innovative newspaper coverage of elections do not reach the average citizen. Ironically, these rich sources of political information reach the voters who need them the least.

DELIVERING INFORMATION
TO THE VOTERS WHO NEED IT MOST

For the electorate to reject unresponsive representatives, it is critical that even the less-attentive voters judge candidates effectively. Not only do these voters need better candidate information the most, they are also sometimes the most pivotal subgroup of the electorate. Because voters of low and moderate sophistication are less attached to political parties, they are often more independent. In close races, these swing voters can decide the outcome of an election. In the 1998 New York Senate race, for instance, polls conducted a month before election day showed Republican Senator Alfonse D'Amato in a statistical tie with his Democratic opponent, Charles Schumer, with 10 percent of voters undecided. Just a week before the election, the results were the same, with the same percentage undecided.[43] Though voter turnout and other factors influenced Schumer's victory, his modest victory margin suggests that the undecided voters determined the outcome of the election. To take another example, a study of the 1992 general election in California found that late voters were the least partisan. Seventy-one percent of those who made up their minds before the election was well under way voted for candidates from the same party in the presidential and two U.S. Senate races that year. Only 56 percent of those who selected candidates during the campaign voted along party lines, and only 35 percent of those making a last-minute decision did so.[44]

If these critical voters do not have a reliable and efficient mechanism for candidate evaluation beyond simple partisanship, their electoral choices are unlikely to ensure accountability. Incumbents will win reelection on the strength of their familiarity, and challengers will normally defeat incumbents only when they can mount effective—albeit often unscrupulous, irrelevant, or single-issue—attacks on incumbents. To address this problem, chapter 7 presents a more effective method of providing useful information to even the least politically aware voters. Before doing so, however, it is necessary to consider the public's second form of response—its voice.

CHAPTER 5

Public Expression in American Politics

As it is essential to liberty that the government in general
should have a common interest with the people, so it is particularly essential that the [House of Representatives] . . .
should have an immediate dependence on and an intimate
sympathy with the people.

> The Federalist, *No. 52*
> *(attributed to James Madison)*

From 1970 to 1977, Richard Fenno traveled with and interviewed eighteen members of Congress to study their interaction with local constituencies. Fenno discovered that successful representatives devote considerable energy to developing positive relationships with the most active residents of their districts. The most time-consuming activity for a congressional office is constituent service, which includes everything from helping a small business navigate the tax code to rushing a visa application for a forgetful traveler. At district meetings, moreover, representatives spend much of their time with individual citizens and groups of constituents. Members of Congress use these services and meetings to build up the name recognition, general favorability, and positive personality attributions that win votes in low- and medium-intensity elections. Fenno observed the representatives present themselves "in such a way that the inferences drawn by those watching will be supportive." The representatives themselves called these inferences "trust." According to Fenno, a constituent who trusts a representative is saying:

> I am willing to put myself in your hands temporarily; I know you will have
> opportunities to hurt me, although I may not know when those opportuni-
> ties occur; I assume—and I will continue to assume until it is proven other-
> wise—that you will not hurt me; for the time being, then, I'm not going to
> worry about your behavior.[1]

To earn the trust of their constituents, successful representatives meet regularly with their constituents and gladly respond to specific concerns that have only minor policy implications. When future voters speak in a whisper about local or even private concerns, the representative listens carefully because a constructive response can earn that voter's trust and, come election day, support. These representatives seek to build up the loyalty of voters, because the greater their loyalty, the less likely they will be to attempt collective electoral rejection. Instead, when a loyal constituent has a substantive concern about a policy decision that may harm his or her interests, the loyal citizen uses some form of public voice.

When these direct contacts take the form of a letter, for example, congressional representatives reply using any of a number of available computer programs that generate relevant and often detailed responses. One Wisconsin congressman, Republican Scott Klug, permitted a reporter to scrutinize his mail operation in 1992, and the reporter found that Klug's staff had thousands of sentences and paragraphs it could piece together for any given reply. On the topic of agriculture alone, there were more than nine hundred separate responses.[2] As more and more citizen input comes in the form of e-mail, citizens (and interest groups that organize them) are increasing the speed and volume of their correspondence and increasing the likelihood that replies will be automatic and standardized.[3]

Some letter writers might appreciate a form reply, but this is not the kind of responsiveness that is central to the model introduced in chapter 2. In that model, *effective voice causes substantive changes in the behavior of an elected representative.*[4] In contemporary American politics, many public and private institutions aim to give voice to public concerns. In this chapter, I examine four different forms of public voice: public opinion polls, public hearings, talk radio, and direct lobbying. These forms of voice are by no means exhaustive of the institutions that citizens can use for political influence, but they illustrate the range of mechanisms the public uses to make itself heard.

In evaluating these modes of expression, it is useful to consider the characteristics of a fully democratic public voice.[5] When thought of as a collective entity made up of many individual perspectives and concerns, the public's voice should have four basic qualities in a democratic political system: voice should be representative, deliberative, articulate, and influential. The public's voice is *representative* when it brings into harmony the many voices among subgroups of the larger public, or it can be representative simply by incorporating separate views in a dis-cordant but inclusive voice. A *deliberative* public voice emerges only after a period of informed discussion and reflection oriented toward discerning a clear and mutually acceptable policy direction. When de-liberation arrives at a general decision, the public's voice needs to be-come *articulate* by pointing toward concrete public policy options. Without such clear direction, the public's voice remains strong in spirit but vague in intention. Once articulated, the public's voice needs to prove *influential* if it is to serve its original purpose. Only when voice affects actual policy decisions does it serve the public interests that sparked it and reinforce the civic habits and institutions that gave rise to it. As I argue below, different conventional modes of public expres-sion illustrate each of these features of ideal democratic voice, but none brings all four together.

PUBLIC OPINION POLLS

When citizens contact their representatives, they normally speak as in-dividuals or members of a subgroup of the larger citizenry. By letter, phone call, postcard, or e-mail, an individual asks to be heard among all other voices. Public opinion polls, which purport to speak for the whole, in the form of a stream of percentages, are an unusual but pop-ular form of public voice. In *Numbered Voices,* the political communi-cation scholar Susan Herbst explains that only in the modern era has our political culture equated the abstract concept of public opinion with a specific form of measurement—the mass opinion survey. Previ-ously, straw polls, crowd counts, and other methods were used to gauge public opinion. Public opinion surveys have become conventional be-cause they are more consistent with the Western cultural obsessions with rationality and quantification.[6]

SURVEYS AS REPRESENTATIVE AND ARTICULATE VOICE

Many observers, including Herbst, have criticized public opinion polling as a form of public expression, but well-designed polls have one dramatic advantage over nearly all other forms of voice: they provide a representative portrait of the public's views. This is a result of both the design and the conducting of polls. Most modern public surveys in America are conducted by telephone, by mail, or through door-to-door interviews, and these survey methods usually provide relatively balanced samples of public opinion. Telephone surveys are probably the most common, because they are quick and relatively cheap, and they obtain adequate response rates. The best phone surveys use random-digit dialing to reach both listed and unlisted numbers, and they provide a relatively random sample of the public. This technique misses the fraction of the American public without phones and oversamples households with multiple phone lines, but it also misses people who refuse to answer calls from interviewers and those who are rarely at home. The net result is a happy coincidence of complementary sampling errors—the systematic undersampling of both the low and high ends of the socioeconomic spectrum.[7]

A more subtle reason for the representativeness of mass opinion polls is the intimate setting of a survey interview. Whether face-to-face, on the phone, or via mail, survey respondents have a privacy quite unlike more public forms of voice. The interviewer assures the respondent that all responses are confidential and that the researchers will report only aggregate results or anonymous verbatim responses. For many respondents, this allows a candor that they rarely consider appropriate or socially acceptable. Respondents also understand that the survey gives them a certainty that their voices will be counted among others. An inarticulate or reserved citizen called on the phone by an interviewer suddenly has a chance to speak honestly and directly to all who care to listen without fear of reprisal or recrimination. The result is that mass opinion polls sometimes uncover a balance of public opinion that political life obscures. Michael MacKuen gives a straightforward example of this phenomena in one American city:

> St. Louis is a Catholic town. It is also pro-life. All three members of Congress and both Senators are pro-life. Members of the state legislature have continuously voted measures intended to circumvent *Roe v. Wade*. When an enormous sign advertising that "God is Pro-Life" was argued to be larger than allowed by city ordinance, the city council ruled it was not advertising but instead a work of art. That St. Louis is pro-life is a simple social fact. Yet, public opinion surveys of the area show that residents of St. Louis are much like Americans in general, marginally favoring the *pro-choice* position.[8]

MacKuen sees the implications clearly: "When portions of the public are silenced, then politics may ignore their preferences and plainly violate elementary democratic norms. Being unable to open discussion, current losers cannot even hope to persuade fellow citizens for the future."[9] By contrast, when public opinion polls thrust contrary views into the public debate, an unnoticed minority or even a genuine "silent majority" can begin to speak with a distinct voice.

Were public opinion polls representative in their sampling of public opinion but inarticulate in their expression of it, they would have little value. Part of what makes polls so valuable is that they provide succinct statements of the public's views. When interviewers ask their questions in a straightforward manner and provide respondents with simple, balanced response scales, one can succinctly summarize the survey results. For example, in 1994, the National Opinion Research Center asked Americans, "Do you favor or oppose the death penalty for persons convicted of murder?" Seventy-four percent said that they favored use of the death penalty, 19 percent opposed it, and 6 percent said they didn't know or gave no response. Though the meanings of words shift over time, one can have some confidence that support for this form of penalty has increased since 1974, when the same question resulted in 63 percent supporting "the death penalty for persons convicted of murder."[10]

Some polling organizations have tried to make poll results even more policy-relevant by routinely linking their questions to specific public policy proposals and injecting their poll results into ongoing debates. One of the most ambitious efforts in this spirit was the ten-year experiment conducted by the Americans Talk Issues Foundation (ATI). ATI conducted a series of studies on diverse domestic and foreign policy issues in an effort to "know and to disseminate what the public itself wants for governance."[11] By asking probing sets of questions with varied wording, ATI found that very large majorities of the public supported numerous policies that had not yet been adopted or even entered the public debate. For example, the ATI found strong public support for using the United Nations as the primary response mechanism in cases of international aggression, limiting campaign contributions to residents of representatives' own districts, and adopting uniform international standards for toxic waste. Though ATI's surveys have not always had the desired impact, this may stem in part from the idiosyncratic, iconoclastic style in which it presents itself and its results. In any case, the ATI surveys provide a detailed record of the general public's views on important public issues.[12]

CRITICISMS OF PUBLIC OPINION SURVEYS

Conventional polling is by no means a perfect method of eliciting the public's voice, although only some of its failings are inevitable. Public opinion polls do not, in fact, provide perfect random samples of the public, and their failure to do so is most serious when the undersampled population's views differ from those of the general public. To take an extreme example, the homeless population has needs and worries of a kind and degree that most Americans do not share, yet every form of survey—even the U.S. Census—has great difficulty including this group in its sample of respondents. If a survey tried to measure general support for publicly financed free toilets in parks, it might find some support among those who hoped such facilities would reduce the visibility of the discomfort of the homeless, but the homeless themselves, despite their more direct stake in the issue, would mostly not be heard.

Another problem with even elaborate surveys is that they measure public opinion without extensive deliberation. Typical surveys last fewer than thirty minutes and address many issues in rapid succession. A survey might ask a set of five-to-ten questions on an issue to get a general sense of the public's views, or a survey might ask a single question to address a broad issue. Surveys that try to go into greater depth on a concrete policy debate sometimes devote ten minutes to an issue and juxtapose policy questions with a relatively long preface to give respondents background information. A few exceptional surveys go one step farther and give interviewers scripted lines that permit them to engage in a structured debate with respondents, such that one response elicits a counterargument and follow-up question from the interviewer. For instance, a national survey on the government's role in preventing job discrimination used counterarguments to shift respondents' views: when initially asked if the government should "see to it that blacks get fair treatment in jobs," two-thirds supported government action; after hearing both liberal and conservative counterarguments to respondents' initial policy choices, the net result was only 42 percent support for government intervention to prevent job discrimination.[13] Such surveys reveal the importance of delving beneath surface-level public opinion, but they cannot simulate sufficient discussion to measure the public's fully informed or enlightened interests adequately. Without deliberation, public opinion polls risk oversimplifying the public's views and misrepresenting both the depth of disagreement and potential common ground.

Ironically, it is the danger of willful and careless misrepresentation that makes this most representative form of public voice hazardous. In some cases, the public survey sample is nonrandom. Though familiarity with sample bias may make the public and the media more cautious in their interpretation of surveys, it is remarkable how often and to what effect such surveys are used. Politicians routinely survey their districts to accomplish many purposes, and their mail surveys generally obtain very low response rates and unrepresentative samples. Nonetheless, officials sometimes refer to those biased polls to defend their policy votes. Interest groups and other political organizations conduct similar surveys to show support for a particular policy or simply to raise money. Even virtuous organizations and public entities regularly cite the "interesting results" of nonrandom public opinion surveys that they concede are "nonscientific."

Though a sample may be randomly drawn, its responses may still mislead because of the way in which the survey questions were asked. Volumes have been written on the methods by which pollsters misrepresent public opinion through biased questions, tricky phrasings, unbalanced response scales, and clever item-ordering. Political campaigns, for example, sometimes give opponents unflattering descriptions in their surveys, then claim imminent victory by revealing their candidate's strong showing in the biased poll. (Campaigns are rarely forthcoming about the full wording and methodological details of their surveys.) The apparent public support for the Republicans' 1994 "Contract with America" was also based upon willful misrepresentation of public opinion, although that egregious case included distortion even of the poll results themselves.[14] More commonly, however, survey results are misleading because of poorly worded questions, typified by Alan Kay as equivalent to: "Would you like a free lunch?"[15]

In the long run, these biases in survey sampling, question design, and the reporting of results undermine the credibility of even well-crafted surveys. This has a direct effect on the influence of public opinion polls, which are hamstrung by the common perception that one cannot trust survey results. Every time public officials and citizens learn of fraud or deception in a poll, especially when they discover it firsthand, it makes them less likely to believe the next survey findings they read or hear. Given the widespread use of biased and false surveys in political and commercial ad campaigns, it is not surprising that considerable skepticism has accumulated regarding surveys as a whole. More indirectly, this skepticism may erode response rates in surveys, as the most cynical subgroup of citizens becomes unwilling to participate when asked to do so. This could result in a genuine bias in survey samples over time.[16]

On the other hand, some critics fault public opinion surveys for being too powerful. Some critics argue that surveys can foreclose inclusive political debate and other forms of public expression. Elizabeth Noelle-Neumann argues that public opinion polls (and similar mechanisms) can create a "spiral of silence." When polls reveal a majority view, the most malleable members of the minority shift over to the majority view or simply silence (or lie about) their own views. The next poll then shows an even larger majority, which similarly influences the next-most impressionable subset of the remaining minority. As this cycle continues, the majority view spirals outward to absorb, or at least silence, more and more of public opinion.[17] Research on opinion shifts in response to information about the views of others, however, provides only mixed support for the "spiral of silence" thesis. Hearing about public opinions does prompt people to reflect upon their own views. For less informed voters, the result can be a shift toward the more popular view. Among more involved and informed voters, this same self-reflection process often results in the strengthening of their original views, even if those clash with majority public opinion.[18]

Another criticism is that surveys limit the range of ways in which the public expresses its views. Anointed the one, true king of public opinion measures, random-sample surveys make even large-scale demonstrations and civil disobedience seem unrepresentative, if not irresponsible. By mediating citizens' opinions through forced-choice questions and statistical summaries, surveys also dampen the strength and volume of the public's voice, which can speak more boldly at a rally or in a public meeting. In this view, a political system should recognize survey research as nothing more than one among many worthy methods for measuring the public's sentiments.[19] Benjamin Ginsberg points out that the commercial and political origins of poll data compound this problem:

> Given the commercial character of the polling industry, differences between the polls' concerns and those of the general public are probably inevitable. Polls generally raise questions that are of interest to clients and purchasers of poll data—newspapers, political candidates, government agencies, business corporations, and so on. . . . Because they seldom pose questions about the foundation of the existing order, while constantly asking respondents to choose from among the alternatives defined by that order, . . . polls may help to narrow the focus of public discussion and to reinforce the limits on what the public perceives to be realistic political and social possibility.[20]

Notwithstanding that some academic and interest group surveys address questions that commercial and government polls ignore or avoid, there is merit in this view. Public opinion surveys can create a representative and articulate public voice, but they have difficulty spontaneously capturing the public's underlying priorities. This is partly because of the institutional problem highlighted by Ginsberg, but it is also because surveys are not deliberative. Because public meetings are open-ended and permit extended discussion, some citizens look to them as a more deliberative form of public expression.

FACE-TO-FACE MEETINGS WITH ELECTED OFFICIALS

In a sense, public opinion polls bring together the numerous, discordant voices of a large public into a statistical arrangement. Sometimes the voices come together in a harmony of public consensus; sometimes the survey juxtaposes opposing views in a clear counterpoint. The orchestration permitted by closed-ended questions and quantitative summaries, however, can obscure the real dynamics and diversity of public voices on a given issue. A public hearing or meeting can bring these many voices into a single room and record their interplay.

When this exchange of ideas and perspectives is inclusive of different perspectives, and involves attentive listening and clear articulation, it often amounts to genuine public deliberation. A sincere meeting between a school board and a group of concerned parents can change the way both parties view an issue, as well as how they see one another. Careful discussion and debate can cause people to critically examine the problem they face, their own perspectives, and the views of their opponents. This leads citizens toward a more enlightened understanding of their interests and a more accurate understanding of the policy problem under discussion. This, in turn, can lead to an articulate presentation of the public's shared and divergent interests.[21]

In practice, many public meetings fail to achieve deliberation. The public hearing is an especially notorious form of public dialogue. Often required by federal, state, or local statutes, public hearings give citizens the opportunity to express their concerns and address questions directly to public officials. At a typical hearing, citizens take turns speaking before a panel of government agency employees and elected officials. The experience of Thomas Webler and Ortwin Renn, who have witnessed countless hearings in the United States and abroad, suggests that neither citizens nor policymakers value the public hearing process:

> To a citizen, the thought of attending a public hearing immediately conjures up negative images. Citizens often picture the public hearing process as disempowering. Typically, attendance is slight. To regulatory officials, experts, and project sponsors, the public hearing hall is a battle zone. Legal obliga-

tions must be met, hopefully without raising the hackles of the local populace. A well-attended meeting is bad news.[22]

Webler and Renn suggest that public hearings usually fail to produce deliberative and influential public deliberation both because of their timing within the policymaking process and the "structure of discourse within the public hearing process."[23] When public officials schedule hearings late in the process after they have reached a preliminary (or final) decision, the hearing only permits citizens to complain or implore a change in plan. Under those circumstances, the process becomes adversarial, because citizens perceive that those "hearing" their input have already chosen to ignore it. A former county council member in Maryland explained that elected officials are no less cynical about hearings:

> One of my fellow council members would occasionally start a public hearing by announcing that he already knew what position each witness would take. And he was usually correct. I figure I spent nearly 2,000 hours in formal public hearings over the last eight years. It was not time well spent. Public hearings may give the appearance of public involvement, but they are unsatisfactory to citizen and official alike.[24]

The structure of discourse at public hearings is a more subtle problem. Even when an elected official convenes a hearing before making a decision, the typical public hearing encourages a nondeliberative process by restricting public expression to a series of statements and limiting official response to periodic counterpoints. Hearings also tend to have unduly technical issue framings that make it difficult for well-meaning citizens to address officials in their own language.[25] Daniel Fiorino, the director of the Waste and Chemical Policy Division at the U.S. Environmental Protection Agency, acknowledges that when agency hearings are held, they "usually do not allow interested parties much of a chance to engage in full discussions with the agency and other parties or to influence the outcome" on issues before the agency.[26]

One increasingly common form of quasi-hearing is what public officials call a "town hall" or "town meeting." Officials invite the general public to these meetings to discuss a particular issue, and depending on the topic, timing, and advance publicity, the meeting rooms typically become either empty meditation chambers or rousing political theater houses. When attendance is light, there can be a pleasant informality at such affairs, but there is little discussion. The attendees include friendly party activists, one or two strangers who saw a note in the paper, and possibly a fretful lobbyist who has had trouble getting a one-on-one meeting with an official. The poor attendance can give representatives the impression that the public does not care about an issue, or that it endorses whatever position the official might have.

Other town halls draw large crowds and often result in bedlam.[27] When a group of elected officials in Madison, Wisconsin, held a public meeting in 1990 to discuss responses to Iraq's invasion of Kuwait, hundreds of antiwar protesters dominated the meeting. In one impassioned speech after another, citizens demanded that their representatives take any actions they could to prevent a full-scale war between Iraq and the United States. "All of the oil in the Persian Gulf is not worth the life of one American man or woman," exclaimed one veteran from Green Bay. When an Army officer from Whitewater spoke in support of President Bush, the crowd hissed, booed, and heckled her. In the end, however, the overwhelming opposition to war swayed none of the hawkish representatives present. One congressman even dared to defend his unchanged position. Republican Scott Klug, who had taken office just weeks before by carrying suburban towns and areas outside of Madison, argued that the public in attendance did not represent the views of voters in the surrounding areas. "I would have liked to have done this in Cross Plains or Stoughton," he said. Given poor weather and treacherous highways, the meeting was dominated by antiwar activists, he believed, because few outside the city of Madison were able to attend.[28]

Residents of Minnesota gave similar antiwar speeches at a series of town meetings held by another newly elected representative, Democrat Paul Wellstone. The liberal senator agreed with the pacifist sentiments of the speakers he heard, and he used the meetings as the basis for an editorial released to the nation's newspapers. In the *Seattle Times,* Wellstone's comments ran under the headline, "Minnesota Message: War on Iraq Would Be a Terrible Mistake." In the editorial, Wellstone explained that in response to his meeting announcements, "large crowds overflowed auditoriums in the cities of Minneapolis, Duluth, Rochester and St. Cloud and in the rural communities of Chisolm, Virginia and Marshall." The meetings were not "scientific opinion polls," but they served as a "lightning rod that attracted those with strong feelings about our nation's policy in the Gulf." Wellstone's editorial describes the specific pleas of diverse attendees but never acknowledges any disagreement with his antiwar position. These meetings provided political ammunition for Wellstone, but they did not demonstrate a deliberative and influential public voice.[29]

Not all public meetings resemble these extreme examples. Even if one looks only at the town meetings on the Gulf War, at least one member of Congress appeared to be swayed by such gatherings. The Virginia Democrat James Moran had argued that war with Iraq was justified, but he reversed his position following a public meeting in Alexandria. After the meeting, Moran told a reporter that he was surprised to hear the antiwar sentiment in a district peppered with military bases. "There's a balance we in Congress have to strike between leadership and representation," Moran explained. "I'm convinced the vast majority of the constituency that elected me to represent them is not prepared to go to war."[30]

Few public meetings prove both deliberative and influential, but almost none are also representative. The voices that might have swayed Representative Moran were not heard from every corner of his district; rather, the few electric cries he heard were drawn by the "lightning rod" of a public meeting. He did not hear the flickering thoughts and soft voices of less involved, aroused, or mobile constituents because they did not take part in the public meetings. Many people, in fact, rarely resort to any form of active public expression, whether it be writing a letter to the editor or demonstrating in front of a government building. Most public representatives recognize this fact and, like the Wisconsin congressman mentioned above, dismiss contrary sentiments expressed at public meetings on those grounds. As an anonymous county commissioner remarked to one investigator, "I think frequently you get your vocal minority there instead of a balance of opinion."[31] Even if the vocal minority's voice proves influential, it does so at the cost of being unrepresentative.

TALK RADIO

Face-to-face public meetings of citizens hardly make a sound compared to the clamor of daily debates in the mass media. For some democratic theorists, this is as it should be. As Benjamin Page argues, the sheer size and technological complexity of modern society

> almost certainly necessitate a *division of labor* in political expertise, policy-making, and communication. This is why we have professional policy experts, at universities, research organizations, and elsewhere, who deliberate about policy in a multitude of small groups of their own. It is also why we have professional politicians and why we have a representative, rather than direct, democracy.[32]

In a sense, Page argues, the United States and similar nations rely upon
a representative system of public deliberation. Thus, "The perennial
problem of how to ensure that legislators properly represent their constituents has an analogue in the . . . problem [of] how to ensure representativeness by professional communicators," who include "reporters,
writers, commentators, and television pundits, as well as public officials
and selected experts from academia or think tanks."[33]

Even advocates of representative deliberation, however, acknowledge that this system of public expression does not always function
properly. As I argue in chapter 3, the mass media, intellectual elites, and
public officials often pursue agendas that conflict with the public's interest.[34] Page recognizes one problem in particular:

> The most prominent journalists, television commentators, and public offi-
> cials tend to have much higher incomes than the average American and to
> live in very different circumstances. On certain class-related issues, it seems
> possible that these professional communicators may interpret events in ways
> that do not take the public's values into account and may recommend poli-
> cies contrary to those values.[35]

Because of this class difference, representative deliberation sometimes
fails when there is little or no disagreement among policy elites, such as
when the United States has a bipartisan foreign policy. Under these circumstances, the public often remains unaware of an important issue or
its ramifications for the general population, and public tragedies like
the wholesale collapse of savings and loan associations in the 1980s can
follow a period of elite consensus, media indifference, and public ignorance.[36]

Even in these situations, the mass media can solve their own problems by providing alternative communication outlets, such as talk
radio. To illustrate the importance of this form of public voice, Page offers the example of the Zoe Baird nomination. President Clinton had
nominated Baird to be attorney general, and her confirmation appeared
likely, despite the revelation that she and her husband had hired two il-
legal aliens to help with driving and baby-sitting. Baird's bipartisan
support eroded, however, and Clinton withdrew her nomination after
a firestorm of public opposition. The criticisms of Baird flowed through
call-in radio programs that encouraged listeners to talk about current
issues. Callers to programs across the country were outraged that a
law-breaker would serve as the highest-ranking law-enforcement official. Baird's decision was sympathetically viewed by fellow members of
the elite, but not by the general public. As one Boston talk-show host

remarked, "I don't think the average schmo says, 'Hey, I know 15 people who have Peruvian live-in nannies.' " The evidence suggests that the criticism of Baird was a case of genuine popular backlash, rather than the result of behind-the-scenes orchestration.[37]

If talk radio is an important forum for the expression of the public's voice, the next question concerns who takes part in this form of discussion. As anyone who has listened to talk radio knows, the host's perspective is more important than those of the callers, because the on-air personality sets the topic and tone of a show.

Although Jerry Brown, the former Democratic governor of California, created the *We The People Radio Show,* successful liberal hosts are rare in the upper echelons of talk radio. Political conservatives, however, have large followings. Table 8 shows that there is not one clear liberal among the most popular shows in the nation. The top-rated political programs include only conservatives, some of whom proudly wave the flag for the Republican Party (Rush Limbaugh, G. Gordon Liddy, Michael Reagan), while others express conservative views without the party label (Dr. Laura, Art Bell, Jim Bohannon). One might mistake Howard Stern and his forerunner, Don Imus, for quasi-liberals because of their openness to unusual points of view. These "shock jocks," however, rarely dwell on political matters. Stern, Imus, and their innumerable local imitators devote their shows to perverted or simply strange guests and topics, and when their talk becomes political, they identify themselves as libertarians as much as anything else.

Not only do the hosts of the political talk radio programs in the United States consistently present issues from a conservative perspective, they are also notorious for their intolerance of opposing views. The on-air personalities of Rush Limbaugh and G. Gordon Liddy, two of the most successful and trend-setting conservative hosts, include a macho arrogance inhospitable to sustained counterargument and self-criticism. There is no spirit of debate in Limbaugh's aptly chosen book titles, *The Way Things Are* and *The Way Things Ought to Be.* On his radio program, Limbaugh's assertions never face serious criticism, even though many of his most outrageous and frequently repeated claims have been debunked in mainstream newspapers and popular writings, such as Al Franken's best-selling tongue-in-cheek rebuttal, *Rush Limbaugh Is a Big Fat Idiot.* Passing up an opportunity for lucrative national television exposure, Limbaugh declined Franken's invitation to debate the proposition that, in fact, he is a "big fat idiot."[38]

TABLE 8
PROFILES OF TALK RADIO PROGRAMS WITH
THE LARGEST AUDIENCES (1988)

Listeners (Millions)	Host	Political Ideology	Description
15.8	Rush Limbaugh	conservative	Most influential national host; strong Republican supporter; coined the term *feminazi*
14.5	Dr. Laura Schlessinger	conservative	America's "Mommy" gives a "Judeo-Christian" perspective; strongly anti-gay; co-wrote *The Ten Commandments: The Significance of God's Laws in Everyday Life* (1998)
9.3	Howard Stern	libertarian	This "shock-jock," a.k.a. the "king of all media," has run for office as a libertarian; quite sex-obsessed
6.3	Art Bell	quasi-conservative	Discusses parapsychology and alien abductions; more anti-government than pro-Republican
6.3	Dr. Joy Browne	nonpolitical	Relationship advice program
5.0	Don Imus	libertarian (if anything)	This "shock jock" promotes himself as "the man who says whatever hideous things pop into his head"
5.0	Jim Bohannon	conservative	Self-described as a "militant moderate" but celebrated by the Heritage Foundation as a conservative
5.0	Bruce Williams	nonpolitical	General advice program
3.3	G. Gordon Liddy	conservative	Made famous by his role in Watergate; strongly pro-Republican and conservative
2.5	Ken and Daria Dolan	nonpolitical	Financial advice program
2.5	Dr. Dean Edell	nonpolitical	Health advice program
2.5	Michael Reagan	conservative	Son of President Ronald Reagan; pro-Republican

SOURCE: Ratings estimating total number of cumulative weekly listeners come from *Talkers Magazine*'s (1988) sampling of Arbitron reports. *Talkers* updates the list every six months at http://www.talkers.com/talkaud.html. Program descriptions come from hosts' promotional materials and program summaries.

Conservative though the hosts may be, talk radio's listeners appear to be diverse. A comprehensive survey of national talk-radio audiences since 1989 suggests a profile that defies the stereotype of the white, male, conservative "ditto-head." Because the survey is methodologically schizophrenic—integrating focus groups with mall surveys and caller interviews, its exact audience estimates are unreliable, but it suggests that talk-radio audiences are surprisingly diverse. Arbitron data, which collapse news and talk-radio listenerships, indicate that 57 percent of adult news/talk listeners are men. A more methodologically rigorous but geographically narrow survey of radio listeners in San Diego, California, found that the frequency of listening to talk radio was unrelated to every major demographic variable. In other words, talk-radio listeners come from all bands of the demographic and political spectrum, even though the talk-radio listenership overrepresents conservatives.[39]

Research also suggests that those who *call* talk-radio programs come from diverse backgrounds. A study of callers in Prince's County, Maryland, for example, sought to learn the makeup of talk-radio users in a county that had a relatively large African-American middle-class population. The investigators found that social class did not predict call-in use, even though past research had shown it to be a factor in general media use. In addition, call-in use was unrelated to perceptions of public officials' responsiveness and trustworthiness. Instead, those who called talk-radio programs were distinguished by their high levels of political self-efficacy. Those with greater confidence in their ability to take meaningful political actions were more likely to pick up the phone and interact with talk-radio hosts.[40] In other words, the people calling talk-radio programs come from a wide variety of backgrounds but tend to have a degree of political self-confidence.

This minimum of diversity and political initiative give talk radio some potential as a medium for repressed public expression, but the hosts and program formats of the top-rated programs make talk radio an inhospitable setting for liberal political viewpoints. Conservative and libertarian voices closed out of mainstream debates may make themselves heard through these programs, but progressive and liberal ones do not. The expansion of talk radio may provide avenues for these voices, but those views may not be suited to the macho, aggressive character of talk radio in its present incarnation.

More generally, the talk-radio format that has taken hold in American political culture does not permit open-ended political deliberation. No popular program attracts listeners through the to-and-fro of honest political debate between intellectual equals. Mutual respect between a sincere host and a critical listener is not the hallmark of talk shows, which have earned the moniker "hate radio." For many political observers, it is enough for a diversity of voices to exist, but deliberative democratic theorists ask not just for a diversity of views but for a genuine exchange and debate among those perspectives.[41]

LOBBYING AS A MEANS OF ARTICULATION AND INFLUENCE

Each of these forms of public voice—opinion polls, public meetings, and talk radio—present officials with the views of the citizenry, but they have relatively little direct influence on the policymaking process. Politicians do read newsworthy polls, attend pivotal public meetings, and notice when talk radio has generated an uproar, but those forms of voice rarely receive more than recognition. There may be many reasons for this unresponsiveness, but the analyses of voting in chapters 3 and 4 suggest that the primary problem is that public voice is not tethered to a credible threat of collective rejection of unrepresentative incumbents. Individual citizens may threaten to vote for an opponent if their advice goes unheeded, but an elected official has no reason to believe that the average voter can organize a successful opposition campaign.

By contrast, effective lobbying can change actual votes on upcoming legislation, and it can prod officials to change what bills they introduce or what causes they champion. By "lobbyists," I mean the full universe of influential interest groups, which includes policy institutes and think tanks (e.g., the American Enterprise Institute, Brookings Institution, Heritage Foundation) and, more commonly, special- and public-interest groups (e.g., the American Medical Association, American Association of Retired Persons, National Right to Life Committee, Mothers against Drunk Driving, People for the American Way, Conservative Caucus, National Federation of Industrial Businesses League, Sierra Club). Often, the actual individuals and firms representing these interests are professional lobbyists and public relations mercenaries (e.g., Hill & Knowlton), and it is increasingly common for lobbyists and their firms to represent multiple interests.[42] Before examining why these groups and their lobbyists have success influencing elected officials, it is useful to briefly relate the criteria for political voice to the practice of lobbying.

Influential though it may be, lobbying is far from the democratic ideal of voice. Lobbyists and advocacy groups generally present narrow or partisan viewpoints, earning them the name "special interests." Some public-interest groups do advocate policies supported by the general public, but even those rely upon their professional experts for guidance more than on random samples of the public or diverse grassroots memberships. More generally, lobbying is not a representative form of public voice because its influence depends largely upon the wealth that funds it.[43] "One dollar, one vote" is a closer approximation to lobbying's ethic of representation. Even the most influential individual-donor lobbyists are not evenly distributed across different social groups: a recent study of federal campaign contributions of $200 or more cross-referenced donor zip codes with census data and found that donations disproportionately came from predominantly wealthy, white zip codes.[44]

In addition, lobbying is not an inclusive, deliberative form of public voice. The most public-spirited interest groups sometimes promote public dialogue on an issue by convening public meetings or engaging in televised debates, but the purpose behind such activities is to increase the amount public support for a preset policy position. Persuasion through argument is an important part of the deliberative process, but orchestrated public discussions often become manipulative. For example, Murray Edelman argues that policy advocates attach themselves strategically and psychologically to a particular plan of action and then cast about for problems that justify their prefabricated solutions. Thus, an organization might promote public meetings to discuss a problem only to lead the public to support a particular solution.[45]

Most interest groups lack even internal deliberation. As Jane Mansbridge observes, "Few interest associations in the United States or Europe institutionalize any formal deliberative processes among their membership, let alone deliberative processes designed to promote identification with the public good." Mansbridge's own research on the movement for an Equal Rights Amendment found that "even in this democratic and public-spirited movement, the elites never learned what the grass-roots activists would have formulated as good public policy if both elites and activists had taken part in a more extensive process of deliberation."[46]

Lobbying does not usually involve a representative and deliberative public voice, but it does present an articulate one. Lobbyists focus on concrete agendas and specific policies. If defeating a single amendment or obtaining a particular ruling means outright victory for a lobbyist, his or her lobbying campaign will speak unambiguously on that specific point. As one example among thousands, Boeing's $5.2 million lobbying campaign in 1996 focused on tax "mitigation" and "avoidance." Though costly, the campaign succeeded in winning the company deductions and credits resulting in a $33 million rebate—the equivalent of a negative 9 percent tax rate.[47] The articulate quality of the lobbyist's voice is one reason it is so effective. By contrast, other forms of public voice often result in general preferences, vague policy preferences, or specific demands unaccompanied by awareness or acknowledgment of the difficulties of meeting those requests. In this sense, the lobbyist's reasonable and precise criticism of an incumbent's actions is closer to Albert Hirschman's understanding of voice as a complaint about a specific product defect.

Aside from the fact that it is clear and realistic, why does a lobbyist's request receive a response? The exit, voice, and loyalty model suggests that the lobbyist must be making a credible threat of collective rejection of an incumbent. Most policymakers are busy people, and although they might appreciate the technical assistance and professional experience of a lobbyist on an issue, in the long term, lobbyists would have little tangible influence if they did not give elected officials a more powerful reason to heed their voices. The reason that lobbyists give, often implicitly, is that they have the power to influence electoral outcomes in incumbents' own districts. Whether in the form of a public-interest nonprofit organization, a private special-interest association, or a partisan political organization, lobbyists can shape elections in three ways: through campaign contributions, independent expenditures, and voter organizing and mobilization.

Standing behind many lobbyists are political action committees (PACs), which can contribute up to $5,000 per election to a candidate for federal office. A group such as Handgun Control Inc. can give a candidate $5,000 in the primary and another $5,000 in the general election, to be spent at the candidate's discretion. Indirectly, Handgun Control can encourage unaffiliated individuals and other PACs to make similar contributions, so it may leverage a much larger total contribution. Many congressional candidates receive the maximum legal contribution from multiple members of a family whose commercial or ideological interests are represented by a single lobbyist or lobbying organization. At $1,000 per person, this can mean $10,000 or more per election from a single family. Even more indirectly, PACs and individuals can contribute "soft money" to national parties, who then send the money to candidates or spend it on their behalf. In this way, PACs can even support candidates who publicly refuse to accept PAC money.[48] In the course of a primary and general election, a PAC can give $30,000 to a national party, and individuals can give $40,000. As an extreme example, during the health care debate of 1993–94, a cluster of PACs affiliated with insurance companies donated a total of $8,764,815 to individual candidates and $801,863 to national political parties.[49] Direct contributions can exceed these federal limits in the many state and local races that have no constraints on individual and organizational donations. By making campaign contributions conditional on incumbent responsiveness, lobbyists can buy a measure of influence, especially from candidates concerned about reelection.

Indirect spending, however, can prove even more powerful. To aid its lobbying efforts, an organization can directly attack or praise candidates, and some incumbents respond to the promise or threat of such action. For an incumbent who has irked powerful interests, turning to competing interests can become the only way to fend off those attacks. The example of the Republican Congressman Philip English is instructive. English won a close race in 1994 for Pennsylvania's Twenty-First District seat, which is anchored in Erie. With only 49 percent of the vote in 1994, and a district that had given President Bush just 34 percent of the vote in 1992, English had to triple his campaign funds to win reelection in 1996, and he took all the direct contributions he could get. Favorable ads run by the American Hospital Association and the U.S. Chamber of Congress bolstered English's position, but those ads had to counter a strong series of attacks sponsored by the AFL-CIO. The *Almanac of American Politics* notes that "during one 20-hour stretch in November, more than 500 political ads aired on Erie television" and that noncandidate organizations "appear to have spent at least $1.4 million, and quite possibly more" on the race.[50] In the end, English won with 106,875 votes to 104,004 votes for his Democratic opponent. For local, state, and national public officials like English, the lesson is clear: lobbyists have the potential to spark an electoral defeat, and they often have the power to prevent one. Indirect expenditures are a clear manifestation of that power.

Other lobbying organizations have both money and members. Behind them stand not only a well-funded and media-savvy public relations arsenal but also a large membership and a skilled organizing staff. One of the most striking examples of this lobbying tool is the membership of the American Association of Retired Persons (AARP). Through a system of incentives, the AARP has built a membership exceeding 30 million, and the organization has become skilled at mobilizing its members to contact specific officials who might fail to respond to the AARP's voice. "Those millions of letters, postcards, and phone calls that arrive on Capitol Hill and at the White House promise revenge at the next election" if officials do not protect Social Security or other policies backed by the AARP, Lance Bennett notes.[51] Elected officials recognize the importance of these letters because they represent more than diffuse constituent concerns; rather, they are a clear reminder of AARP's ability to influence thousands of votes in any single district. In a congressional district where an incumbent has difficulty winning re-election, such as the Pennsylvania district described above, those votes could prove decisive. In a smaller state or local district race in which turnout is low, a few hundred votes can make the difference. If a lobbyist's organization has proven that it can register new voters sympathetic to its cause, bring its otherwise nonvoting supporters to the polls, or even change the votes of its membership, the lobbyist can then speak to elected officials with a powerful voice backed up by serious threat.

Sometimes political groups go much farther than the AARP and other mainstream lobbying organizations. Civil disobedience and other forms of protest can prove effective mechanisms of expressing dissent if the actions are timely, well-attended, and articulate. Even protest, however, has the same problems of other forms of lobbying: the participants in protest politics are unrepresentative of the general public. Those who participate in protest politics, as well as other demanding forms of political expression, are disproportionately white and wealthy.[52]

Whether the voice of a lobbyist is backed by people or money, much of its influence derives from the ability to shape electoral outcomes. Other factors contribute to the influence of a given lobbyist: real policy expertise, refined social skills, cordial or intimate relationships with officeholders, and even powerful moral persuasion can have an independent influence on policymakers. Nonetheless, it is the implied threat of retaliation (or promise of aid) that makes elected officials more responsive to lobbying than other forms of public voice.

LISTENING FOR AN AUTHENTIC PUBLIC VOICE

Whatever their failings may be, public opinion polls can create a relatively representative and articulate recording of the public's voice. Public hearings allow some degree of deliberation among citizens, often in the company of policymakers, and talk-radio debates permit a dispersed population to participate in public discussion. Lobbying, by contrast, often results in articulate and influential citizen input directly into the policymaking process. These forms of expression demonstrate how to generate representative, deliberative, articulate, and influential citizen feedback, but they do not provide a means for integrating those qualities into a single democratic public voice.

This creates a dilemma for even the most well-intentioned public official. After an ideal democratic election, a representative remains uncertain about the needs and concerns of his or her constituency, let alone the larger public as a whole. The best of all possible elections give offices to individuals who understand and respect the general interests of their constituents, but without periodic guidance, elected officials have difficulty knowing how to act in the public's best interest. Officeholders can not *re*present the public's policy judgments to their decision-making body until the public *presents* those concerns to them. In practice, policymakers often act without knowing how the general public might view an issue, and citizens who find fault with such actions routinely state their views after the fact by criticizing officials for the actions they have taken. On a given issue, an elected official might hear the public's voice as a warning, a request, praise, criticism, or simply a notice. Under these circumstances, it is not surprising that public officials respond to lobbyists, who underscore the real consequences of following their advice and offer a measure of genuine policy expertise.

The situation might be different if the public could express itself in a way that was representative, deliberative, and articulate. If an elected official heard such a voice and knew it was genuine, he or she might be inclined to respond to it. At the present time, however, no such voice exists. "The biggest problem facing Americans is not those issues that bombard us daily. . . . *The crisis is that we as a people don't know how to come together to solve these problems.* We lack the capacities to address the issues or remove the obstacles that stand in the way of public deliberation," lament Frances Moore Lappé and Paul Martin DuBois.[53]

Contemporary American politics lacks this means of discovering and articulating the interests of the general public, but some democratic reformers believe they have found it. The following chapter introduces these ideas and judges their effectiveness as a means of creating a representative, deliberative, articulate, and influential public voice.

CHAPTER 6

Glimpses of the Deliberative Public

The often tumultuous, always unstable democratic urge does
not introduce a workable notion of the people, or of the
public interest. . . . It leaves behind the underlying conditions
it found: a political economy of self-seeking interests pushing
ahead within a complex welter of political rules that advantage some citizens, disadvantage others, and seem almost invisible to all.

James A. Morone, The Democratic Wish

American government embodies different political traditions. In the
view of the historian James Morone, the clash between Thomas Jefferson's democratic populism and James Madison's liberal republicanism
has continued through two centuries of political debate. Morone argues
that American government embodies the Madisonian vision, yet the
public periodically acts upon a "democratic wish" for "reform and
change, a legitimate, populist counter to the liberal status quo." When
successful, democratic reform begins with a political stalemate, in
which existing institutions and elites thwart any efforts at change. Different social groups then answer a call for the people to come forward,
and these diverse groups converge on a single set of ideas or symbols of
change. The resulting institutional changes create the image of a united
public, but that soon "evaporates into the reality of classes and interests scrapping for partisan advantage. . . . When the people and their
consensus fail to materialize, the aspirations of the democratic wish are
done in." The new institutions, however, remain. The new political con-
figuration may temporarily break up the preexisting stalemate, but the
fundamental Madisonian rules remain the same—"a political economy
of self-seeking interests pushing ahead within a complex welter of political rules that advantage some citizens, disadvantage others, and
seem almost invisible to all."[1]

Any attempt to discern a truly democratic public voice must recognize the history of failed populist reforms catalogued by Morone. Thus far, the call for a deliberative public voice falls into the conventional pattern. Interest in public deliberation in the United States grew in response to an emerging critique of American politics: advocates of deliberation claim that elections have become shallow popularity contests that push "the people" out of the political process, and government has become tangled in gridlock because of the intense cross-pressures of interest groups and the partisan posturing required by conventional electoral strategy. The deliberative reform process is now in the second stage, in which various groups answer the call for "the people" and suggest different reforms of the political process. To add another chapter to Morone's history of failed populist reforms, the deliberative movement must now produce political institutions that reinforce liberal Madisonian political traditions, albeit unintentionally. New institutions and political processes that create additional layers of bureaucracy and complicated, ineffective avenues of public expression would fit nicely within the historical pattern.

These could be the results of the deliberative reforms under development, but this outcome is not inevitable. I argue in this chapter that modern experiments in deliberative discussion suggest that new forms of public voice could create more educated and active citizens and reveal popular and effective solutions to pressing national and local policy problems. What might such deliberation look like, and how could it avoid the pitfalls of past efforts to discern the public's will? To answer those questions, it is best to see how advocates of deliberation have tried to translate their democratic theories into practical methods of public discussion. I have grouped those efforts into three categories: deliberative civic education, community deliberation, and random sample forums. Each of these forms of discussion offers insight into the promise and problems of deliberative democratic reform.

DELIBERATIVE CIVIC EDUCATION

From the time of the colonies to the present day, educators and civic leaders have developed a variety of programs to create a democratic citizenry.[2] Many of these have used group discussion methods, because face-to-face talk provides direct experience with the deliberative element of the democratic process. Group discussions in America on local, state, national, and international policy issues include those sponsored by the Lyceum, the Chautauqua Assembly, Great Books, and many others, both small and large.[3] The communication scholar Ernest Bormann argues that the "public discussion model" of political dialogue became so commonplace in the United States that it achieved the status of a "special model of communication" embedded in America's larger cultural norms and practices.[4]

Modern examples of these programs include the projects of the Study Circles Resource Center and the National Issues Forums.[5] Established by the Topsfield Foundation, the Study Circles Resource Center (SCRC) promotes citizen education in the United States and believes that study circles are an ideal method for such education. The number of people who annually participate in SCRC's study circles is not known, and the SCRC's promotional literature is more interested in the widespread use of all varieties of study circles than the use of SCRC materials per se.[6]

By the SCRC's definition, a study circle is "a participatory, democratic discussion group that focuses on a social or political issue."[7] Ideally, "individual members take responsibility for the study circle and ultimately control both the content of the discussions and the group process."[8] The SCRC hopes that organizing and participating in study circles will provide individuals with a broad range of skills and values conducive to democratic citizenship.

The SCRC conceives of study circles as a series of three to five small group discussions among five to twenty people focusing on a particular issue. Each session has a discussion leader who (a) ensures broad participation, egalitarian communication styles, mutual respect, and careful listening, (b) keeps the discussion focused and incisive, and (c) maintains a neutral posture in the discussion. Print and audiovisual materials provide a framework for each topic and are designed to spark spontaneous discussion.[9] For example, in 1994, the SCRC joined with ACCESS: A Security Information Service to publish *In Harm's Way,* a discussion guide on the use of U.S. military forces in international conflicts. The book is divided into four sessions, each of which outlines alternative views and introduces relevant facts and issues.[10]

As for the educational benefits of participation, the SCRC claims that "the study circle . . . has a long track record of enhancing individual self-esteem, increasing communication skills, and encouraging self-directed adult learning." Participation in study circles triggers "feelings of power and the capacity to effect change through education." The

SCRC also claims that discussion has direct political effects: "The study circle . . . helps citizens to develop the capacity for self-government and leadership by helping them to acquire the knowledge and skills to participate actively in public life." In sum, the SCRC believes that study circles have broad effects on political attitudes and knowledge, and these effects are presumed to result in sophisticated political deliberation beyond the study circles themselves.[11]

The National Issues Forums (NIF) has much in common with the SCRC's method and mission, but it is more ambitious. The NIF is the flagship of current programs in deliberative civic education, and it has caught the attention of scholars who study political communication. According to an NIF self-study, by 1993 several thousand potential NIF conveners had received training in the NIF method at the annual Summer Public Policy Institute and similar regional institutes. The same study showed that many of these potential conveners had chosen to adopt the NIF approach: during 1993, for example, forums were probably convened by approximately 1,440 adult literacy programs, 2,600 high schools, and 1,360 civic organizations.[12]

Individual organizations and conveners use the NIF system for their own particular educational and institutional purposes, and this diversity is actively encouraged by the Kettering Foundation, which initiated the program in 1982. The foundation prides itself on the diversity of NIF settings and has published different NIF pamphlets for use in the Catholic community, colleges, and high school and adult education programs.[13]

The NIF's basic guidebook, *Hard Choices,* argues that the NIF serves many of the goals that participants themselves have when they attend forums. Citizens want to "overcome a personal sense of being without voice or power." They seek to play a more direct and effective role in politics by acting on "pressing problems in their communities" and changing the way "local, state, and national governments understand the public interest." Citizens hope to "learn how to make difficult choices" and "increase and improve the quality of public deliberation" by making it "more sensible and constructive."[14]

As an educational process, the NIF has two basic aims: to help participants develop more informed and reflective judgments on current policy issues and, more generally, to teach the art of public deliberation. If it is successful, the NIF approach gives citizens the cognitive and social tools they need to build reasoned public policies upon real common ground.[15]

To achieve these educational goals, the NIF uses face-to-face group discussion. The guidelines in NIF manuals leave much room for variation, and the *NIF Leadership Handbook* openly acknowledges that "there is no one best way to organize a Forum." NIF discussions "can take many forms ranging from community-wide town meetings attended by the general public to small study circles sponsored by individuals or local organizations, such as book clubs or church groups, for their own members." NIF forums come in many shapes and sizes, but the approach may be best suited to a series of study circles with five to twenty people, "especially since we place some stress on encouraging participants to 'work through' an issue."[16]

No matter what the size of the group, the first step in the NIF process is reading an "issue book" prior to the forum or the first study circle. Each issue book provides relevant factual information, but the most important reason for reading the book is that it frames the issue in terms of three or four contrasting policy choices. For example, the *Freedom of Speech* issue book outlines three choices: government censorship, private industry self-censorship, and unfettered speech.[17] The book on American foreign policy distinguishes three options: abandoning global leadership to address domestic concerns, focusing on U.S. national security, or promoting democracy and human rights abroad.[18] In practice, not all NIF participants take the time to read the book. For this reason (and to refresh the memories of other participants), moderators often begin forums by reading a brief summary of the issue book or by showing a fifteen-minute videotape that comes with each book.

Next, the moderator establishes ground rules and explains the deliberative process to participants. The ideal NIF moderator will "explain the expectation that all those present will be both active listeners and active participants—it is their program."[19] This is crucial, because, as one NIF convener has lamented, "Citizens always come to forums expecting to vote on something. . . . They always want solutions—it's hard for them to accept the idea of just discussing the issue."[20] The NIF Institute provides a variety of wall posters outlining the NIF process, but moderators also can remind participants that after the forum, everyone should be able to:

(1) identify the range of realistic alternatives and move toward a choice; (2) make a good case for those positions one dislikes as well as the position one likes, and consider choices one has not considered before; (3) understand others have reasons for their choices and that their reasons are very interesting—not dumb, unreasonable, or immoral; (4) realize that one's knowl-

edge is not complete until one understands why others feel the way they do about the choices; (5) consider the underlying values of each choice; and (6) leave the forum/study circle "stewing" over the choices. (Sometimes this is called "thinking.")[21]

Some moderators then move participants through one more introductory stage before discussing the policy choices. These moderators encourage participants to identify their personal stake in the issue by asking questions such as, "Is this an important issue to you?" Or, "How does the issue affect people?" Questions such as these draw participants into the discussion and make abstract issues more concrete. For example, forum participants discussing the U.S. economy might tell brief stories about their own financial straits or the economic injustices they have witnessed in their communities.[22]

Moderators then lead the group into deliberation. During this phase, the moderator remains neutral, guiding but not directing the direction of discussion. Moderators encourage participants to connect choices with values, illustrate their ideas with stories or examples, consider hypothetical dilemmas, and explore the consequences of actions for different people. The discussion moves through each of the choices outlined in the NIF issue book, and participants weigh the pros and cons of each policy option.

After the moderator guides the group through one to three hours of deliberation, the forum or final study circle comes to the last stage. At this point, the moderator encourages participants to identify any common ground that they have discovered on the discussion topic. In the lingo of the NIF, this process is "harvesting a public voice." The *NIF Leadership Handbook* asks moderators to think of harvesting, "not as concluding, but as giving meaning to what you are doing. Participants describe the experience they just had, not report results." Moderators might ask participants, "What trade-offs are people willing to make to get what they want?" Or, "What makes this issue so difficult to decide? What is really at issue? . . . Is there enough common ground for action? What is unresolved?"

NIF moderators and conveners attribute a wide range of effects to the NIF process. They believe that the forums have the potential to change the way people view particular issues, as well as the way they view politics and their role as citizens. Open-ended and informal research on the NIF suggests that participation in deliberative forums can (1) change participants' political opinions, (2) increase participants' political self-efficacy and their sense of community identity, (3) widen and diversify participants' political communication networks, (4) make participants more "deliberative" in their political conversations, (5) raise participants' interest in politics, and (6) increase the frequency of participants' political information seeking and political activity. Marjorie Loyacano concludes with regard to NIF literacy programs: "While the degree of NIF's effects may vary, the program has had a dramatic impact on the lives of some adult learners."[23]

More systematic research has followed up on some of these claims about the NIF's educational impact. A questionnaire survey of 51 NIF participants in forums on public education found evidence of some of the self-reported cognitive effects identified in earlier qualitative studies. Fifty-seven percent of respondents said that their "interest in education issues" increased after the forum, and 49 percent said that the discussion increased their "understanding" of those issues. With regard to opinion change, the modal responses were that respondents "changed their mind" about an aspect of education policy "once or twice" (51 percent) or had "second thoughts about a policy option" once or twice (61 percent). Forty-seven percent of respondents, however, said that they did not change their mind on the education issue. Overall, this study suggests that between one-third and one-half of forum participants do not perceive changes in their political opinions as a result of participating in NIF forums, and it also shows evidence of an increased interest in learning more about the discussion topic after the forum.[24]

The 1990–91 "research forums" sponsored by the NIF also found evidence of a cognitive impact. The research forums used three discussion issues—economic competitiveness, racial inequality, and abortion. A comparison of participants' pre- and post-forum responses to questionnaire items showed three patterns: an increase in knowledge about the issue, a greater willingness to compromise, and movement toward a more "moderate" policy choice.[25]

Further evidence of changes in participants' political opinions is provided by a study of the standard NIF questionnaires administered before and after many forums. This study reviewed the pre- and post-forum ballots completed by several hundred NIF participants for seven different issues. The authors found that the NIF process had a significant influence on the sophistication of participants' political opinions: after forums, participants' views were more refined and internally consistent, and they exhibited less attitudinal uncertainty.[26]

A fourth study measured the behavioral and psychological impact of NIF participation by examining a sample of 149 adult literacy students, half of whom had participated in a brief NIF forum in the course of their studies. This study found that NIF participation was associated with greater political efficacy, a more diverse political communication network, and a decrease in "conversational dominance" during political discussions. However, NIF participation also appeared to reduce confidence in the efficacy of group political action, and it may have reduced the intensity of participants' political group memberships. The group efficacy and intensity findings are particularly noteworthy, since one clear purpose of the NIF is to *increase* citizens' confidence in group deliberation.[27]

Taken together, these studies show that the actual effects of NIF participation are not as far-reaching as the qualitative studies might have suggested. The NIF process does generally increase the sophistication of participants' political views, and it has other anticipated effects on political communication and some political attitudes. In addition, the studies suggest that NIF participation may inadvertently turn some people away from group-based political involvement.

Because the more "educational" forms of deliberation often remain disconnected from official policy debates and elections, they risk disconnecting participants even further from the workings of government. In the case of the NIF, some forum conveners have started to work with elected officials, and the Kettering Foundation, which originated the NIF program, has begun to examine how NIF conveners make those connections.[28] The SCRC has also begun to make a direct connection between study circles and government through its "community-wide programs" and congressional exchange initiative.[29] The civic educational orientation may have great value, but sponsors of both the NIF and study circles recognize that full deliberation requires a more direct connection between public discussion and public policies.

COMMUNITY DELIBERATION

Although deliberation might prove effective in the long run as a means of civic education, other deliberative forums have had more immediate goals. In cities across the United States, citizen groups have formed to deliberate on current public problems and suggest solutions. One example among many is Chattanooga Venture, which began a "visioning process" in 1984. For twenty weeks, a group of fifty citizen activists and volunteers deliberated about the most pressing problems in Chattanooga, Tennessee. Their final list of priorities and solutions included diverse structures and initiatives, such as a shelter for abused women and a riverfront park. To realize those goals, Chattanooga Venture organized neighborhood associations, nurtured new nonprofit organizations, and spurred investment in the city. By 1992, the group had achieved most of its objectives. For this group, deliberation both developed coherent collective interests and built strong bonds among the citizens who pursued those interests together.[30]

Whereas the Chattanooga group illustrates the use of deliberation among a core of concerned citizens, a nonprofit organization in Oregon demonstrates the potential impact of a more broadly based deliberative public voice. In 1980, a group of participants who met at a state health council conference decided that the state's health care problems required extensive public discussion. With the help of thirty community volunteers, they organized neighborhood forums to discuss health care rationing and curative versus preventive care. Over the next ten years, this group facilitated hundreds of face-to-face discussions across the state. In 1990, the state legislature created the Health Services Commission, which used the same process to obtain more "official" input into health care policymaking. A year later, the commission produced a list of health care priorities generated from citizen discussions.[31]

When deliberation emerges spontaneously within a community, it usually begins in the manner described in Chattanooga and Oregon. A group of concerned citizens come together to talk about their community, and their discussions radiate outward to friends and neighbors and other active citizens. The public voice that comes from these deliberations is often well-reasoned and articulate, but it is not always representative. To address this problem, some public officials and citizens organizing deliberative discussions make great efforts to draw into the conversation people who might otherwise not attend or speak up at public forums.

For example, when the city of Cupertino, California, contracted the Public Dialogue Consortium in 1996 to convene a series of open-ended public meetings, the consortium began with focus groups. It recruited focus group participants at random from lists provided by the city, and it structured the small-group discussions to maximize opportunities for both prolonged self-expression and attentive listening.[32] The focus groups set the agenda for the subsequent meetings, which addressed cultural diversity and public safety. Though relatively small numbers of citizens participated in the meetings, the intensive focus groups at least oriented the discussions toward the concerns of the larger community.[33]

Another difference between the Cupertino project and the ones in Oregon and Tennessee is that the Cupertino program began as a public project, funded in part by tax dollars. Some deliberative projects are *entirely* funded by public agencies, as was the case in Chelsea, Massachusetts. A failed local government led the city toward bankruptcy, and the state legislature placed Chelsea in receivership. Lewis Spence, the state receiver appointed in 1991, led the city through a charter development process that included many of the deliberative methods described above, including town meetings and small discussion groups. Just as the Cupertino project tried to balance intensive deliberation among the most active citizens with representative focus groups, so the Chelsea process used a random survey to check the findings of its planning meetings.[34]

Some public deliberation bridges the grassroots and government approaches. Perhaps the best example is the Community and Education Workshop that took place in Birmingham, Alabama, in 1997. The Birmingham Community Education Department convened the workshop to bring together the perspectives and resources of citizens, nonprofit organizations, school officials, and the media. Principals from four schools put together neighborhood teams that included "a parent, a non-parent neighborhood representative, a PTA or PTO member, a neighborhood business leader, a student or teacher, and one or two others." The four groups met separately to discuss questions such as, "What must our neighborhood become or look like in order that our children have a greater chance of success in school?" and "What human capacities and strengths do we have to help us achieve our goals?" The groups tried to act on the ideas that these questions generated, then they regrouped four months later to assess their performance.

The Gate City neighborhood group, for instance, met many of its initial goals and decided to continue meeting every month, even after the official workshop had ended. Since the workshop, the Gate City group's continuing deliberations and collaborations have resulted in many small successes, such as those shown in box 2.

Box 2

Recent Achievements of the Gate City Neighborhood Team

A Summer Sports/Day Camp: Held for Gate City youth in the Gate City School gymnasium. Operated in the first part of the summer by New Life Harvest Ministries, a husband and wife team that lives in the Marks Village housing site. Run the second part of the summer by Holy Roses Church.

A Vocational/Literacy Training Center: Mt. Moriah Baptist Church is acquiring a vacant warehouse in the neighborhood to turn into a youth job skills center. Holy Roses has agreed to donate carpentry equipment and other materials.

A Gate City Cleanup Effort: Seventy-five Gate City students along with ACT members filled 120 garbage bags with litter from the streets of Gate City. Being An Apostle Foundation donated the bags. City Councilman sponsored food and door prizes. Holy Roses designated cleanup routes. Local auto dealer provided each child with $5 gift certificate to Toys 'R' Us.

The Gate City School Career Day: In the past, career day had been run entirely by Gate City school officials. This year, ACT team members reached out to area businesses and brought in eight additional presenters.

A Gate City Home Repair Effort: The team obtained money from the city to purchase paint and materials for home improvements in the neighborhood. The Metro Changers, a group of skilled tradesmen affiliated with the Baptist Association, painted six homes, put on one roof, and made one home handicap accessible.

A Neighborhood Business Owner's Breakfast: The team organized and convened a breakfast for Gate City business owners. They will discuss economic development efforts taking place throughout the city and invite in officials to discuss the kinds of steps Gate City might take to strengthen its economic base.

SOURCE: Higgins 1998: 9.

Damon Higgins, who developed a case study of the Gate City neighborhood, summarized it this way: the Gate City "team" illustrates "what can happen when the citizens of a neighborhood and their school officials think of ways to partner together. . . . The team appears to be creating the conditions required for a sustained culture of civic participation around education in its neighborhood."[35]

Though I make a clear distinction between community deliberation in Gate City and more educational programs, like the NIF and the SCRC, the actual method of deliberation is not always so different. Many towns have conducted "living room meetings" resembling informal study circles to reflect upon their community's future.[36] Other cities and towns, such as Trinidad, Colorado, have used an NIF choice format and discussion process. This was the model for a 1994–95 community convention on economic development. Dozens of citizens from the small town of Trinidad came together to discuss possible paths for the town's future. After weighing the costs and benefits of controlling growth, the citizens looked at a variety of directions in which they might guide their economy: revitalizing mining and ranching, recruiting new employers, promoting recreation and tourism, becoming a trade center, and building an entrepreneurial mecca. The multiple-choice discussion format guided the citizens through numerous alternatives and brought into the conversation a wide range of perspectives. The net result was a rejuvenated core of citizen activists, who improved the quality of discussion in Trinidad regarding the town's economic future.[37]

These examples of community deliberation demonstrate how face-to-face meetings among neighbors and fellow citizens can build effective coalitions among active citizens and public and private organizations. In small but important ways, these groups can improve community life through coordinated voluntary activities, philanthropy, and policy initiatives. Some of these groups even attempt to influence public representatives. Steeped in the tradition of adversarial labor organizing, Communities Organized for Public Service (COPS) in San Antonio, Texas, combines internal deliberation with grassroots lobbying. By introducing local elected officials to the group's large and activist membership, COPS gives representatives an explicit or implied threat of collective rejection before asking them for assistance. Though the rhetoric of such organizations might not explicitly link their "accountability sessions" with public officials to elections, officials seeking reelection cannot fail to see the connection. COPS has used this approach to improve San Antonio's infrastructure, schools, and job-training programs, all of which required government assistance.[38]

Even when public meetings are deliberative, articulate, and potentially influential, this form of public voice usually is not representative. More precisely, the informal gatherings and official meetings described above could not make strong claims that they represented the perspectives of the larger public. Their deliberations were by no means exclusive: they used focus groups, numerous statewide meetings, and extended neighborhood social networks to draw in diverse participants, and none of the examples cited above actively excluded any interested citizens. On the other hand, those who participated in the deliberations were usually members of the public known for their civic interest and involvement. What if these citizens have values and concerns that are different from those who are more withdrawn, uninterested, alienated, or simply busy? Even if the two groups have similar interests, would the "inactive" citizens trust their more active peers to reach the same deliberative conclusions as the inactives would, if they had deliberated? Without a fully inclusive group of participants, community deliberation raises these questions about the accuracy and legitimacy of collective judgments.

RANDOM SAMPLE FORUMS

To address the representation problem, some advocates of public deliberation have created what I call "random sample forums." In this view, the virtue of public opinion polling is its reliance upon representative random samples of large publics. If deliberation wishes to meet the modern standard of representation, which has been set by such polls, it needs to incorporate the same principle of random sampling.[39]

In the 1970s, public policy planners and citizen activists in the United States and abroad experimented with different forms of random sample forums, largely unaware of one another's efforts. In Minnesota, Ned Crosby developed the Center for New Democratic Processes to promote the use of the Citizen Jury deliberation process. In Hawaii, Ted Becker and Christa Slaton used their concept of a "televote" to present a quasi-deliberative public opinion to delegates at the Hawaiian Constitutional Convention. In Britain, Granada TV used face-to-face random sample assemblies, called the "Granada 500," to deliberate upon candidates and current issues. In Germany, Peter Dienel developed random sample "planning cells" to bring representative, deliberative citizen input to government agencies and officials drafting rules and laws.[40]

Contemporary experiments in deliberation with random samples range from simple one-day local events to national spectacles. Ordered from the most modest to the most elaborate, the three U.S. examples I discuss below are citizen conferences, citizen juries, and the National Issues Convention.

CITIZEN CONFERENCES

In 1996, the New Mexico State Highway and Transportation Department commissioned a public opinion survey on the state's road system. The poll provided the Transportation Department with insight into the public's views on many important planning issues, but the department wanted to develop a deeper understanding of how the public thinks and talks about transportation. In the past, the department had held numerous public meetings, but few people attended. Those who did attend usually had specific, personal concerns about potholes, truck routes, bike paths, and other narrow issues.

The University of New Mexico Institute for Public Policy (IPP) suggested that the department sponsor a series of random sample forums on long-range transportation planning. The "citizen conferences" were intended to provide a clear window into how average New Mexicans think about transportation when provided with essential background information, exposed to diverse perspectives on the issue, and given time to deliberate upon a set of policy options. To achieve this purpose, each conference was designed as a day-long public meeting centered around a group of six to twelve adult citizens, selected at random to represent the diverse views and demographics of a region of the state. Each of these "citizen advisers" voluntarily agreed to participate at the conference and received a $200 honorarium.[41]

Before coming to the conference, each citizen adviser read a brochure outlining the purpose of the conference. The brochure explained that the conference would give citizens the chance to tell the Transportation Department how it should spend "$40 million of each annual budget from 2005 to 2020." The three main spending options presented were (1) minimal maintenance of the maximum number of highway miles, (2) major improvements of key stretches of highway, and (3) development of regional and statewide public transportation. Box 3 shows the details of these policy options, as the brochure described them.

Box 3

Issue Framing for Citizen Conference on Long-Range Transportation

The majority of the budget of the New Mexico State Highway and Transportation Department (NMSHTD) is committed to road maintenance, and the budget has already been set through 2005. However, the Department has not yet decided how to spend $40 million of each annual budget from 2005 to 2020, and the Department is asking for advice on how to spend that money, which amounts to a total of $600 million spent over fifteen years.

The NMSHTD has explored several different ways it could use this $600 million to address New Mexico's transportation problems. As required by federal law, the Department has tried to find solutions that respect the needs of commercial and recreational motorists, pedestrians, and bicyclists. The Department must also respect the concerns of rural communities, metropolitan areas, and Indian tribal governments in New Mexico, as well as the impact of transportation policies on society, the economy, and the environment. Taking these issues into consideration, the Department can use its available funds in at least three different ways. Each of these three policy choices comes with certain advantages and disadvantages.

Choice 1: Extending the Life of State Highways

If the NMSHTD followed Choice 1, New Mexico would maintain as many highway miles as possible. Given current budget projections, the State would probably be able to maintain 5,000 miles of highways at minimum standards. When necessary, these 5,000 miles of roads would be reconstructed, a procedure that completely rebuilds a road to ensure its long life.

Choice 1 would also continue to resurface 3,000 miles of state roads to extend their lives for several more years. Because these roads would not be reconstructed, they would eventually wear out, but the process would be more gradual. However, there would not be enough funds to resurface the remaining 4,000 miles of state roads. The NMSHTD would only be able to repair these roads, filling potholes and making other minor repairs.

This choice might be most valuable for those parts of the state that want highways maintained for as long as possible. All three policy choices acknowledge that 7,000 miles of state road will ultimately wear out, but Choice 1 maintains the health of these roads for a greater number of years.

Critics of Choice 1 point out that the State has more than enough highway to meet its current needs. The population of New Mexico is moving toward the metropolitan areas along the Rio Grande River, and it is unwise to devote so much of the Department's highway funds to the roads with the least traffic. Other critics point out that this choice continues to rely on roads as the only solution to New Mexico's transportation problems. In the end, it only delays the decay of roads the State can't maintain forever.

Choice 2: Improving Major State Highways

If the Department picked Choice 2, it would turn 3,000 miles of road over to local and county governments, which may or may not be able to maintain them. The Department would repair another 4,000 miles of road, which would eventually wear out and become local or county roads.

These actions would save the State millions of dollars, which it could then devote to improving the 5,000 miles of most heavily traveled roads in New Mexico. Choice 2 would improve these roads by widening their lanes and shoulders, straightening some curves, adding safety rails, and conducting more regular maintenance, such as road resurfacing and repairs.

Smoother and safer roads would reduce traffic congestion, wear-and-tear on vehicles, and highway accidents. Wider shoulders would also make highway travel easier for bicyclists.

Some critics of Choice 2 argue that local and county governments will not maintain the roads turned over to them by the State of New Mexico, so the State should continue to resurface and repair these roads as long as possible. Other critics say that improving the major roads will only encourage more people to use them, so the highways will remain congested.

Choice 3: Improving Statewide Public Transportation

The difference between Choice 2 and Choice 3 is that the third choice would reconstruct but not improve the 5,000 miles of major roads in New Mexico.

Instead, Choice 3 would devote millions of dollars to improving the statewide public transportation system.

The primary civilian means of transportation is a car with one driver and no passengers. These are called "single occupancy vehicles" or SOVs. An alternative to the swarm of SOVs on our roads is a strong statewide public transportation system. This system would use vans to connect cities and towns to a stream of busses that would travel along the interstates and principal highways. Many people would drive a short distance to "park and ride" lots, where they would board a bus for the rest of their journey. The NMSHTD might also promote "ride pools" in which people regularly driving to the same destination share a single car or van.

Although this choice would not improve the quality of New Mexico's major roads, it would make long-distance transportation more affordable for people without cars. It might also make roads safer because every bus or van on the road might replace a dozen cars.

Critics of Choice 3 argue that the state has a responsibility to maintain its roads—the transportation system that New Mexicans know best. Habits change slowly, and if citizens do not use the new public transportation system, the state will have wasted millions of dollars on something travelers don't want. In addition, a public transportation system does nothing to improve the roads that trucks and other commercial vehicles rely upon. Rather than investing in new kinds of transportation, critics argue, we should improve the road system we already have.

Each citizen conference began with a morning question-and-answer session in a public auditorium. There the citizen advisers asked policy questions of a panel of experts and concerned citizens. The panel members were selected by the Transportation Department in consultation with the IPP to ensure that the panelists represented a broad range of opinions and expertise on transportation in New Mexico. At the end of the morning session, advisers heard brief comments from members of the audience who wished to add to the dialogue between advisers and panelists.

After taking a break for lunch, the citizen advisers then retired to a deliberation room for the afternoon. Aided by an IPP moderator, the advisers reviewed the three different long-range transportation policies that the department could pursue.[42] When they chose to do so, they also had the chance to consult further with any panelists or department officials, who were seated in an adjoining room and watching the deliberation on closed-circuit television. Toward the end of their afternoon session, the advisers attempted to develop a set of written policy recommendations, which they drafted with the assistance of the moderator.

Advisers were encouraged to reach consensus on their long-range transportation policy suggestions, and they were able to do so at each of the six conferences.

At 4 P.M., the advisers returned to the public auditorium and held a press conference to present their recommendations. One of the advisers read aloud the citizens' recommendations, then the advisers answered questions from the public and media in attendance. Advisers responded to queries about the details of their recommendations, the policy options that they did not choose to recommend, and the nature of their experience at the citizen conference.

The most common view expressed at the citizen conferences was that New Mexico should focus its energy on maintaining the existing network of state highways. As the Gallup citizen advisers said in their final recommendations, "We believe that the State of New Mexico should maintain as many of the state roads as possible through resurfacing and repairs. Many state roads need improvements, but first we have to maintain the road system we have. Even the least traveled state roads are still serving a purpose and are important to people living in rural parts of the state." The citizen advisers in Albuquerque, Roswell, and Las Cruces shared this view.

However, at the Taos and Santa Rosa citizen conferences, the citizen advisers recommended that New Mexico devote more funds to improving major highways. "The Transportation Department should focus on improving its most heavily-traveled state highways and pay for these improvements through a gradual reduction in its maintenance of less critical state roads," the Taos advisers wrote.

Two other recommendations emerged from the citizen conferences. First, advisers recommended that the State of New Mexico enlarge the road fund through increased revenues (e.g., an increase in the gasoline tax, increased trucking fees, etc.) or by permitting the Transportation Department to buy goods and services without paying gross receipt taxes. Second, some citizen advisers recommended reducing truck weight limits on New Mexico's highways.

What was the ultimate impact of these conferences on policy and public officials? Because the conference participants opposed planning and funding public transportation at the state level, it is likely that their recommendations undermined the efforts of government officials and activists who promote state-level public transportation programs. Prior to the conferences, advocates of such programs might have claimed that a deliberative public would endorse state-level transit, but the failure to win such support at the conferences suggests otherwise.

James Kozak, the Transportation Department official who oversaw the conferences, argued that their main impact on public officials was to restore their faith in the competence and wisdom of the general public. The citizens arrived at policy recommendations that, from the department's perspective, were realistic and clear expressions of the public's basic concerns about highway transportation.[43] Because the conferences were not linked to elections in any way, however, they had no appreciable influence on public officials beyond their persuasiveness as the only clear recording of a representative, deliberative public voice on transportation policy.

CITIZEN JURIES

From the perspective of the Transportation Department, one of the virtues of the citizen conferences was that they were a quick and inexpensive method of public deliberation. By contrast, the inspiration behind the conferences was the citizen jury model, which uses a much more elaborate deliberative process.[44] In a citizen jury, participant selection follows a carefully designed set of demographic and attitudinal quotas, deliberation takes place over four or five days, and sometimes regional juries select members for subsequent meetings.

The citizen jury process earned its name because it was "based on the analogy of a jury," as opposed to a public opinion poll, explains its founder, Ned Crosby. Just as juries can resolve criminal and civil disputes by hearing evidence and argument, deliberating, and presenting verdicts, so citizen juries go through the same stages to suggest resolutions to public policy problems. The Jefferson Center for New Democratic Processes, which Crosby founded, has conducted dozens of innovative citizen jury projects on a wide range of local, regional, and national issues, ranging from organ transplants to the federal budget.

A 1995 jury on hog farming in Rice County, Minnesota, is a good example of the citizen jury process. Faculty and students at Carleton and St. Olaf Colleges, with Crosby's assistance, designed a jury to address the contentious issue of how the county government should regulate the private large-volume pig feedlots common in the area. Specifically, the jurors answered six questions:

1. What aspects of hog feedlots are beneficial to, or appropriate for, Rice County?

2. What aspects of hog feedlots are detrimental to, or inappropriate for, Rice County?

3. Should hog production in Rice County be regulated? If so, how and why?

4. If hog production should be regulated in Rice County, should the number of animal units per farm be limited? If so, should the limit be 500, 750, or 1000 (or more) animal units?

5. What should be the future of hog production in Rice County?

6. What should be the role of local government in the regulation of animal production?[45]

Twelve paid jurors, selected at random within Rice County, were asked to answer those questions after reflecting on the issue for a full week. On Monday, they listened to testimony from academic experts and administrators on hog production methods, demographics, zoning, and regulations. Jurors had the chance to ask questions of these witnesses, and the jurors also met with their moderator to make certain that they understood the six questions they would have to answer. Tuesday and Wednesday, jurors heard from farmers, community members, professors, and administrators, who discussed the economic, environmental, and social effects of hog farming, as well as local zoning and regulation. Thursday morning, jurors deliberated on the six questions, and in the afternoon, they reviewed and then presented their final recommendations.

In the end, the jurors reached agreement on every question put before them. They recognized a wide array of costs and benefits associated with hog farming, and they believed it was essential to regulate feedlots, both large and small. In effect, the jury rejected the question, "How large is too large?" Instead, the jurors wrote, "It doesn't matter how many animal units you have; it's what you do with them and the manure." According to the jurors, hog farms of any size should be subject to random on-site inspections to ensure compliance with state guidelines, inspect manure management practices, and to check the health of the pigs. In answering their "charge," the jurors also made other specific recommendations about zoning, permits, and ownership.

Though representative, deliberative, and articulate, the citizen jury on hog farming shared the same problem as the citizen conferences: it is difficult to influence elected public officials when jury deliberations have no direct electoral implications. In the case of this jury, one Rice County commissioner who attended the jurors' press conference was dismissive of the recommendations: "The jurors don't have the responsibility for citizens of Rice County. I do. . . . Why should I make the decision to compromise the welfare of the majority for the benefit of a few?" The other commissioner who attended the press conference promised to "sit down and read through the written document" jurors prepared and "take them into consideration" when making a decision on the issue.[46] An editorial in the local paper praised the jury process as a "starting point for discussion" but opined that "the jury's recommendations will probably not make it through the political process intact—and perhaps it shouldn't."[47]

Some citizen juries, however, have focused directly on elections and candidates. A 1976 presidential jury evaluated the issue stands of Jimmy Carter and President Gerald Ford. Teamed with the Minnesota League of Women Voters, the Jefferson Center also held juries on the 1989 St. Paul, Minnesota, mayoral race and the 1990 Minnesota gubernatorial primary and general elections. In 1992, the center also joined with the Pennsylvania League of Women Voters to convene citizen juries on the views of Republican Senator Arlen Specter and his Democratic opponent, Lynn Yeakel.[48]

The Pennsylvania effort was the most ambitious and influential. Specter used its findings in television campaign ads, and the *Philadelphia Inquirer* praised the process and presented its findings in detail even though it endorsed Yeakel. On election day, Specter prevailed with 49 percent to 46 percent of the vote despite a vigorous Yeakel campaign, which spent over $5 million dollars and attacked Specter's actions during the confirmation hearings for Supreme Court Justice Clarence Thomas. It is impossible to determine the extent to which the jury results influenced the election, but the important point is that the Pennsylvania citizen jury demonstrated how a random sample forum can have direct electoral implications.[49]

DELIBERATIVE POLLING AND THE NATIONAL ISSUES CONVENTION

James Fishkin had an even more ambitious plan when he created the 1996 National Issues Convention (NIC) to showcase his method of deliberative polling. Fishkin argues that the best way to bridge a large national public with the deliberative ideal of face to-face-democracy is to use random sampling to *simulate* nationwide deliberation. Public opinion surveys provide an effective mechanism for getting a representative sample of public views, but if the poll follows a period of deliberation among the respondents, the interviewer will hear a more deliberative and articulate public voice. In *Deliberation and Democracy,* Fishkin observed: "Deliberative opinion polls offer direct democracy among a group of politically equal participants who, as a statistical microcosm of the society, represent or stand for the deliberations of the whole. The institution is, in that sense, a direct face-to-face society for its participants and a representative institution for the nation state." The results of a deliberative poll are "something that begins to approximate what the public *would think,* given a better opportunity to consider the questions at hand."[50]

Fishkin failed to engineer a "deliberative poll" in the 1992 U.S. presidential election, but with the help of Granada Television, he conducted such a survey in Manchester, England, in 1994. Drawing on the success of the 1994 poll, Fishkin succeeded in orchestrating a national poll in the United States. On January 18, 1996, 459 randomly selected strangers from across the United States converged on Austin, Texas, to attend the National Issues Convention. Participants spent most of the next three days in small group discussions of U.S. foreign policy, the economy, and "the American family." In face-to-face groups of ten to twenty persons each, participants shared their perspectives and weighed the pros and cons of alternative policy choices that had been spelled out in a preconference briefing book.[51]

The deliberation that took place in these small groups of citizens was not remarkable. Having observed three of the small groups in person, I witnessed both searching discussion and unfocused rambling, as one finds when observing other forums and study circles.[52] Box 4 shows one of the many exchanges that took place during the NIC, and the only noteworthy aspect of the dialogue is that its participants came from different backgrounds and had different points of view. Given that citizens tend to engage in political conversation with like-minded peers, this fact alone is important.[53] Beyond mere conversation, however, analysis of transcripts of NIC discussions shows that participants spent much of their time weighing conflicting facts, ideas, and policies. More than one-third of the comments recorded included some form of self-examination or criticism, and 7 percent "examined the group through the eyes of some other party."[54] The small group discussions at the NIC sometimes lacked focus, but they gave participants the opportunity to present, hear, and consider diverse views, and such talk is an important part of the deliberative process.

Box 4

A Glimpse of a Small Group Discussion at the National Issues Convention

At one point, two assertive and conservative white participants, Scott and Ron, shifted the discussion to macroeconomic problems. Scott argued that unemployment can be good because it holds down inflation. As he elaborated on this point, his choice of terminology revealed a formal background in economics. Ron added to Scott's comments by stating this view more starkly: "Poverty is good. It creates an incentive—something to strive for."

Jason, the most vocal African-American participant, was stunned. As he retorted, the three young African-Americans sitting across from him nodded and made it clear that they shared his disbelief. "This must be a cultural difference," Jason said with intentional understatement. Trying to reframe Ron's words to make them compatible with his own view, Jason asked, "Are you saying that the rich need to have poor in order to stay rich?"

Scott rejected this awkward invitation to agreement and simply added, "The rich get to keep their loot. That's democracy. It's in our constitution." Stepping out of her neutral role, the moderator joined in the discussion as a participant. She said, with obvious cynicism, that the basic purpose of the U.S. Constitution was to protect property rights.

Lewis, a young African-American man who had not spoken previously, said that it's not easy to find work. In his own case, he explained, he has to go through a job service to look for work, and he often winds up with temporary jobs.

Alan, another relatively quiet participant, picked up on the emerging theme of greedy business people and referred to his own boss (and the boss' son, who is rising in the ranks "faster than seems fair"). Alan said that his boss spends profits on expensive trips to clubs and resorts. "Why can't he invest those dollars back in the employees and the company?" Alan asked.

"But he made the company," Mark answered the rhetorical question. "He earned the right to do that."

"Okay, but it's rude," Alan responded. On this point Mark agreed: it may be legal to brag about one's riches and squander them on luxuries, but that doesn't make it right.

With others making a brief comment at times, Jason and Scott continued to disagree, slowly moving their focus toward progressive versus flat tax rates. After Scott asserted that taxes on the wealthiest five percent of Americans provide forty-three percent of all federal revenue, Jason began to understand that he and Scott agreed about what a "fair share" of the tax burden means. Jason said that he could now support the flat tax—so long as the rich pay their percentage just like everyone else.

With this final topic, Scott, Jason, Lewis, and the other active group members had steered the group all the way from a discussion of human greed to the flat tax. Although the rambling group conversation sometimes wandered into a thicket of irrelevancies, its innocent meandering permitted participants to stumble upon points of agreement. A conservative participant acknowledged the problem of corporate greed, but not due to the force of an unrelenting colleague's argument. And a liberal came to see virtue in the flat tax, which just popped into the conversation.

SOURCE: Gastil 1996. Pseudonyms are used for the NIC participants.

The actual deliberation—or lack thereof—at the NIC merits careful study. Scholarly writing about what took place at the NIC has, however, focused almost entirely on the method and results of the deliberative poll of the participants. The poll began with a traditional door-to-door survey of a random national sample of households, and 72 percent of those initially contacted by interviewers took part in the pre-NIC survey. Of those 600 respondents, only 50 percent made the trip to Austin. That resulted in a 36 percent response rate, which falls well below the standards of professional polling organizations in the United States.[55] The National Opinion Research Center, which administered the survey, made a concerted effort to persuade a higher percentage of respondents to come to Austin, but the free round-trip ticket, a $325 honorarium, and regular contacts by paid liaisons were not enough for many respondents, some of whom remained skeptical about the NIC's purposes.[56]

Though the low response rate raised questions about the representativeness of the sample, demographic and attitudinal data suggest that the NIC attendees were similar to the national population in most respects.[57] Given this resemblance, one might infer that changes in the attendees' attitudes reflect what the larger public would believe if it had deliberated in the same manner. Deliberation did have a modest effect on the attendees' views, when taken as a whole. Of the 81 survey items asked before and after the NIC, the direction of majority opinion shifted seven times, and a total of twenty items showed statistically significant changes in overall response.[58] For example, the flat tax fell out of favor, with support dropping from 44 percent to 30 percent. Before the NIC, 63 percent said that the states should take charge of welfare programs, but only 50 percent maintained that conviction after the convention. Support for no-fault divorce dropped from 57 percent to 36 percent. Participants also became, on average, more accurate in their beliefs about the percentage of Americans receiving AFDC (Aid to Families with Dependent Children), the identity of the main U.S. trading partner, the unemployment rate, and the ideological orientations of the major political parties in the United States.[59]

Beyond these issues, changes were also apparent in attendees' attitudes toward public officials. After deliberating on issues and addressing questions directly to Republican presidential candidates and Vice President Al Gore, the percentage of attendees who believed that "public officials care a lot about what people like me think" rose from 41 percent to 60 percent. Remarkably, even audiences who watched the NIC from the comfort of their living rooms experienced a slight boost in political efficacy, as evidenced by their increased disagreement with the statement, "People like me don't have any say about what the government does."[60] After studying the survey of NIC participants' experiences, an observer, Tom Smith, concluded: "For almost all of the delegates, the NIC was a positive, moving experience. For some it was an epiphany that they felt would transform their lives, making them better citizens, changing them into more complete Americans. . . . Overwhelmingly, it was empowering, making them believe that they could and should make a difference."[61]

As envisioned by Fishkin, the results of the NIC deliberative poll are important because they could set the course of the primary election for president. By revealing the policy views and priorities of the deliberative public, the NIC could influence how the media covers the election and how candidates campaign. Daniel Merkle, director of the Voter News Service, found that 194 stories mentioning the NIC appeared in major U.S. newspapers during the two weeks following the convention, and NIC sponsors ultimately tallied over 500 articles. PBS devoted several hours of live coverage to the convention, and although NBC and CBS ignored the convention, CNN and ABC ran in-depth segments on it. Nielsen ratings for the convention were low and well below those of comparable presidential debates; overall, the NIC did not have a clear, direct effect on the conduct and media coverage of the primary election.[62]

INTO THE REALM OF THE POSSIBLE

Nevertheless, the NIC had a significant effect on how the media think about citizens and public forums. The NIC demonstrated that, under the right circumstances, average American citizens can ask useful questions and interact respectfully with candidates. Even if it did not draw a large general audience, academics, media professionals, and political activists noticed the NIC and learned its approach to recording a democratic public voice. It was probably not a coincidence that during the general election, one of the televised presidential debates and many other political news programs used random sample audiences to generate questions and guide discussions. Since 1996, many organizations have conducted deliberative polls, quasi-juries, and similar events, and the organizers of these public forums know of the NIC but often remain unaware of its forerunners and other spin-offs.[63]

Above all else, the NIC has brought random sample forums from the world of science fiction into the realm of the possible. The underlying concepts and purposes, as well as the practical methods, of deliberation with random samples of a general public are now well known in many academic and professional communities. Though random sample forums differ considerably from civic education programs and the numerous community forums across the United States, the NIC has also helped to legitimize these more spontaneous and informal methods of public deliberation. In return, as the SCRC directors Matt Leighninger and Martha McCoy explain, the "small, heroic changes" that take place in study circles and community forums "show us that bigger changes are possible."[64] Because of these programs, hundreds of thousands—perhaps millions—of U.S. citizens now recognize careful, respectful deliberation as a legitimate and often desirable method for addressing community and political conflicts.

What has yet to happen is for public deliberation to find its way into the mainstream electoral process. Experiments like the NIC and citizen juries have proven that citizens can deliberate meaningfully on candidates as well as issues, but deliberation and elections remain largely unconnected in American politics.[65] In the next two chapters, I argue that this separation is neither ideal nor inevitable. By combining the electoral reforms introduced in chapter 3 with the deliberative methods presented above, it is possible to record a public voice that is not only representative, deliberative, and articulate, but also influential in contemporary American elections. If the strong voices of deliberative forums can tie themselves to a credible threat of collective rejection of unrepresentative elected officials, government will hear those voices as clearly as any other.

CHAPTER 7

The Citizen Panels Proposal

[In] a neighborhood where the quiet kids are being bullied
by a few big kids, . . . there are all kinds of rules parents and
teachers can adopt to try to restrain the big kids, but if the
neighborhood is a fairly free and open place, these are going
to have limited success. Bullies are very inventive in how to
get their way when the only thing to restrain them is a set of
rules enforced by parents and teachers. . . . The key lies in
getting the quiet kids to find a way to band together and
take care of themselves.

> *Ned Crosby, "Citizens Election Forum:*
> *A Proposal for Electoral Reform"*

A successful reform of the U.S. political system must deal with the "bullies" in Crosby's analogy. Citizens need a mechanism that ensures relatively quick and decisive electoral action against unrepresentative officials. Chapter 4 explained why current reform proposals for American
politics would not meet that need. Radical changes in the voting system
might better incorporate minority publics, but they would not facilitate
better overall representation. Public financing and term limits might
make elections more competitive, but they would not improve voters'
candidate evaluations. Regulations on the messages candidates send to
voters are either unenforceable or unconstitutional, and efforts to provide voters with neutral guides have not gone far enough to change fundamentally how citizens vote.

This chapter proposes an electoral innovation that effectively helps
"the quiet kids" to take care of themselves on election day. But, following Crosby's metaphor, the electorate first needs a way to band together. So long as the public's voice is barely a whisper, both public officials and citizens themselves will have difficulty acting upon it.[1]
Chapter 5 showed that conventional forms of public expression do not
create a democratic public voice, but the experiments in public deliberation reviewed in chapter 6 suggest how one might develop. Between

elections, a powerful and authentic public voice would provide public officials with guidance as they draft, implement, and evaluate rules and policies. On election day, the public could listen to its own voice and use it to select the best representatives.

The reforms I propose would also meet another challenge—the low motivation of the electorate. Many advocates of deliberation envision a deliberative process that requires considerable effort and drive. In one view, intensive, ongoing deliberation should take place in small groups and organizations that are part of larger social movements, which will develop citizens' abilities, self-awareness, and sense of responsibility.[2] Others imagine enlivened communities and neighborhoods in which people regularly talk about politics and public problems in local institutions, grassroots civic associations, and informal interactions.[3] Technophiles envision a virtual community in which Internet surfers— better known for treading water in virtual hobby shops and idly swimming through the sea of sites—would dutifully step into electronic political discussions to deliberate upon complex issues and current candidates.[4] In the long run, each of these efforts might slowly change the abilities and attitudes of the larger public, just as the civic education and community deliberation programs discussed in chapter 5 inspire and empower their participants. In the meantime, however, I propose a political reform that can bring all of the "the quiet kids" together, even if they remain quiet for the foreseeable future.[5]

Another way in which the general public remains quiet is in its increasing social isolation, and effective political reforms must take this fact into account. Chapter 3 documented the decline in party loyalty among the electorate, but that is part of a larger decline in group-based political participation. Robert Putnam, who brought this decline to the attention of the larger scholarly community, blames eroding public life on the influence of electronic media, particularly television, which moved people from their porches to their parlors.[6] In a critique of Putnam, Lance Bennett suggests that group politics simply does not fit the modern U.S. economy, in which two-income families lacking economic and geographic stability act as individuals more than community members. He also sees the emergence of "lifestyle politics" as a force toward more individualized political action.[7] This trend toward individualistic politics undermines the effectiveness of reforms centered on strengthening political parties and other ongoing associations. By contrast, the reforms I propose would deliver information to individual voters, only a small fraction of whom are asked (with strong financial incentives) to join together briefly to deliberate upon political matters.

Drawing upon the random sample forums described in chapter 6 and the voting guides reviewed in chapter 4, my basic recommendation is that voters should have access to the results of representative citizen deliberation on the candidates and issues that appear on their ballots. Using random samples of the general public, government institutions could sponsor deliberative citizen panels on past legislative actions, individual candidates, and ballot measures.[8] Panel participants could summarize the results of their deliberations, and federal election officials, secretaries of state, and county clerks could communicate those results to voters through elaborate Internet sites, printed voter guides, and simple information printed on the ballots themselves. Average voters would spend no more time researching candidates than they do today, but they would have the chance to check their impressions against those of a deliberative body of their peers. If the citizen panels proved influential in elections, public officials might also use them as a legible signpost pointing toward the public's policy interests.[9]

The remainder of this chapter outlines the forms that deliberative election panels might take, and chapter 8 reviews the potential benefits and limitations of this approach to electoral reform. Deliberative citizen panels can take many shapes and still realize the same basic purpose. I propose five different forms of citizen panels: priority panels could identify key legislation to aid voters in comparing candidate voting records; legislative panels could rate legislators' performance; advisory panels could weigh in prior to important legislative decisions; candidate-selection panels could evaluate candidates for executive, judicial, and administrative offices; and referenda panels could review ballot referenda, initiatives, and propositions.

PRIORITY PANELS

I have chosen a priority panel for U.S. House and Senate elections as an illustration because Congress is the most powerful legislative body in the United States and discussion of political reform largely focuses on congressional elections. As shown in box 5, the basic purpose of such a priority panel would be to identify the ten most important pieces of legislation introduced in Congress over the past two years. The results of these panels would permit voters across the country to see how incumbents and their opponents voted, or would have voted, on a limited number of key issues.

Box 5

Steps in Implementing a Priority Panel for Congressional Elections

1. Panel Selection and Preparation

   a. The Federal Election Commission (FEC) pays a nonprofit polling organization to select a national random sample of 400 citizen panelists.
   b. Congressional party leaders identify potential bills and amendments to examine and name witnesses to testify in favor of each bill.

2. Deliberation on Pieces of Legislation

   a. Witnesses present testimony to citizen panel and engage in cross-examination.
   b. Citizen panelists deliberate and vote to select ten pieces of legislation.
   c. In small groups, citizens write brief summaries of the bills.

3. Implications for Elections

   a. Candidates who have not cast official votes on those ten pieces of legislation report their unofficial votes to the FEC.
   b. Through printed and on-line voter guides, secretaries of state provide voters with the official and unofficial votes of congressional candidates on the ten key pieces of legislation.

Before describing priority panels in detail, however, I wish to address two aspects of their implementation. First, the following description assumes that the priority panel process would be written into federal law by Congress itself, and at this point I ask the reader to postpone questions about the likelihood of such action until the next chapter. My present purpose is to describe how the panels would work, not the process by which they might become law. In chapter 8, I return to this question and suggest how citizen panels might develop in the United States.

Second, fidgety taxpayers and deficit hawks might insist upon examining the cost of citizen panels before anything else. Cost is a real

concern, and I suggest panels that use manageable numbers of participants deliberating for just one week. Nonetheless, convening citizen
panels would be expensive. The printed voter guides that would follow
the panels would also have a significant cost for those states not already
printing and mailing voter guides, although awarding grants to the
League of Women Voters to incorporate panel results into its existing
voter guides might prove cost-effective. In any case, the cost of panels
would be only a fraction of the cost of public financing for state and
federal elections, and it is probably no greater than the cost of adminis-
tering other regulatory reforms.[10] In any case, the cost is unproblematic
compared to the real practical challenge of designing and implementing
government-sponsored citizen panels.

RANDOM SELECTION OF PANELISTS

The first step in convening a priority panel would be selecting a national
random sample of four hundred citizen panelists.[11] The federal government would not do the sampling itself, but instead contract with a professional nonprofit organization, such as an academic research institute
at a public university. The recruiters would use quotas and financial incentives to ensure a relatively random sample of the nation's population. Demographic quotas would use census data on the entire adult
population, including those not registered to vote, so that the panelists
would represent the nation as a whole.[12]

Once demographic quotas and random sampling identify potential
panelists, recruiters would contact citizens in person or, when possible,
by phone or mail. Excepting those citizens unable to deliberate for
medical reasons, or due to incarceration, recruiters would seek as high
a participation rate as possible and only pursue new citizen panelists
when unable to persuade initial recruits to participate. Some citizens
would no doubt gladly seize the opportunity to talk politics with a
small group of their peers, but others might only participate with the
right incentives. The simplest positive incentive would be payment,
which might be free travel and accommodation plus a $600 honorar-
ium.[13] In the same way that jury duty laws protect employees, the law
that enacts the priority panels could prohibit employers from pressur-
ing employees to decline to participate. Some might take the jury example a step farther and compel participation on the panels, but I prefer permitting citizens to make their own decision. So long as adequate
incentives are provided to potential panelists, self-selection should

exclude only those citizens so preoccupied with other matters that they would be unable to make a significant contribution to deliberation if they did attend.

Even if one accepts that it would be possible to recruit a representative sample, one might object to the very idea of using a national sample to judge senators and representatives elected in geographic districts. Why should conservative voters in Utah or liberal voters in Massachusetts care what a national sample views as legislative priorities? Is not the point of the Senate to represent the genuinely distinct interests of different states, just as the individual House districts within those states represent the varied interests within them? These questions reflect long-held beliefs about the district system of election popular in the United States, and I am sympathetic to critics who embrace the idea of priority panels but want to convene a state or district panel instead of a national one. Nevertheless, I wish to make an argument for using national sampling to create a single priority panel for Congress (or, for that matter, one statewide panel per state legislature).

As I argue in chapter 2, the point of deliberation is to bring together conflicting views to seek out points of agreement, if not full unanimity, on pressing public policy problems. The job of congressional representatives is not only to represent their respective districts but also to create policies that serve the best interests of the nation as a whole. Joseph Bessette, in *The Mild Voice of Reason* (1994), used a careful study of legislative history to demonstrate that some members of Congress do act in this manner and have considerable influence over their peers. Even Bessette, however, sees an ominous trend in federal policymaking: "The demise of so many Congressional constraints on mere self-seeking suggests that the Congress as a whole has become a less deliberative institution in recent decades. Less and less do the members of the House and Senate seem willing to sacrifice their private advantage for the sake of responsible lawmaking."[14]

Similar concerns about the chaos that comes with individual districts has led some critics of Congress to propose a unified national election system, such as the "universal representation" scheme outlined in chapter 4. In a way, the priority panel takes the middle course by leaving voters with district elections but giving them a shared set of policy priorities that they can use to evaluate their unique sets of candidates.

IDENTIFYING A PRELIMINARY SET OF LEGISLATION

Since the priority panels would be held only during election years, two years of legislation would be eligible for consideration.[15] Legislation would include any bill or amendment introduced in either the House or Senate, including those that never came to a vote on the floor or in a committee. I include amendments because those sometimes have more powerful implications than the bills themselves, and individual amendments often have a clearer focus. Citizen panelists may often choose amendments because larger bills have too many conflicting, unrelated provisions to permit straightforward evaluation. The more cumbersome bills, however, may also make the citizens' list of key legislation because of their overall impact. To avoid the phrase "bills and amendments," however, I shall refer to all legislation simply as "bills" for the remainder of this chapter.

Using legislative votes as the basis for evaluating representatives is problematic but useful. Every two years, the *Almanac of American Politics* compiles its own list of noteworthy votes, and it concedes that listing key votes "grossly oversimplifies the legislative system where months of debate, amendment, pressure, persuasion, and compromise go into a final floor vote. However, the voting record remains the best indication of a member's general ideologies and position on specific issues."[16] The 1998 *Almanac* lists twelve votes in the Senate and House, but the priority panels would produce one set of legislation—some of which only one chamber will have voted upon—to avoid splitting into separate panels for the House and Senate.

Each political party with a representative serving in the House or Senate would have the opportunity to present pieces of legislation for review by the priority panel.[17] To keep their task manageable, the panelists would consider no more than roughly thirty bills. Each party would be permitted to introduce for consideration an equal fraction of the total. (Independent legislators would, for this purpose, constitute one "party.") In other words, a party with only one seat in Congress would suggest just as many bills as one of the major parties. This system, which I repeat elsewhere, defies the logic of even proportional representation, but I believe it serves the pursuit of full deliberation. In a deliberative body, the goal is to give each perspective equal and adequate opportunities for expression. If one hundred people in a room represent five viewpoints, and there are only fifty minutes for discussion, it is better to hear the full range of arguments than to give more time to just one or two views. The citizen panel faces the same dilemma because of its limited time and energy, and I would prefer that the citizens hear about the legislative priorities of political groups with substantially different views.[18]

DISCUSSION AND VOTING

Once all the panelists have been selected and all proposed bills identified, panelists would receive summaries of each bill and statements from their authors about the bills' significance. After a period of weeks to consider these statements on their own, panelists would come to Washington, D.C., to deliberate jointly upon the bills. Each bill would have an author (or author-appointed stand-in) who would argue for its significance for fifteen minutes, and panelists would have the chance to ask questions of the witness for an additional fifteen minutes. In two days, citizens would have had the chance to review all of the bills before them, and they would then begin to deliberate on the bills in roughly twenty small groups, with twenty panelists in each one.

Just as jurors and the participants in random sample forums have a clear purpose or "charge" for their deliberations, so would the priority panelists. Their goal would be to select ten pieces of legislation using these three criteria: breadth, clarity, and significance. The citizens would seek to assemble a set of ten bills that addressed different policy issues so that voters could later learn about the views of their representatives (and other candidates) on a range of important national issues. The panel would also choose clearer bills over others to permit straightforward interpretation of votes on issues. This criterion might exclude some bills that include too many unrelated provisions, and it would lead citizens to choose bills voted upon by both the House and Senate over earlier versions so that voters can look at the official votes of both representatives and senators. Finally, the significance criterion would recommend the inclusion of complicated but powerful bills, and it might lead panelists to include multiple influential bills on a single issue that happened to receive sustained attention during a particular session of Congress.[19]

Working with these criteria, the priority panel would deliberate for two days on the different pieces of legislation. Small group deliberations would take place in a room spacious enough to accommodate a large group seated at desks in a circle only one row deep, like a discussion circle in a typical college classroom. That arrangement is important because it enables all participants to make eye contact with one another and gives no participants spatial advantages over others that might influence leadership emergence, speaking frequency, or floor management.[20]

When the citizen panelists moved from discussion to voting, the four hundred citizens would come together to vote in three phases. First, to simplify matters, citizens would go through the bills and quickly decide, one bill at a time, whether each bill was a candidate for further consideration. Any bill receiving less than a one-third vote would be rejected. (If fewer than fifteen bills received one-third of the votes, the fifteen with the most votes would remain under consideration. If more than twenty bills remained, those with the fewest votes would be dismissed.) Second, a panelist could identify any pair or cluster of remaining bills that he or she thought addressed the same issue. If a majority agreed to select one bill from the cluster, then each panelist would name his or her preferred bill and the top vote-winner would remain for consideration. Third, after reducing some bills through this process, the citizen panelists would individually rank the ten bills they found most important, and the ten with the highest average ranking would be used in subsequent deliberations.[21] Though somewhat complicated, this process makes the final rankings more meaningful by removing clutter and redundancy before requiring final ratings. If it was found to be too cumbersome or confusing to citizen panelists, they could simply rank the bills after their deliberations without any preliminary votes.[22]

These votes, as well as all other votes taken by citizen panels, would be conducted using secret ballots. Deliberations themselves would need to be public, lest they appear secretive and undemocratic. Keeping the votes secret, however, would take some pressure off of citizens shy of taking public stands, and it would reduce the potential for lobbyist influence. Even if citizens were somewhat sequestered during their deliberations, any creative lobbyist or special-interest organization would be able to reach citizens before or during their deliberations. Such groups might manage to influence what some citizens think about issues, and that is a natural part of the larger process of political debate. If votes are taken in public, those same groups might be able to tie votes to tangible rewards; secret votes make it impossible for a group to know whether any particular panelist voted in its favor (except in the case of unanimous votes against the group's position).

In any case, at the end of their deliberation period, the citizen panelists would break into ten groups of forty. Each of these groups would have one bill assigned to it, and the groups would write brief summaries of the bills, which would then be used in voter guides. Individual panelists would try to agree upon neutral phrasing for the summaries, possibly starting from one suggested by the bill's author, and majority votes would be used to resolve any disputes about wording.

IMPLICATIONS FOR ELECTIONS

If the priority panels stopped at this point, they would provide some insight into the national public's general policy priorities, although the panelists would indicate only that they thought bills were *important*— not whether they thought they were *good*. The point of their deliberation, however, would be to identify a limited range of concrete issues that voters could then use to compare candidates. To make those comparisons, voters would need to know where candidates stood on the issues chosen by the priority panels.

For that reason, it would be necessary to obtain the official and unofficial votes of congressional candidates. Once the priority panel named the ten key bills, the FEC would ask every registered candidate to provide their unofficial votes, accompanied by brief rationales. Incumbent senators and representatives would need to provide unofficial votes as well, because they probably would not already have voted on some of the pieces of legislation. Elected representatives would not have the opportunity to vote unofficially after failing to make an official vote without cause; this would provide representatives with one more reason to vote on controversial but important bills, rather than dodging the vote to avoid offending voters or interest groups.

Some candidates would have difficulty making these unofficial voting decisions, and challengers with limited political experience would spend some of their time examining the set of ten key bills before voting and providing rationales. No matter how busy or indifferent a candidate might feel, there would be a clear incentive for voting on the ten bills: failure to do so would make a candidate appear undecided on what the public considered a critical issue.

Once it had compiled the voting data, the FEC would pass the information to secretaries of state, who would deliver it to the households of registered voters through printed and on-line voter guides. The online guides could include the full text of all thirty bills initially considered, the priority panel's votes, and the candidates' votes and statements on the ten bills. An official Internet site could describe the citizen deliberations in detail, including video records of witness testimony and the deliberation on every bill. Printed information in official state voter guides would be more limited to hold down printing costs and to provide less interested voters with a simple document. The printed voter guide would give summaries of each of the ten key issues and show candidate votes and rationales.

Of the citizen panels I discuss, the priority panel is the tamest. It asks citizen panelists only to identify key bills for further discussion and scrutiny. By showing voters candidates' positions on ten specific issues, the panels help the electorate compare candidates using objective criteria with direct relevance to voters' policy interests. That is a significant improvement over the status quo, but I believe that citizen panel deliberation should go one step farther by asking panelists to deliberate and vote upon legislation and candidates.

LEGISLATIVE PANELS

In effect, the priority panels set the agenda for legislative panels (box 6). To move this hypothetical example from the national level to the state level, let us say, for example, that the Ohio secretary of state has already convened priority panels on the state legislature. The secretary of state would then use a nonprofit polling firm to select a new set of ten representative legislative panels, each of which would consist of fifty citizens.

Box 6

Steps in Implementing a Legislative Panel for State Legislative Elections

1. Preparation and Deliberation on the Agenda

    a. The secretary of state pays a nonprofit polling firm to select a statewide random sample of five hundred citizen panelists. Panelists are randomly assigned to groups of fifty, each of which will deliberate on one of the ten pieces of legislation.
    b. Party leaders in the state legislature recommend witnesses to provide testimony.

2. Deliberation on Legislation

    a. Witnesses present testimony to citizen panel and engage in cross-examination.
    b. Citizen panelists deliberate, vote for or against ten pieces of legislation, and write rationales for their votes.

3. Implications for Elections

    a. Secretary of state and county clerks provide voters with the citizen panelists' recommendations and the official and unofficial votes of legislative candidates through printed and on-line voter guides.

    b. On the ballot, county clerks print a number beside each candidate that indicates the percentage-agreement between each candidate's votes and those of the citizen panels.

    c. Using these same agreement scores, candidates are listed on ballots in descending order (i.e., highest score listed first).

Although a large sample would be more representative, it would also prove quite costly, and I think an argument can be made for smaller groups. (Those who cannot stomach this idea should read on and simply substitute larger samples as necessary.) The point in convening fifty citizens is to ensure that the sample includes the full range, if not the exact distribution, of viewpoints in the larger population. Panels with just fifty participants cannot perfectly represent a large population in the statistical sense, but quotas can make the sample sufficiently representative. By combining demographic quotas (for age, ethnicity, etc.) and possibly attitudinal quotas (for party affiliation, basic opinions, etc.), each panel of fifty citizens can be made a microcosm of the larger state population.[23]

DELIBERATION ON LEGISLATION

The ten legislative panels would come together to Columbus, Ohio, but they would deliberate and vote independently. Each panel would be assigned to a single bill, and the panels could either deliberate simultaneously (but separately) or in sequence. The latter might prove less chaotic, and it could permit serial media coverage of the bills during the election season.[24]

Prior to arrival in Columbus, citizens would receive information about the bill assigned to them. To promote continuity in judgments over time, panelists would also receive copies of the judgments of past panels who deliberated upon related legislation. Undoubtedly, many of these citizens would discuss their bills with friends and family beforehand, and such discussion could only benefit the overall process. Indirectly, it would involve many more people in the process, and it would have a positive average effect on citizens' knowledge and the quality of subsequent panel deliberation. Because the citizens are geographically dispersed prior to arriving for panel deliberations, this initial period would give them the chance to hear the quiet voices of average citizens from across the state. Some panelists will undoubtedly make reference to those interactions during panel deliberation.

To ensure that citizen panelists do share a common knowledge base, however, the first day of deliberation would consist of testimony from witnesses chosen by the highest-ranking members of the legislature in favor of and opposed to the bill that each panel considers. The structure for such testimony, cross-examination, and question-and-answer could take many possible forms, drawing on the examples set by the random sample forums described in chapter 6. At the National Issues Convention, pro and con experts each made statements and then took turns answering questions from the audience. At the New Mexico Citizen Conferences, each of five or six expert witnesses made a brief statement, then citizens asked questions, which experts answered in a free-for-all format. Citizen juries have used many discussion methods, including a straightforward succession of witnesses, each of whom devotes half of his or her time to presentation and half to a question-and-answer session. A new approach taken in a recent citizen forum used a panel of witnesses in which one speaker would make a presentation, then the others would give balanced critiques of the speaker's arguments.[25]

This process of cross-examination is important because it exposes witnesses to professional scrutiny. Those testifying before the legislative citizen panel will be more reluctant to make false statements if they see it as a high-risk strategy. At a minimum, witnesses risk the erosion of their credibility if cross-examination reveals that they have used fabricated survey data, lied about their prior knowledge, or otherwise sought to deceive the citizen panel. Following the courtroom analogy, one might even want make these witnesses "subject to penalties for perjury" if cross-examination "reveals that a witness made false statements."[26] I would stop short of placing a judge in the panel room, but witnesses guilty of perjury might be subject to civil lawsuit after the fact.

Whatever particular format is used, it is important that the number of witnesses remain manageable, that the citizens be able to guide the direction of the discussion, and that either a paid moderator or a citizen-chair maintain decorum and keep the panel on schedule. My own preference is for a paid, professional moderator to manage the meetings under the direction of the citizen panelists. Following the example of the citizen juries, the moderator would be responsible for establishing and

maintaining the ground rules for the discussion and keeping the event
on track. Moderator duties would include stopping quarrels among
witnesses, helping panelists clarify questions and get direct answers,
and cutting off witness answers that run too long. The panelists would
first meet the moderator during a brief orientation session, during
which the moderator would go over the discussion guidelines sent to
participants. This brief training would be more advanced than typical
jury training, in that the moderator would openly discuss common
group problems, such as inattention, communication style differences,
and the formation of cliques. During panel deliberation and the question-and-answer sessions with witnesses, moderators would also keep
track of speaker time and periodically invite quiet participants to speak
up if participation rates became greatly unbalanced.[27]

After the first day of testimony, citizens would have a day to deliberate on their bill. The course of the deliberation itself is impossible to predict, but it could be structured to ensure full participation and conformity to the preset schedule. A trained moderator could have the
responsibility of periodically reminding a panel how much time it had
and what it needed to do. The moderator could also intervene if verbal
conflict moved toward physical confrontation, which, incidentally, has
been a rarity at random sample forums conducted in the past. The moderator would also call for three or four "round-robins" at roughly preset
intervals. In a round-robin, each participant has a chance to speak for a
minute, and speaking turns move from left to right without interruption.
Its purpose is to draw out quieter participants, and it can cause an otherwise silent voice to shift the emphasis or direction of deliberation.

After deliberating through most of the second day, the citizen panelists would write what they considered to be the strongest arguments
for and against the bill. This set of arguments would be as inclusive as
possible, and it would provide a succinct written record of the facts,
ideas, and considerations influencing in their deliberation. Aside from
this listing of arguments, the panel would not take anything resembling
a preliminary vote or straw poll on the issue.[28]

On the third day, expert witnesses would return and have the opportunity to respond to the arguments of citizens for and against the
bill. Again, this process could follow many formats, but during this
stage, it would be important that the lead witnesses be able to direct
discussion toward their most pressing concerns. This day would be
their last chance to bolster arguments, correct factual errors, and remove confusion or misunderstandings.

As citizens undertake their final deliberations on the fourth and fifth days, the debate they have heard on the previous day should give the panelists more confidence in their final votes. Citizens will have had a chance to be second-guessed by outside observers prior to reaching their final decision. By the end of the fourth day, the moderator will require the panelists to take their first formal vote by secret ballot.[29] If two-thirds or more of the panelists agree on the issue (with abstentions counting as "no" votes), they will then divide into pro and con subgroups to write one-paragraph rationales for and against the bill. If there is not a two-thirds majority for or against the bill, deliberation will continue until the middle of the fifth and final day, with the moderator calling for periodic votes. If still deadlocked, the citizens will divide into pro and con groups to write rationales, but their verdict would be recorded as "undecided."[30]

Just as a priority panel would have guidelines for its deliberation on the legislative agenda, so legislative panels would have preset goals. Their task would be to reach agreement (two-thirds majority or greater) on the bill before them. Also, they would be asked—but not required—not to take a solid "yea or nay" position on the bill until their vote on the fourth day of deliberation. In the case of a statewide legislative panel, citizens would also be encouraged to try to base their vote upon their final judgment of what is in the interest of the state as a whole. Prior to arriving at that point, however, participants would be invited to contribute their own unique perspectives and experiences. Ultimately, citizen panelists would manage to combine genuine self-expression with the pursuit of a larger public judgment, but as Lynn Sanders points out, it is also important "to ensure that those who are usually left out of public discussions learn to speak whether their perspectives are common or not."[31] Most civil and criminal jurors manage to take on the role of the "neutral judge" briefly, and most past participants in past random sample forums have taken their jobs very seriously.[32] So might the participants in a legislative panel.

IMPLICATIONS FOR ELECTIONS

Because they involve substantive judgments about specific bills, the legislative panels could have far more powerful electoral implications than the priority panels. When secretaries of state present these panel results to voters, they would show candidates' votes on key legislation, but they would also permit voters to compare each candidate's vote with a democratic public voice—the verdicts of a representative, deliberative, and articulate body of fellow citizens (see box 7). This would make it possible for voters unfamiliar with issues to judge candidate votes more critically by moving past their own surface-level judgments and using those of the legislative panels. In effect, the voter guides distributed after legislative panels would permit a voter to *simulate* deliberating about ten national issues and comparing final deliberative judgments to candidate positions.

Some might wish to stop at this point, having provided interested voters with detailed printed and on-line information about candidates for the Ohio state legislature and the views of a deliberative sample of the state's population. I suggest going one step farther by providing a very simple piece of information that reduces the detail of the voter guide to a single numeric symbol—the percentage of agreement between the votes of each candidate and those of the legislative panels. The rationale behind this number is that past voting research has found that the typical voter prefers to choose candidates using only simple bits of information, as explained in chapter 3. Voters "tend to make use only of information that is incidental" or available information "for which there is virtually no cost, such as names and parties on ballots."[33] Even when voters lack reliable clues that permit confident deduction of which candidate would best represent them, they can find highly suggestive "cues" that tell them how to vote.[34]

Box 7

Sample Voter Guide Showing the Results of the Legislative Panel and the Votes of Legislative Candidates on a Hypothetical Bill

Issue #1. Welfare Reform (HR 3734, signed into law July 1996)

Bill imposed a five-year limit on welfare benefits and a required welfare recipients to find work within two years.

	Republican	Democrat	Libertarian
Citizen Panel	*John Dorshuck*	*Rhonda Schulman*	*Orlando Morales*
For	For	Against	For
(25–5 vote)	(official vote)		

Citizen Panel Argument For: Many people need welfare at times in their lives, but five years is long enough. Also, people who receive welfare should be able to find jobs. Pushing people out of the welfare system will hurt some, but most will fend for themselves once they are forced to find work.

Citizen Panel Argument Against: This bill was too severe. It provided no safety net for the poorest of the poor. It also forces single parents to work instead of caring for their own children.

Dorshuck Argument For: The government cannot afford to pay for our overburdened welfare system. This bill will force people to fend for themselves after years on welfare, and it provides some child care benefits for working mothers.

Schulman Argument Against: Republicans stereotype welfare recipients as lazy cheaters, but that's just not true. Nobody wants welfare, and recipients take jobs when those jobs are available. Turning our backs on the neediest is cruel, and we should offer job training and assistance to those who need it.

Morales Argument For: The only legitimate purpose of government is national defense and policing our streets. This bill did not go far enough, but it was a step in the right direction. We should eliminate all government handouts to both the rich and poor.

In candidate selection, as in most mental activities, people are cognitive misers. Considering the likelihood of one vote deciding an election, plus the finite difference between a typical pair of candidates, citizens attribute little value to making a correct voting choice. Consequently, voters give low priority to candidate selection relative to the more immediate concerns they must attend to in their daily lives. This may be truer of less sophisticated voters, but when cues such as a candidate's party affiliation are present, even more involved voters can overlook complex candidate characteristics and make decisions solely on the basis of simple heuristics.[35]

In low-visibility elections, where the average voter has heard little about the candidates, many voters lack solid data upon which to base their choice, so they make their decision using simple facts, such as the candidate's party and sex.[36] When voters know *nothing* about candidates prior to entering the voting booth, they must either make random choices or respond to the scant information that appears on the ballot itself. Assuming even the slightest sense of responsibility, voters are likely to take the latter course by voting based upon at least some information, no matter how mundane. Sometimes this means voting based on party, although that cue is often unavailable. Other times, voters choose candidates because their first name sounds male or female or their last name suggests a particular ethnic background.[37]

The political scientist Arthur Lupia considered this problem in a study of insurance reform elections in California. As others have observed in national elections, Lupia found that some unsophisticated voters were able to make complex judgments by relying on cues from like-minded elites. Transferring the lesson of that election to the larger political process, Lupia recommends improving the quality of cues rather than pursuing wholesale civic education: "While scholars and pundits propose that we educate the public about politics in order to lessen the impact of uninformed votes on the responsiveness of democratic decision-making institutions . . . directing our efforts into the provision of credible and widely accessible 'signals' may be a more effective and cost-efficient way to ensure the responsiveness of electoral outcomes."[38]

I suggest providing voters with a new cue—a candidate rating that shows the extent to which each candidate's unofficial and official votes correspond to those of the legislative panels (see box 8).[39] The cue has the same virtue of other ballot cues, in that it is simple and readily available to even the least active voter. What sets it apart from all other ballot cues, except sometimes political party, is that it carries a tremendous amount of information. Particularly when one candidate has an agreement percentage (or "rating") well above the other candidates, a voter can use that cue to decide that the highest-rated candidate stands a much better chance of representing the public's interests. The cue is not flawless, but it provides uninformed, confused, or undecided voters with one simple fact to consider before marking their ballots.

Box 8

Sample Ballot Showing Legislative Candidate Ratings

This August, a randomly-selected panel of Ohio residents voted on ten bills that came before the Ohio state legislature during the past two years. The ratings by each candidate's name show the percentage of the time that each candidate agreed with the citizen panel's votes. For example, a rating of 100% shows that a candidate agreed with the citizen panel on every issue, and a rating of 50% shows that the candidate and citizen panel voted the same on half of the issues. For more details, refer to your official Voter Guide.

Ohio House of Representatives (District 6) Choose One

John Dorshuck REPUBLICAN	[75% rating]	❏
Rhonda Schulman DEMOCRAT	[60% rating]	❏
Orlando Morales LIBERTARIAN	[30% rating]	❏

Finally, county clerks can use the candidate ratings to order the names of candidates on the ballot. Many candidates believe that the order of names on the ballots influences the outcome of elections by a small percentage. A rigorous study of this problem found name-order effects in 48 percent of 118 Ohio elections. In races where there was an ordering effect, the candidate listed first almost always benefited, and the average impact was 2.5 percent. Partisan races and elections in counties with higher levels of political information were less likely to demonstrate ordering effects.[40] It is discouraging to imagine that innumerable close races have been decided by the order of candidates' names on the ballot. Even if one doubted the necessity of convening citizen panels for all elections, one might still see wisdom in obtaining panel judgments in competitive races just to remove this problem. By listing candidates in descending order, with the highest-rated candidate first, clerks can assign this advantage in a manner that is less arbitrary than random ordering.

ADVISORY PANELS

Priority panels and legislative panels could be used for many elections besides congressional and state legislative races. City councils, county commissions, and school boards could use similar panels, and the more local the political unit, the cheaper these would become. (In addition, these panels could apply to candidates for executive offices, although the nonlegislative duties of executives might recommend the use of the candidate selection panels, which I describe later.) At the city and county level, however, it might be preferable to use a different form of panel that involves the public more directly in the policymaking process. This "advisory" approach shares much in common with the legislative panels, but has some important differences, which I shall now describe.

One of the greatest drawbacks of the legislative panels is that the citizens usually vote *after* bills have received a vote in committee or on the floor. Most of the time, this means that the panel votes will chiefly function to eliminate bad representation, and they will thus serve as a voice of the public only in the long run. A legislative panel vote might reveal some unrepresentative officials, but those officials will have already taken action on the bills they considered. Even if the officials had wanted panel guidance on those bills, the advice will come too late, for by the time the panel votes, officials will already be on record—unofficially, if not officially.

To address this limitation, the advisory panel changes the process by convening a random sample of citizens to deliberate and vote on legislation *prior* to official votes by governing bodies. Box 9 illustrates the advisory process using the example of a city council. The process would begin whenever a special city council vote or citizen petition delays official action on a piece of legislation, pending citizen deliberation. (Enactment of an advisory panel law would stipulate the circumstances under which the council or a petitioner could take this action.) A local courthouse would then provide the city council with fifty citizens previously selected for jury duty.[41] In a sense, this first review panel would serve as a "grand jury," examining the relevance of a bill to determine whether it merits the sustained attention of a full advisory panel of citizens. For just one day, the citizen review panel would hear arguments from city councilors (and petitioners, if applicable) on the importance of the piece of suspended legislation. The review panel would deliberate and vote, and if a majority recommended full deliberation, then the process would continue. (Otherwise, the legislation would return to the city council for a vote.)

Box 9

Steps in Implementing an Advisory Panel for a City Council

1. Initial Review Panel and Agenda Setting

   a. A city council vote or petition delays official action on a piece of legislation.
   b. The municipal (or county) courthouse provides the city council with fifty citizens who had been previously selected for jury duty. For just one day, these citizens will serve on a review panel.
   c. City councilors (and petitioners, if applicable) argue for the importance of the piece of legislation to the review panel.
   d. The review panel deliberates and votes on the importance of the legislation. If a majority recommend full deliberation, then the process continues; otherwise, the legislation returns to the city council for a vote.

2. Advisory Panel Preparation and Deliberation

   a. The city or county courthouse provides the city council with fifty citizens who had been previously selected for jury duty. These citizens will serve on an advisory panel.
   b. City councilors (and petitioners, if applicable) select witnesses to provide testimony on the legislation.

c. Witnesses present testimony to advisory panel and engage in cross-examination.
d. The advisory panel deliberates, votes for or against the legislation, and writes a rationale for its votes for and against. If two-thirds reach agreement for or against a bill, the decision is recorded. Otherwise, the panel is labeled "undecided."

3. Public Expression by Advisory Panel

The city clerk reports the results of the advisory panel's deliberations to the council prior to its vote on the legislation.

4. Implications for Elections

a. Candidates not serving on the council report unofficial votes to the city clerk.
b. The city clerk provides voters with the oversight panelists' recommendations and the official and unofficial votes of council candidates through printed and on-line voter guides.
c. On the ballot, county clerks print a number beside each candidate that indicates the percentage-agreement between each candidate's votes and those of the citizen panels.

After a bill passed the review panel, the local courthouse would provide the city council with a new set of fifty citizens previously selected for jury duty. This advisory panel of citizens would follow a process similar to that of the legislative panels, hearing testimony from witnesses chosen by city councilors (and petitioners, if applicable), deliberating on the matter, hearing a critique of their preliminary findings, then reaching a final decision and writing a rationale. Because of the size of the advisory panel, a two-thirds majority would be required for a decision. If citizens were unable to reach a final decision, they would be labeled "undecided," but they would still split into subgroups to write rationales for supporting and opposing the bill in question.

After the conclusion of the advisory panel's deliberations, the city clerk would inform the council of the panel's recommendations. At the next official council meeting, the panel's vote would be read before the council members took a roll-call vote on the bill. Depending on one's viewpoint, this would provide public-spirited elected officials with a high-fidelity recording of the local community's deliberative voice, and it would put pressure upon self-interested officials, who might otherwise follow the guidance of special interests. What makes the advisory panel powerful in the latter case is that it would carry electoral implications: citizens would receive ratings of incumbent councilors through the same voter guides and ballot ratings as in the case of legislative panels.

The timing of the advisory panel is its most distinctive quality, and that is also its limitation. The advisory panel would prove impractical at larger levels of government because it requires the spontaneous assembly of citizen panels and witnesses. Unless a form of video-conferencing were used, it would be difficult and expensive to quickly create panels as issues arose. In addition, the advisory panels would convene several times between elections, and candidates for office not presently serving would be able to cast their unofficial votes weeks, months, or years after the panels had already voted. Newcomer candidates could simply give themselves a 100 percent rating, and nobody would know whether their adopted views were sincere. Challengers with political histories might have more difficulty squaring their 100 percent ratings with past actions, but their opponents could only question the honesty of their unofficial votes. (Because of this problem, county clerks would not use the final candidate ratings to determine candidate order on the ballot.)

CANDIDATE-SELECTION PANELS

When candidates run for nonlegislative offices, neither the legislative nor the advisory panels would be suited to consider their election. Mayoral and gubernatorial candidates might receive ratings from legislative or advisory panels, but the responsibilities of mayors and governors extend far beyond signing and vetoing bills. Those two forms of panels would also be useless as mechanisms for helping voters evaluate judicial and administrative candidates, such as those running for sheriff, corporation commissioner, or state supreme court justice.

What distinguishes these candidates from the legislative ones is that they do not have voting records per se. Judicial and administrative rulings sometimes have profound implications, but they are not the same as legislative action. Judges and administrators interpret and enforce laws, rather than drafting and enacting them. To evaluate the past and future performance of candidates for these offices requires a citizen panel that can rate the candidates only after it determines the criteria by which it evaluates candidates.

Box 10 uses the example of a state supreme court election to show the two stages in which a candidate-selection panel would deliberate. First, the panel would consider candidates' testimony on the appropriate criteria for selecting justices, deliberate on the matter, then vote on a set of specific criteria using a two-thirds majority voting rule. Second, in front of the selection panel, the judicial candidates would testify and cross-examine one another in relation to their satisfaction of the aforementioned evaluative criteria. Citizens would then deliberate on the candidates and reach their verdicts, using a two-thirds majority decision rule. When comparing more than two candidates, votes failing to reach a two-thirds majority would result in dropping the candidate with the fewest votes.

Box 10

Steps for Implementing a Selection Panel for State Supreme Court Candidates

1. Panel Selection

> The secretary of state pays a nonprofit polling organization to select a statewide random sample of fifty citizen panelists.

2. Deliberation on Evaluative Criteria

> a. In front of the citizen panel, candidates for the state supreme court testify and cross-examine one another on the appropriate criteria for selecting justices.
> b. The citizen panel deliberates and, using a two-thirds majority decision rule, identifies the criteria that it believes should be used to evaluate judicial candidates.

2. Deliberation on Candidate Selection

> a. In front of the citizen panel, judicial candidates testify and cross-examine one another with regard to their satisfaction of the aforementioned evaluative criteria.
> b. Citizen panelists deliberate, select candidates for each supreme court election, and write rationales for their majority and minority votes using the aforementioned evaluative criteria. Citizens write arguments both for and against each candidate.

3. Implications for Elections

> a. The secretary of state provides voters with the citizen panelists' candidate selections and their rationales through printed and on-line voter guides.

    b. On the ballot, county clerks print the percentage of citizen panel
       votes won by each candidate beside the candidate's names.
    c. Using these same percentages, candidates are listed on ballots in de-
       scending order.

    On-line and printed voter guides would present the rationales given
for each candidate, and a record of the sequence of vote tallies in cases
where there were multiple candidates. In these cases, however, there
would be multiple ways in which one could represent the panel's votes
on the ballot itself. The ballot could show candidate vote percentages
from the final round of voting, but this would obscure the fact that
some panelists initially voted for other candidates in some cases. The
ballot could show no percentages and, instead, would simply place an
"endorsement symbol" by the name of the candidate who won two-
thirds of the panelists' votes on the final tally, if there was a winner. Or
the ballot could simply show the candidates' vote percentages from the
first round of voting.

    The decision about what appears on the ballot could, in turn, change
the decision about what voting procedure to use on the panel. My own
preference is to proceed through the stages of voting until the panel either has a two-thirds majority candidate or reaches a final, two-candidate vote, whichever comes first. Afterward, panelists would then take
a final multicandidate vote with the understanding that this final vote
would be their "published" verdict. The voting stages would have
shown some panelists that their first-choice candidate was not viable,
and they might—or might not—choose to cast their final vote for one
of the front-runners. The county clerk would then publish those panel
vote percentages on the ballot.

REFERENDA PANELS

Because of complexity of candidate evaluation, particularly in multicandidate races, a government could implement panels with much
greater ease when their only task was evaluating a specific initiative or
referendum. Box 11 shows how a secretary of state would convene a
panel on a statewide ballot referendum. The process is analogous to the
deliberation of a single legislative panel, and the voter guides and ballots would show how the panelists voted. This is more straightforward
than candidate evaluation, because there is a one-to-one correspon-

dence between the decision panelists make and the choice that voters must make. This form of panel might improve citizen deliberation in direct democratic processes, but it does not ensure the accountability of public officials.

Box 11

Steps in Implementing a Panel on a Statewide Referendum

1. Preparation and Agenda Setting

   a. The secretary of state pays a nonprofit polling organization to select a statewide random sample of fifty citizen panelists.
   b. State legislative party leaders (and petitioners, if applicable) select witnesses to provide testimony.

2. Deliberation

   a. Witnesses present testimony to citizen panel and engage in cross-examination.
   b. Citizen panelists deliberate, vote for or against referendum, and write rationales for the votes for and against.

3. Implications for Elections

   a. Secretaries of state provide voters with the citizen panelists' recommendations through printed and on-line voter guides.
   b. On the ballot, county clerks print a number beside each referendum that represents the percentage of citizen panel votes it won.
   c. Using these same percentages, referenda are listed on ballots in descending order.

One could extend this idea beyond statewide referenda to more local ballot items, such as municipal bonds and school levies. These measures usually ask voters to decide whether or not to spend public money on schools, fire stations, and other services and projects. Unfortunately, deliberation on these measures is rare, even in the parts of the United States with traditions of "town meetings." In Meredith, New Hampshire, for example, 400 citizens attended meetings on school, road, and library budgets, but a majority of the 4,000 who eventually voted on those issues rejected every spending proposal. As Joseph Zimmerman argues, "If you walk into the voting booth and know nothing more than so much money is recommended for a purpose, you may have a tendency to vote against it."[42] On the other hand, if voters had read recommendations and rationales from citizen panels, they might be more inclined to consider each bond or levy on its merits, instead of defensively rejecting them all (or, for that matter, mindlessly supporting each one).[43]

For the severest critics of representative democracy, such as Simon Threlkeld, the purpose of referenda and other ballot measures is to enact "laws supported by the informed will of the citizenry . . . even if opposed or ignored by elected governments." Because of elections' failure to put responsible public officials in office, Threlkeld also doubts the quality of referenda elections. For that reason, he suggests using citizen panels not as a source of voter information but as decision makers. He envisions juries of 100 or more paid citizen jurors meeting for the "days, weeks, or months needed to become fully informed" about individual referenda. Like the referenda panels, the jurors would hear testimony, deliberate, then vote, but in Threlkeld's system, the jurors would act with full authority as randomly chosen representatives.[44]

The referenda panels I propose stop short of this because I believe it is important that elections give all voters the chance to have a direct say on specific pieces of legislation. Blending representative government with direct democracy in this way keeps all voters connected to the process of lawmaking, whereas a citizen jury with final decision-making authority would replace a direct democratic process with another form of representation.

DEVILISH DETAILS

This chapter has shown ways in which official random sample panels could extend a transmission belt from deliberation to voting, from the expression of the public's deliberative voice to its ability to reject unrepresentative public officials. Different panels would serve different purposes, but the basic structure is the same: each panel would involve drawing random samples of citizens, selecting witnesses, convening deliberative sessions among citizens, and using decision rules to record summary votes and statements of the citizens' views.

I have discussed each of these critical components, but the actual implementation of any one of these panels would require considerable refinement to ensure fair, open, and well-informed deliberation. I have not specified these processes in greater detail because I wish to emphasize the *general* properties of deliberative citizen panels. If the reader finds the idea palatable, I encourage further discussion of the particulars. In practice, the structural details of citizen panels could vary considerably, although I would hope that these variations would still share the same abstract features I have outlined.

CHAPTER 8

The Political Impact
of Citizen Panels

Developing a sense of the public interest requires a level of
cognitive engagement with the political world that is both
broader and deeper than that found today. . . . Gauging the
impact of today's political choices on the future and influencing those choices . . . requires political knowledge.

Michael Delli Carpini and Scott Keeter,
What Americans Know about
Politics and Why It Matters

Any successful reform of the American political system must offer a
means by which citizens can broaden and deepen their understandings
of the most pressing national issues. Effective reform must also sharpen
voters' evaluations of the candidates who seek to act upon those issues
as elected officials. The citizen panels presented in chapter 7 can provide the information that voters need without requiring a tremendous
effort on the part of the average citizen.

For the panels to achieve this purpose, however, they must produce
high-quality decisions, and citizens must be willing and able to use
panel judgments when voting. If subject to self-deception, groupthink,
and other decision-making illnesses, the citizen panels would reach unwarranted conclusions and promote the election of unqualified or unrepresentative candidates. If voters found the panel results to be irrelevant, elitist, or confusing, the panels would also fail to have their
intended impact. These dangers merit discussion, and in this chapter, I
explain why the panels would be likely to reach sound and influential
judgments. If they succeed in these two respects, the panels could
change many other features of American politics. Institutionalized citizen panels could reduce civic neglect, dampen the cynicism of public officials, promote deliberation, and change the nature of American political campaigns.

THE QUALITY OF CITIZEN JUDGMENTS

For many reasons, the citizen panels I propose would make policy judgments of varied quality. Sometimes the panels would see an issue clearly, connect the policy options to their underlying values, and reach a decision in sync with the public's most enlightened understanding of its own interests. At other times, however, the panels might make decisions based on imperfect reasoning, low self-awareness, and possibly even faulty information. In those cases, the citizen panels would write flawed rationales for their policy decisions, and their decisions would often be contrary to the public's best interests.[1] No process can remove the possibility of such mistakes, but I have designed citizen panels to increase the likelihood of deliberation and sound judgment.[2]

The psychologist Scott Tindale raises concerns about the quality of deliberation in programs like the 1996 National Issues Convention. "Small groups," Tindale explains, "can sometimes lead to unexpected and occasionally problematic outcomes." In the worst groups, participants will polarize into extreme and possibly irrational points of view, and the majority will wear down the minority through pressure to conform and its superior numbers, which produce more speaking time and arguments for the majority position.[3] Separating out these problems, there are four hazards that merit examination: a flawed or unduly limited information base; low motivation to deliberate thoroughly; excessive social pressure to adopt the majority position; and a countervailing possibility of internal divisions that prevent the discovery of common ground.

INFORMATION

Insufficient or flawed information can result in suboptimal group decisions.[4] Groups that convene to discuss an issue can make outrageous statements and reach ridiculous conclusions because the group participants lack necessary information. In a group with a poor knowledge base, a single idea or assertion can hold sway, especially if there is no procedure for testing participants' beliefs against some external information source. For that reason, all of the deliberation programs presented in chapter 6 have some mechanism for infusing basic facts and important arguments into group discussions.

The citizen panels proposed in chapter 7 would be no different: participants would gain relevant information from informal discussions among friends and neighbors, formal witness testimony, and joint deliberation among the panelists.[5] The lead witnesses, who orchestrate the arguments that panelists hear, will have powerful incentives for providing the most compelling testimony possible, and by presenting opposing viewpoints with cross-examination, it is likely that the panelists will develop a solid base of information on the issue before them. By using round-robins and active moderation during deliberation, the uneven participation rates typical in small group discussion would not preclude meaningful participation from the quieter panel members.[6] In addition, exposing each panel's deliberations to second-guessing on the third day of deliberation would address the problem of the panel moving too far without external criticism. These procedures provide mechanisms for verifying or challenging important facts and other "validity claims."[7]

MOTIVATION

Good information is useless, however, if panelists choose to ignore it. Citizen panels will fail if the participants lack sufficient motivation to deliberate. As explained in chapter 2, deliberation is hard work. Even with its alternative choices predefined, a panel must carefully examine a problem, establish a set of criteria for judging alternatives, and then weigh the pros and cons. Only a highly motivated group can simultaneously sustain high levels of attention, critical scrutiny, and self-awareness over a period of days. If the panels cannot sustain a sufficient level of motivation, their final judgments are likely to suffer some of the same weaknesses as superficial survey responses.[8]

The sources of motivation for citizen panels are straightforward. First, participants would be paid a considerable honorarium to demonstrate that panel organizers respect the time and effort required to participate. In past random sample forums, participants have appreciated this gesture, and citizen panelists would receive even greater compensation for their efforts. Second, panelists would be asked to perform for only a limited number of hours over a limited number of days. No citizen could sustain a high level of deliberation indefinitely, but a clear deadline and a structured series of activities would make it possible for most participants to remain alert and constructive throughout their deliberations. Third, since some panelists might tend to become distracted and produce uncritical judgments if left to their own devices, the panel organizers would be present throughout the event. Motivation can be contagious, and with large panels, there would always be someone to serve as a model of the motivation that other panelists need to maintain. Finally, and most important, if the panels achieve their intended goal and influence the outcomes of elections, panelists would see clearly the importance of their judgments. Citizens may appear apathetic about politics, but they obviously care about public issues. "Americans seem to overcome the obstacles to participation when they believe that they might have an effect—that there is some opportunity to create and witness change," David Mathews concluded after watching a series of focus groups on political alienation.[9]

PRESSURE TO CONFORM

Panelists might push each other to maintain a high level of motivation, but the panels are also designed to reduce the pressure to conform to a particular group viewpoint. Groups are more likely to arrive at a premature and low-quality consensus if (a) the discussion concerns an ambiguous object or issue, (b) only one group member holds the minority view, (c) the group members are required to present their final judgment in public, and (d) the group is close-knit.[10]

First, the ambiguity of the panelists' discussion topics would be inevitable, for truly political dilemmas never have straightforward solutions. If there were an objective standpoint from which one could judge public decisions, society would have no need for politics. Psychological research suggests that this inherent ambiguity can increase pressure to conform, because of the difficulty of knowing the accuracy or appropriateness of one's own views.[11] To alleviate this pressure somewhat, the citizen panel process would present participants with clear task requirements and focus their discussion on relatively narrow issues, such as a single piece of legislation or one set of candidates.

Second, using citizen panels with fifty or more members reduces the likelihood that lone individuals will favor the minority position. Past research on small group behavior shows that even the encouragement of just one fellow dissenter can bolster the confidence and independence of a minority group member, who will then continue to present arguments in favor of his or her minority viewpoint. For this reason, minority influence is common in jury deliberation. In one study (Hastie, Penrod, and Pennington 1983), the final jury verdict did not correspond to the original judgment of a majority "verdict-favoring faction" on thirteen out of sixty-nine mock juries. Four wound up as hung juries, and nine reached agreement on a verdict opposite the initial majority preference.

This kind of reversal is somewhat analogous to the shifts in opinions that James Fishkin has witnessed at the National Issues Convention and other deliberative polls.[12]

Third, the use of secret ballots in citizen panel discussions would alleviate the pressure produced by the public presentation of a minority viewpoint. For this same reason, panel moderators would also prohibit public straw polling and encourage panelists to refrain from publicly stating early verdicts. In the same jury study cited above, Hastie found evidence that the postponement of preliminary judgment can aid deliberation in just this manner: "Juries that deliberate with an evidence-driven style, starting deliberation with a discussion of evidence rather than law and deferring formal voting until later in deliberation" tend to produce "more thorough and impartial assessments" and a better "integration of the evidence."[13]

The fourth source of group conformity pressure is high group cohesion. The political psychologist Irving Janis fingered cohesion as the culprit in *Groupthink*.[14] Countless scholars, organizational consultants, public figures, and citizens have accused cohesive decision-making bodies of engaging in groupthink, as if the phenomenon were a common and almost inevitable result of group decision making. On the contrary, Janis found that groupthink only arose under particular circumstances and that many groups escaped it through well-crafted procedures. According to Janis, a group is more likely to engage in groupthink when it is cohesive, flawed in its organizational design (i.e., a homogenous membership isolated from other people and no neutral leader and procedures), lacking in self-esteem, and under extreme external pressure.

To protect against groupthink, the citizen panels would have a diverse membership, neutral procedures, and a professional moderator. The most important procedure regarding groupthink might be exposing the panel's deliberation to outside scrutiny on the third day of deliberation. In addition, whenever a panel's deliberations appeared to converge on a consensus ahead of schedule, the panel moderator could randomly assign a citizen to play the role of devil's advocate to spark critical examination of the panel's emerging decision.[15] Some citizen panelists may lack self-esteem and feel outside pressure, but not to the degree that Janis observed in his case studies of groupthink. In addition, the panelists are likely to form cohesive bonds, as have the participants at past random sample forums; however, social psychological and small group communication research has found that there is no simple correspondence between cohesion and the quality of group decisions. Some research even suggests that moderate cohesion can *increase* group productivity.[16]

Differences among participants in communications skills and style are also relevant to conformity. Individuals vary in their abilities to express themselves and process new information rapidly, and they also have different styles of listening and speaking. Were these variances randomly distributed across the population, they would reduce the quality of deliberation but produce no pressure toward conforming to a particular viewpoint. Eloquence would come from all directions. Some critics of deliberation, however, argue that "status inequalities and regular patterns of social oppression might intrude when Americans deliberate." In this view, males, whites, and more highly educated participants tend to dominate in juries and classroom discussions, so groups might conform to their views by force of social power more than argument.[17]

Evidence supporting this view comes from jury trials, however, and citizen panels differ from juries in many important respects. Jury discussions are shielded from public view, have a relatively loose structure, and do not use an outside moderator. Each of these features makes it easier for dominant social groups to wield power. Citizen panel deliberations are subject to external review and comment, so they lack the insulation that facilitates unjustified judgments. Because panel deliberation has guidelines and structured activities promoting debate, it is harder to silence opposition. Like all random sample forums, citizen panels also employ a moderator, who reinforces discussion rules and encourages broad participation.[18]

Mitigating factors such as these are important considerations when considering the power of social status on group conformity and bias. Careful study of group interaction has found that the impact of social status varies tremendously across different groups. For example, a careful meta-analysis of seventy-five studies of group leadership found that males emerged as leaders more often than women, but this effect was reduced if groups met outside a laboratory, undertook a gender-neutral task, or had complex social relations among participants. If groups had more than one meeting, the effect of gender on leadership emergence all but disappeared.[19] In sum, social status differences in communication styles and skills are real, but carefully designed group activities can diminish—or eliminate—their potential to force group conformity to a particular viewpoint.

FINDING COMMON GROUND

While guarding against conformity, the citizen panels will need to avoid the personal conflicts and internal schisms that can polarize groups into extreme factions and create a deadlock. This problem is especially important in the case of political deliberation, because American politicians, the media, and citizens share a cultural tradition of adversarial democracy.[20] Interest groups tenaciously defend their positions in public debates, and giving ground is more a sign of weakness than a virtuous gesture. Candidates for public office—and the parties backing them—create a climate of hostile conflict through irrelevant personal attacks, exaggerated or misleading policy contrasts, and empty but evocative symbols.[21] The media plays its part by giving undue attention to posturing and demagoguery, as opposed to more respectful dialogue. By framing politics as the competitive pursuit of self-interest, the media feed into a spiral of political cynicism.[22] From the right come such soothing pet names as "baby killer," "feminazi," and "tree hugger," and the left replies with "woman hater," "Bible thumper," and "greedy capitalist," among others.[23]

How could deliberation and consensus-building take place in such a climate? Citizen panels would engage in meaningful discourse and careful listening because of the nature of their participants. Though immersed in a culture of political conflict, most citizens show a willingness to speak and listen respectfully in face-to-face interactions with strangers. Personally, I have found that even at the most bloodthirsty public rallies, I can strike up a reasoned conversation with an apparent adversary if we can stand just beyond the crowd to hear each other speak. We usually come away understanding one another much better and even agreeing on certain issues. When citizens step into the far more hospitable setting of a random sample forum, such as the National Issues Convention described in chapter 6, they become even more likely to play the sober role of juror. As Roderick Hart and Sharon Jarvis concluded after studying transcripts from the convention, participants "showed themselves respectful of—but not cowed by—the issues of the day and respectful of—and not cowed by—their own heterogeneity. They used a variety of strategies to build bridges to one another."[24]

Despite participants' varied viewpoints, random sample forums usually move toward consensus because participants come together as a group to compensate for the unfamiliarity of their setting. They develop a thin but shared group identity around the very structure and official norms of the jury or public forum, which is all they have in common.

In other words, panel participants would build their group identity using the procedures and purposes of the panel process itself and their shared experiences as citizen-participants.[25] Because one of the central emphases of the citizen panel process is the common pursuit of the best interest of the city, state, or nation, it is likely that the panels, like past random sample forums, usually will avoid excessive internal division and reach the necessary level of agreement.[26]

In sum, citizen panels can be expected to reach reasonable decisions, given an adequate information base and group procedures that mitigate against both conformity and internal polarization. In some respects, the citizen panel design is more elaborate than those used in criminal and civil juries, which deliberate in private without any procedural structure. Despite their lack of safeguards against faulty information-processing and social pressure, conventional juries perform quite well. As Valerie Hans and Neil Vidmar conclude in *Judging the Jury* (1986): "The data from hundreds of studies of jury trials and jury simulations suggest that actual incompetence is a rare phenomenon. Juries do differ sometimes from the way judges would have decided, but it is on grounds other than incompetence."[27] In a similar manner, one could expect citizen panels to deviate from some conventional political judgments, but that is part of their purpose—to reveal the judgments that average citizens reach when provided with roughly the same information base as policy experts and public officials.

PANEL INFLUENCE ON VOTING DECISIONS

Even if citizen panels avoid the pitfalls of group decision making, their final judgments would have little value if they did not influence elections. In chapter 3, I explained how voters routinely use simple information cues when evaluating candidates, but some might question whether voters would be inclined to use the ratings and rationales of the citizen panels to evaluate public officials and their opponents. If voters found the panel judgments to be unnecessary, illegitimate, biased, or too confusing, they would ignore the panels when making their voting decisions.

NECESSITY

A critic of the citizen panel proposal might argue that voters would find the panel recommendations superfluous. Why would voters use this information when they have so many other cues and solid facts upon which to base their decisions? Chapter 3 shows that the way in which a person evaluates candidates depends, in part, upon the intensity of an election and the person's political sophistication. The most sophisticated voters would probably find the panel recommendations an unnecessary guide when voting in moderate- and high-intensity elections, because those races provide information that these voters can readily translate into firm candidate evaluations. Most elections are low-intensity, however, and most voters do not have well-developed political skills and a keen interest in campaigns. Consequently, the majority of voters in the majority of elections would find panel evaluations helpful in choosing candidates.

In addition, most voters lack strong party loyalties that might otherwise determine their voting choices. Unlike many proposed political reforms, the citizen panel proposal would work *because* of the decline in the strength of the traditional American political system. Chapter 3 demonstrates that political parties do not have the power they once had, and only a minority of citizens continue to use them as a dominant voting cue. Moreover, party primaries involve candidates of the same party, and many general elections do not identify candidates by party affiliation. In those elections, even partisans must turn to other sources of information to select among opposing candidates.

Voters often recognize that they lack the necessary facts to make an informed choice. A recent national survey conducted by the League of Women Voters found that 76 percent of voters said they did not have "enough accurate information" to make meaningful decisions in the voting booth.[28] Voters know how to find and follow cognitive shortcuts to compensate for limited and biased information, but many voting decisions do not even use those simple cues. Citizen panel recommendations would improve voters' information base across the ballot and give them a sound, simple way to make choices.

LEGITIMACY

Notwithstanding that voters might need or want more information about their candidates, some may view the panel process as elitist. Though he does not use that term, Frank Newport, the editor-in-chief of the Gallup Poll, presents such a critique in his discussion of a deliberative poll conducted in Britain in 1994. A national survey found that 57 percent of respondents advocated "sending more offenders to prison" to prevent crime, whereas after deliberating, only 38 percent of a similar sample supported that approach. As Newport sees it,

> Since many citizens in a democracy are never going to deliberate and read briefing papers, and since their opinions still count just as much as their deliberating friends, it seems that the 57% number is the more useful. It tells us where the people stand on the issues *as they are*—based on their own life situation and choices about the degree to which they want to be immersed in issues and deliberation. The higher "prison is effective" number reflects the reality of the average citizen's daily life. . . . To rely on the "informed" survey finding of 38% . . . is to turn one's back on the average citizen.[29]

The average citizen does, however, recognize the limitations of his or her own surface survey responses. Giving an answer to a serious policy question in a matter of seconds permits no reflection and even less self-education, and citizens know this. In their personal and professional lives, citizens routinely delegate deliberation to an individual or committee that returns with recommendations. Political representation works with the same premise, although citizens have lost confidence in the deliberative wisdom of their governing institutions, as demonstrated in chapter 3.

There is even direct evidence that average Americans would view citizen panelists as reasonable representatives of their own deliberative judgments. A 1999 survey by the Center on Public Attitudes asked a random sample of American adults whether they would trust the decisions of Congress more than those produced by a randomly selected deliberative body of 500 citizens. Only 15 percent said that Congress would make better decisions, whereas 66 percent said that the group of citizens would do better. In the view of 76 percent, the 500 citizens would be "most likely to show the greatest wisdom on questions of what the government should do."[30]

NEUTRALITY

To be useful, panel recommendations would have to appear both legitimate and neutral. It is conceivable that voters might think of the panels as an appropriate and fair political process yet think of panel judgments as nothing more than another biased and unreliable voting cue. Evidence on public attitudes toward juries suggests, however, that citizens would probably find the citizen panels a relatively neutral source of information about candidates and ballot propositions. Reviewing past research on attitudes toward juries, Valerie Hans found evidence of

public support for the criminal jury process: 79 percent of those surveyed nationwide rated the right to trial by jury as "extremely important," while only 14 percent of respondents said that jury trial "is over-
rated because juries can so often be swayed by a clever lawyer." A more
detailed survey of Cook County, Illinois, residents found that 90 percent rated that jury system as "somewhat fair" or "very fair," and most
reported believing in the accuracy of jury verdicts. "Even though the
public expresses a good deal of negativity over the failings of the criminal justice system at large, public opinion studies of the courts and the
criminal trial process show strong public support for the jury as an institution," Hans concluded.[31]

Public attitudes regarding *civil* juries are more mixed because of
widespread concern about the proliferation of civil lawsuits. Fortunately, the public's concern about this problem focuses "more on the lit-
igants and lawyers than on the jury."[32] Relating this back to the citizen
panels, it is likely that voters would view panel information as valuable
because they recognize the potential for random samples of citizens like
themselves to make competent and informed decisions, particularly
when doing so in the right deliberative setting.

To further safeguard citizen panels against perceived bias, it might be
prudent to place them within a novel institutional architecture and subject them to periodic evaluation. Ned Crosby has proposed that a
quasi-governmental public corporation run the citizen panels. A randomly selected citizen evaluation group could conduct an annual review of the deliberative process employed by citizen panels, and the
evaluation groups could elect the board of directors for the corporation.[33] If the panel process itself were placed under direct citizen control in this way (rather than having a government agency administer it),
the public might be less inclined to be skeptical of the neutrality (or legitimacy) of the citizen panels.

CLARITY

In any case, a voter could still discard the findings of a citizen panel if
unable to understand the panel's recommendations. Even illiterate voters can learn to recognize the name of a party beside a candidate's
name, but what would voters make of complicated voter guides and
numerical panel-agreement ratings beside candidates' names on the
ballot?

A critical factor in the use and interpretation of the panel results would be what voters learned about the panels through public information campaigns and media coverage. If implemented, the citizen panels would be a dramatic change in the electoral process, in part because they would be a political reform sponsored by the government itself. With even modest media coverage, most voters would probably learn the general principle of the panels the first time they were used. Over time, as voters heard more about the panels from citizens, interest groups, and politicians, they would get accustomed to the new information in the voter guide and know what to expect on the ballot.[34] If numerous panels convened to discuss local, state, and federal elections, a significant portion of the population would also gain firsthand experience with the process, and they would share their knowledge with their families and friends.

In sum, if enough voters used the panel-agreement ratings as voting guides, the panels would address the central problem discussed in this book. With a critical mass of the electorate acting in sync, the panels would present a credible threat of collective rejection of unrepresentative elected officials. A legislative candidate's voting record and an executive's past performance would, through the panel-agreement ratings, have direct electoral implications. In other words, the panels would hold public officials seeking reelection accountable for the actions they took as representatives of the public. Even self-serving public officials would have cause to heed the public's deliberative voice. Elected officials would also be less likely to skip an important vote, because if a citizen panel chose to examine that bill, failure to have voted would count against the candidate's panel-agreement rating. In any case, the panels would provide all officials with a democratic recording of the public's voice, and that could greatly benefit officeholders seeking guidance on current policy issues.[35]

REBUILDING PUBLIC TRUST AND REDUCING CIVIC NEGLECT

The regular exercise of a deliberative public vote and voice has intrinsic value for a representative democracy: meaningful public expression and thoughtful candidate selection ensure better representation. The smooth operation of these democratic processes could also reduce civic neglect and restore public trust.

In *Exit, Voice, and Loyalty,* Albert Hirschman encouraged readers to recognize that functional social and economic systems require a mix of exit and voice. When systems permit neither form of response, they can become "permanent pockets of inefficiency and neglect."[36] Some scholars using this model have underscored the long-term effects of the ensuing neglect. In the case of public organizations, when citizens stop responding to perceived failures in public representation and their loyalty toward the system falters, they become cynical and withdrawn. Once they perceive the system as unresponsive, they also begin to reduce their overall concern with public affairs and their local community.[37]

It is not surprising that civic neglect is increasingly common in America. As I show in chapter 3, the experience of voting as a futile form of expression can lead to a near-permanent sense of helplessness and cynicism. For many citizens, this results in chronic failure to vote. Others continue to vote as a matter of solemn duty, but they harbor no hope of unseating unrepresentative incumbents on election day. Chapter 5 shows that only lobbying—the most impersonal (and often inaccessible) form of public expression—has a regular influence on policymaking, and the failure of other mechanisms leads to the sense that public officials don't listen to what the public says.

Even if one believes that the political system is, in fact, responsive to the public's basic values and policy preferences, it is still the case that an increasingly large proportion of U.S. citizens *perceive* their representative institutions to be unresponsive and uncontrollable. In other words, the perception of ineffective elections and muffled public voice can prove almost as important as the actual breakdown of those processes. This is true because civic neglect amounts to more than simply the failure to exercise voice or unwillingness to try opposing an unpopular incumbent: *neglect also damages the social and psychological underpinnings of these political actions.*

As I argue in the preceding chapters, voting and voice should not be envisaged as levers that citizens can pull with ease. In chapter 2, I show how these political responses presume a modest level of civic skills, supportive beliefs (e.g., faith in one's abilities and perceived system responsiveness), and a sense of duty or other strong motivation. Chapter 3 shows that effective electoral action also requires cognitive evaluations that prove quite difficult, and chapters 5 and 6 show that formulating a representative, deliberative, articulate, and influential public voice requires considerable effort and creativity. As citizens withdraw from the political process, these social and psychological precursors of effective vote and voice decline. In this way, even if widespread civic neglect was based upon an underestimation of the impact of vote and voice, that neglect would ultimately erode the public's ability to use those very same mechanisms.

Democracy suffers if those already outside the political process grow even more cynical about politics and do not take the time to vote, let alone to vote after careful candidate evaluation. Were system neglect simply a common cold that afflicted a small percentage of every social group, it might not be so serious. Unfortunately, civic neglect is widespread and unevenly distributed across the population. The decline in political trust and participation documented in chapter 3 has reached the point where a majority of Americans are alienated from politics, refrain from participating in most elections, and decline innumerable opportunities to express their views in public settings. Moreover, political participation is considerably lower among young adults, minorities, and lower-income households than among their counterparts. Important political beliefs supporting participation, such as political self-efficacy and perceived system responsiveness, are also lower for people with less education and income, as well as among ideological moderates.[38] Younger voters and minorities are also less likely to vote than older whites. As Robert Entman writes in *Democracy without Citizens,* "Voters probably do not fully represent those who stay home. Nor do election outcomes accurately reflect what would happen if everyone voted."[39]

As I argue in chapter 1, the public's growing awareness of its weak vote and voice stems from real flaws in the political system. This accurate public perception, in turn, underlies some of the decline in *social capital.* Robert Putnam defines social capital as the "features of social life . . . that enable participants to act together more effectively to pursue shared objectives."[40] Such actions and pursuits are inclusive of voting and voice, as I have defined them, but public life also includes other forms of civic voluntarism and community involvement. Recent critiques of Putnam's diagnosis of declining social capital in the United States have stressed that many aspects of civic life remain healthy.[41] Though the public's trust in the media, politicians, and nearly every public entity is in decline, William Galston and Peter Levine point out that "voluntary activities are on balance healthier than are formal political institutions and processes." Citizens, they argue, "[s]eem to be shifting their preferred civic involvement from official politics to the voluntary sector."[42] The public remains active, but its public activities are moving away from traditional political institutions.

From this perspective, a sound response to declining social capital must begin by reforming "official politics" rather than mending a social fabric that, on second glance, appears strong. Anything short of repairing electoral and voice mechanisms would fail to address the central problem underlying public cynicism and political withdrawal. Because citizen panels create a meaningful and powerful public voice and permit efficient collective rejection of unrepresentative elected officials, they could halt the decline in public trust and participation in formal institutional processes. Voting with the aid of the citizen panel recommendations and rationales could prove satisfying: when the widespread use of panel judgments results in effective collective rejection of flawed incumbents, voters might feel the rare sense of satisfaction that they have knowingly rejected an unrepresentative public official. As voters get the chance to serve on panels, they will also feel at least as much power, pride, and trust in the political process as the people who have already taken part in comparable random sample forums.[43] In this way, the citizen panel process could have a restorative effect by gradually building up citizens' deliberative skills, interest in politics, and confidence in the electoral process.

The strongest connection between citizen panels and public trust is an indirect one. If the regular and effective use of vote and voice improves representation and accountability, government actions might begin to build up—rather than erode—public confidence. "Governments also may be a source of social capital," explains Margaret Levi. "Policy performance can be a source of trust, not just a result."[44] Responsive public policies that have real, positive long-term effects on citizens' lives can restore the public's faith in the efficacy of public action, just as the most effective Depression-era reforms created a measure of popular support for activist government.

After all, well-founded public trust in government comes from the soundness of the justifications of public policies. When elected officials lose their credibility, explains Mark Warren, their "authority can be regenerated only by . . . empowering individuals to demand justifications and rebuild relations of trust. . . . Without challenge, the authority of knowledge becomes hollow." In a representative democracy, "a representative retains authority, he or she is 'trusted,' just to the extent that he or she can be called to account."[45] The citizen panels do precisely this—they require incumbents (and challengers) to account for their past and future policy choices. Successful reelection requires a resonance between an incumbent's accounts and the public's own deliberative voice. When the public returns its representatives to office, it does so with some trust that those officials share the its own reflective judgments.

OTHER EFFECTS OF CITIZEN PANELS

The purpose of citizen panels is to make elections more meaningful, strengthen the public's voice, and reduce the amount of civic neglect, which involves restoring some of the public's trust in government. If citizen panels achieve these goals, they will have succeeded. Beyond these objectives, however, effective panels could have a range of other political impacts. Widespread citizen panels could dampen the cynicism of public officials, stimulate deliberation, and change the nature of American political campaigns and the candidates who embark on them. Some critics might argue that the panels could also have detrimental effects—creating passive voters and undermining leadership. In the remainder of this chapter, I discuss each of these possible outcomes.

DAMPENING THE CYNICISM OF PUBLIC OFFICIALS

By restoring the power of the public's vote and voice, citizen panels might reduce not only the public's growing skepticism about government but also government's cynicism about the public. Though the former problem receives more attention, there is also reason to be concerned about low official confidence in the general public. The Pew Research Center has documented this problem in a survey of members of Congress, presidential appointees, and civil servants. One of the survey questions asked, "Do Americans know enough about issues to form wise opinions about what should be done?" Only 31 percent of congressional respondents, 13 percent of presidential appointees, and 14 percent of civil servants said "yes." When asked how much they could "trust . . . American people on election day," 64 percent of congressional respondents and only 34 percent of all others had "a great deal of trust in the public."[46]

Notwithstanding that a Pew survey of the American public found that 57 percent favored an activist government over a more passive one, government officials do not perceive (or believe in) this public support for their actions. Only 33 percent of congressional respondents viewed the public as pro-government, as did 28 percent of presidential appointees and 25 percent of civil servants. This distrust of the public and its support for government has a direct effect on federal employees: 59 percent of presidential appointees reported that distrust harmed staff morale, and 45 percent said that distrust makes it harder to "hire and retain good people."[47] The perception that the average American does not care about or strongly dislikes politics and government causes elected officials to turn their attention to "the edges of the ideological spectrum," where lobbyists and activists demonstrate a clear interest in policy decisions and elections.[48]

Citizen panels would give public officials the opportunity to meet face-to-face with randomly selected representatives of the larger public. As has occurred during other random sample forums, the officials are likely to come away from the panels with a much more positive view of the public's capacity for deliberation and decision making. While working on the citizen conferences discussed in chapter 6, I found that the public employees who watched the conferences were often surprised and excited by them. They had never met members of the general public who could listen carefully to public officials, ask intelligent questions, and reach well-reasoned policy recommendations. After years of public hearings and meetings, most public officials recognize that the people they meet every day are not a representative cross-section of the general public, yet they remain uncertain about the general public's views and aptitudes.

Witnessing citizen panels in person (or vicariously) would not change the daily lives of public employees and elected officials. They would continue to interact with the public through more conventional forms of public participation, but the panel experience might give them a sense of security that the larger public respects government's role and can judge its work fairly. As a result, public employees might even come to listen more carefully—and respond more vigorously—to a democratic public voice.

SUSTAINING DELIBERATION

If public officials and citizens both change their attitudes toward one another, they also become more likely to create and take advantage of opportunities for deliberation. Citizen discussion programs, like the study circles and National Issues Forums described in chapter 6, can function as civic education programs for whoever wishes to participate, but they have the potential to develop a more representative public voice if they can capture the interest of diverse groups of citizens.[49] If citizen panels reduce the amount of civic neglect, they should bring back into politics the voices that deliberative forums most need to hear.

Changing attitudes among public officials could also stimulate citizen deliberation. Some of the most successful deliberative events have been government-sponsored random sample forums, such as citizen juries. A few bold officials have experimented with these forums based on the belief that the public is capable of reasoned debate and judgment even on complex policy issues. If the citizen panels were to engender similar attitudes among an increasing number of officials, the use of such deliberative means of public input could increase dramatically.

Beyond this increase in quantity, the citizen panels could also improve the quality of public forums. Though the panels would remain a unique part of the political process, they could become a model for political behavior in other settings. The panels would illustrate the virtues of dialogue, debate, and reconsideration of one's initial viewpoint. Individual panelists would, of course, share their experiences with their families, friends, and colleagues, but the panels could have a more indirect effect by simply demonstrating that people can find common ground after listening to one another's views. The very existence of panel judgments on issues and candidates signals to a voter that other citizens were able to reach at least two-thirds agreement.[50]

Finally, participation in panel deliberation might also build up citizens' respect for each other. As Mark Warren argues, increased participation in political discussion on public issues "is likely to encourage substantive changes in interests in the direction of commonality, transforming conflict in the direction of consensus. . . . But even if individuals fail to discover common interests, they are likely to learn about reciprocity; and failing that, they may learn about tolerance." Existing discussion programs, like the National Issues Forums, appear to have some of these same effects. If the citizen panels promote commonality and mutual respect, they will probably make public forums more democratic and deliberative.[51]

CHANGING CAMPAIGNS AND CANDIDATES

The citizen panels might also have a secondary effect on elections through their influence on the strategic choices of candidates and interest groups. During elections, campaign organizations and interest groups do not always pursue rational campaign strategies, but one can often explain their actions in terms of their cost-benefit evaluations of alternative actions in pursuit of the short-term goal of electing particular candidates.[52] For instance, a campaign organization will normally produce and broadcast a vicious attack on an opponent only if the organization believes that the attack will strengthen its candidate's relative position more than other forms of spending. If citizen panels prove influential, they would not change the goals of candidates, but they could change the results of their strategic calculations.

Imagine a local activist who considers running for the state legislature. Under the status quo, she must begin by examining her fund-raising potential and the fund-raising prospects of her likely opponents. Though she might compensate for a financial deficit with a well-trained legion of volunteers or personal charisma, her viability as a candidate depends upon her ability to generate a minimum level of campaign funds. In a system that has citizen panels in place, her viability would also depend upon her prospects for a stronger panel-agreement rating. That, in turn, would require her to consider her actual policy views in comparison to those of the other candidates. If the incumbent state representative has voted in a way likely to receive the support of the citizen panel, she may have great difficulty winning. On the other hand, if the incumbent has missed critical votes or cast votes that would appear unwise under scrutiny, then she may have a chance, although only if she were to take policy stands likely to mesh with the panels' judgments. To understand what the panels might decide, she would need to study the results of past panels and look carefully at the bills scheduled to come before the next round of citizen panels. In other words, candidates would have to consider their actual policy stances as much as anything else when they considered venturing into an election.

Once the panels reached judgments, their verdicts could influence the messages that candidates and interest groups send to voters. In the case of a candidate-selection panel, the candidate who received the panel's support could point to the rationale that the panelists gave for their verdict. Airing that positive message might prove the best way to spend the favored candidate's advertising budget. In addition, the favored candidate and the others might publicize the arguments citizens gave for voting *against* individual candidates. Because those rationales used the criteria selected by the panelists themselves, the negative ads that draw upon them would argue within a reasonable evaluative framework. In this way, the panelists' evaluations could frame the entire debate, and when candidates rejected by the panel tried to make their case for second-guessing the panel, they would have to work within those criteria or contest them directly. In either case, by relating campaign messages to the citizen panels, the panel deliberations could make candidate discourse more relevant and coherent than it is today.

Legislative candidates would also find themselves in a different electoral environment. By identifying the key bills from past legislative sessions, citizen panels would introduce a limited set of specific policies into the public debate.[53] Because the more sophisticated voters would tend to scrutinize candidate votes on these individual issues, candidates might campaign on the relative importance of these issues rather than on the overall candidate agreement-scores. Interest groups running ads might have a simple message for voters: one candidate voted for a specific law, and the other voted against it. The same ad campaign might devote equal effort to raising voter concern about that particular law.

Again, the virtue of the panels is that they give both voters and campaigners a manageable set of legislative proposals to consider, and that makes it more likely that candidates with different views will directly clash during elections.[54] Candidates would still make vague promises about the future and try to draw attention to unrecognized accomplishments from the past, but unless they framed these claims in the context of the panels' deliberations, voters might question the relevance of those statements. Some candidates and interest groups might also try to distort candidates' past records and warn about the dangers of electing their opponents, but voters might be skeptical of such attacks if they contradicted the findings of citizen panels. By getting official candidate positions prior to panel deliberations, the voters would have credible information about different candidates' views on a finite number of issues. Once their views were recorded, candidates would have difficulty dodging those issues or changing their positions during an election.

If campaigns became more deliberative, and voters gave as much credence to panel judgments as they did to the bulk of other campaign activities, this electoral climate might attract new candidates to the political process. The present system rewards candidates for their fund-raising ability, their charisma and physical attractiveness, their ability to make short and evocative statements, their resilience in the face of personal attacks, and their willingness to win at any price. The panels could create a climate that nurtured candidates and elected officials who took consistent and responsive policy stances, could argue the merits of those positions, and had other relevant qualifications for nonlegislative offices. In sum, the panels would reward the professional public representative (focused on the task of representing the public's interests) more than the professional politician (focused on reelection by any means necessary).[55]

PROMOTING POLITICAL PASSIVITY

Up to this point, I have tried to demonstrate the potential impact that the panels could have on voters, the electoral process, and the behavior of public officials. To justify the effort and expense required to implement the panels, I have accepted the burden of proving that they could make a significant difference in the way we govern ourselves. Some critics, however, might accept the likely effects of citizen panels yet oppose them on these very grounds. The problem with the panels, in this view, is that they would change the political process for the worse by making citizens and public officials mindless servants of the will of the citizen panels. In this final section, I consider whether citizen panels would promote political passivity.

If voters become too accustomed to using the panel verdicts when choosing candidates, critics might argue, they would come to depend on them *exclusively*. Voters would ignore other candidate messages, no matter how meritorious. Over time, even the most sophisticated voters would lose their ability to filter political messages critically. By blindly following the advice of the panels, voters would become zombie slaves to their citizen panel masters.[56]

This evolution seems unlikely for many reasons. Those voters who come to rely on the panels would still need to make judgments in those cases when (a) the panelists failed to reach the two-thirds majority required to give a recommendation or (b) there was no difference between candidates' panel-agreement ratings. In every election, it is likely that voters would have some races and ballot issues with no panel recommendations or near-identical candidate ratings. In addition, the two-thirds of voters with at least modest interest in the political process would pay more attention to the detailed panel votes and rationales than to the panels' ratings. Weighing the importance of various issues and considering the rationales behind citizen verdicts would involve voters in more focused and careful deliberation than the present process encourages. An hour spent reading the citizen panel version of a voter guide would do more to sharpen voters' judgment skills than would an equivalent amount of time spent sorting junk mail, watching television ads, or even reading the relatively shallow or confusing voter guides in use today.

Moreover, the establishment of citizen panels in no way precludes the movement toward improved citizen skills, knowledge, and motivation. Chapter 6 reviews some of the emerging civic education programs, community deliberation initiatives, and experiments in integrating citizens directly into state and local policymaking. Nonelectoral civic deliberation would complement the citizen panel process by cultivating the very attitudes and aptitudes that strengthen the public's vote and voice and ensure meaningful participation on the panels themselves.

Though voters are likely to remain independent thinkers even in the midst of uniform panel voting cues, some critics might argue that tying public officials' reelection prospects so directly to panel judgments tethers them to prevailing public opinion. In this view, legislative and advisory panels could preclude effective leadership by removing the healthy distance between electoral outcomes and the policy decisions of public officials. The health of a democracy would decline if its officials did not take controversial stances and lead the public beyond its ignorance, bigotry, and self-delusions.[57] This concern merits attention, although I think it overlooks the other roles of democratic leaders, such as promoting public deliberation.[58]

If voters took the panels' judgments seriously, I believe it is likely that elected legislators would normally vote in a manner they hoped would match the views of the upcoming deliberative panels. Even those who sought reelection through favorable panel-agreement ratings would have considerable latitude. When thinking about taking an unpopular vote, an official would have three reassuring considerations: that particular piece of legislation might not go before a citizen panel; even if the panel disagrees with one particular vote, the overall panel-agreement rating of the official might still be high; and the panel might in any case agree with the legislator's decision.

The latter consideration is the most important one. Because a panel's decisions would come only after days of deliberation, it is quite likely that the citizen panels will often support sound legislative leadership. Past experiments with the random sample forums described in chapter 6 have found that deliberative judgments often differ from the results of public opinion surveys, so citizen panels might actually *promote* departures from surface-level public views when those bold stances can withstand the test of deliberative discussion.

There would be cases, however, in which a public official sought to lead citizens in a direction that even deliberative panels would not support. Sometimes, such leadership would be ill-advised, because it would violate the public's genuine, enlightened interests, but what of those times when the leader simply saw farther than a panel of average citizens? If the panels provide a check on such visionary leadership, they only penalize unarticulated visions, not those that can unfold persuasively during lively political deliberation. Radical critics might worry that this would preclude the election of leaders with revolutionary aspirations. Citizen panels, however, would only oppose such visions when radical leaders failed to answer persuasively the question posed by Robert Dahl—"After the revolution?"

On the contrary, the citizen panels might do more to encourage leadership than diminish it. Benjamin Barber has suggested that America has few leaders because it lacks a strong and articulate public. "It is no good for us to go looking for leaders," he argues. "We must first rediscover citizens. . . . If America is to have leaders, it will have to agree upon goals. If we wish to have leaders to follow, we will have to show them the way."[59] By providing a means of recording a representative, deliberative public voice, citizen panels might inspire public officials and candidates to steer the general public in a direction lit by its own deliberative beacon.

CHAPTER 9

Electoral Experimentation

One of the imperative needs of democratic countries is to improve citizens' capacities to engage intelligently in political
life. . . . In the years to come . . . older institutions will need
to be enhanced by new means for civic education, political
participation, information, and deliberation that draw creatively on the array of techniques and technologies available
in the twenty-first century. We have barely begun to think seriously about these possibilities, much less to test them out in
small-scale experiments.

Robert Dahl, On Democracy

It has been my intention to put forward the most persuasive case possible for instituting citizen panels at every level of government in the
United States. In chapters 7 and 8, I outline the details and virtues of
the panels to persuade skeptics of their potential. I have argued that the
panels could produce sound judgments, influence voters, change the nature of elections, improve relations between representatives and their
constituencies, and, ultimately, spur the development of public policy
that serves the enlightened interests of the larger public. If successful,
the panels would bring the American political system much closer to
the ideal model of representative democracy outlined in chapter 2.

In reality, the panels would surely fall short of that ideal. Political reformers must always acknowledge that their proposals can not make an
imperfect world perfect. Moreover, a self-conscious reformer must remember that tomorrow will improve upon today's reform. I share the
view of Hannah Pitkin, who explains that the tension between ideal
and achievement in representative government "should present a continuing but not hopeless challenge: to construct institutions and train
individuals in such a way that they engage in the pursuit of the public
interest, the genuine representation of the public; and, at the same time,
to remain critical of those institutions and that training, so that they are
always open to further interpretation and reform."[1]

This final chapter embraces Pitkin's sentiment and proposes an experimental approach to developing citizen panels. I begin with a brief comment on the advantages of experimenting with political reforms. In Robert Dahl's words, a healthy democracy must "draw creatively on the array of techniques and technologies available."[2] Small-scale experimentation balances unfettered creativity with realistic assessment, and this makes it possible to sort the best innovations from the worst. Next, I suggest how panels could be systematically tested to measure their effectiveness. At a minimum, the panels must prove cost-effective, but it is also important to gauge their impact relative to alternative reforms. I conclude with a realistic plan for gradually integrating citizen panels into the American political system.

THE EXPERIMENTAL APPROACH

Experimentation requires courage. Scientists must be brave because when they conduct sound experiments, they subject their beliefs to a test. They specify beforehand what they believe (i.e., their hypotheses) and what results would constitute supporting or contrary evidence. Scientific research is exciting in part because its rewards come at the expense of risk. The chance to prove a counterintuitive theory correct only comes at the risk of proving yourself wrong.[3]

In a classic psychological experiment, Stanley Milgram demonstrated that two-thirds of the adults who entered his laboratory were willing to administer what appeared to be near-fatal electric shocks in obedience to the authority of the experimenter, who urged them to continue despite the apparent (but not real) suffering of another person. Prior to conducting the study, Milgram had the foresight to poll his colleagues and found that almost none believed his study would produce such a result. By publicizing his claims prior to conducting his experiment, Milgram increased the risk of professional embarrassment, but he also increased the potential impact of his study—if he proved to be correct.[4]

A healthy scientific community, however, rewards both modest successes and spectacular failures. Ill-conceived studies founded upon faulty reasoning and dubious analytic methods have no scientific merit, but a carefully crafted experiment testing plausible beliefs has value even when its results refute those hypotheses. Such experiments reveal anomalies and force researchers to reexamine long-held beliefs.[5]

At times, the U.S. government has embraced the spirit of experimentation. Cooperative federalism programs, such as the recent Telecommunications Act, have become commonplace. This approach permits state innovation within broad guidelines outlined by Congress. Such programs aim to stimulate creative local solutions to national problems and create "laboratories of democracy."[6] Similar policy experiments have been conducted to address crime, poverty, pollution, and other social, economic, and environmental problems.

It is not a leap to take the same approach to government itself by permitting states to experiment with different election models within the broad democratic tradition. The United States has a long history of experimenting with electoral systems, and it is likely that local, state, and even federal election methods will change in the future. For example, the popular nomination of presidential candidates through primary elections is a relatively new system. The present set of federal campaign finance laws is less than thirty years old, and it is likely that campaign financing laws will change again in coming years.[7] Past political reforms have resulted in some distinctive political institutions, such as Nebraska's unicameral legislature and the presidential caucuses held in Iowa and elsewhere.

Although many Americans do not know it, this country has even experimented with proportional representation. Five Ohio cities used different versions of this system to elect city councilors between 1915 and 1960. Their experience with proportional representation was unremarkable: political conflict rose and fell; citizens appeared neither confused nor inspired by the system; and minority representation improved marginally. Even though it was ultimately repealed, the adoption of proportional representation in cities like Toledo and Cincinnati demonstrates the potential for dramatic electoral innovations in the United States.[8]

In recent years, the public's disenchantment with government has fueled successful reform efforts across the nation. Voters have backed ballot measures limiting officeholders' terms, changing state and local campaign finance laws, and even modifying the structure of local governments. For the reasons outlined in chapter 4, I believe that many of these reforms will neither improve the quality of representation nor restore the public's trust in elected officials. Nonetheless, it is important to implement and test such reforms on a small scale to learn more about their impact. Alternative reforms are not mutually exclusive, particularly

when implemented on an experimental basis by state and local governments. After all, honest critics of a given reform might resist its wholesale implementation, but they should welcome limited experimentation to test—and possibly confirm—the soundness of their criticisms.
In the most extreme case, a skeptic might be encouraged to support
experimenting with citizen panels by the prospect of gloating at their
failure.

TESTING THE EFFECTIVENESS OF CITIZEN PANELS

If one can think of the citizen panels as an experiment, then one must
understand the rationale underlying them, the claims they make, and
the ways in which one might test those claims. The preceding chapters
have explained why the panels might succeed, and at this point it is
only necessary to clarify precisely which political outcomes would constitute success—and which would signal failure.

First, successful panels should show signs of high-quality judgment.
It is impossible to judge objectively the degree to which a panel recommendation represents the true interests of the general public, but citizen
panels should produce the following outcomes:

- Panel deliberation should include periods of debate among the panelists on both questions of fact and more fundamental moral issues.
  The absence of such exchanges would suggest excessive consensus-
  seeking among citizens who surely have genuine differences in experiences and values.

- Panels should be able to work through their differences and reach
  agreements when assessing legislation and candidates. If the panels
  consistently fail to reach large majorities (i.e., the two-thirds majority suggested in chapter 7), it would be necessary to abandon the notion that panels can uncover a general public will.[9]

- While groups may reach joint judgments that surpass the sophistication of any individual participant's view, group deliberation should
  produce changes in the quality of participants' own judgments. After
  taking part in panel discussions, participants should demonstrate
  more informed and coherent views on the issues or candidates they
  have discussed. Participants should be able to give reasons for their
  views, and they should be able to explain the arguments underlying
  other points of view.

- Since there would be little point in deliberating if prediscussion opinions always matched deliberative judgments, panel findings should not always accord with the participants' original views. Narrow majority views may develop into supermajorities, minority viewpoints may prevail, and panels may take positions where none existed before (e.g., when evaluating unknown candidates).[10]

- Chapters 3 and 5 argue that economic elites have a disproportionate influence on public opinion and the political process. Some critics of deliberation contend that the same elites will prevail in face-to-face political discussions. If panelists consider all views equally, however, they should not disproportionately shift toward the views held by economic elites.[11]

- Finally, panel judgments should develop in light of the information presented, the views put forward, and careful, honest discussions among participants. Panel judgments should not derive from the more peripheral features of the proceedings. Minor differences in the characteristics of witnesses, the timing or setting of events, and the backgrounds of the participants should not influence final panel judgments. To test this, multiple panels could convene on the same issues or candidates, and if successful, the panels should arrive at the same judgments on the same questions.[12]

Second, once put in place, successful citizen panels would have to show clear evidence of their influence on the political process. Panel judgments would become just another uninfluential form of public voice if they did not have a measurable electoral impact. Effective panels would thus produce the following results:

- Existing empirical models of candidate selection can predict most electoral outcomes, but the introduction of panels should have two effects on these models: the models should become less predictive to the extent that panel judgments cross party lines and show other deviations from conventional public opinion; also, the addition of panel judgments to these models should improve their predictive value.

- Beyond this general effect, the panel process should be an effective mechanism for unseating unresponsive elected officials. Specifically, when panels give opponents substantially higher ratings than incumbents, the opponents should have a good chance of winning. When the difference between candidate ratings is large, the lower-rated in-

cumbent should lose a bid for reelection, even when competent opponents have relatively small campaign budgets.[13]

If panels are implemented and the evidence shows that they are
reaching sound, influential judgments, that would be enough to war-
rant their widespread adoption. Given their relatively modest cost, any
democratic citizenry would benefit from the powerful voice and electoral muscle that they would provide. Nonetheless, it is important to
examine other potential outcomes. In particular, I have argued that the
panels could halt the decline in public trust—or even reverse this trend.
Trust takes time to build, but the effect should begin to appear in a matter of years. In the long term, panel experiments should be studied to
determine whether they have the following effects:

- Citizens residing in areas using panels should report stable (or rising)
  levels of public trust and signs of reduced civic neglect. Voter turnout
  should increase, and citizens should develop political beliefs conducive
  to participation (e.g., political efficacy, positive political outcome ex-
  pectancies, and a sense of political duty, as defined in chapter 2).

- Voters should demonstrate increased understanding and use of the
  voter guides and ballots that display citizen panel judgments. A majority of voters influenced by the panels may continue to rely upon
  summary ratings, but an increasing number should become readers
  of the voter guides and more detailed on-line information about
  panel deliberations.

- Government officials should develop more favorable views of the
  judgments that voters make during elections (see chapter 8). Officials
  should also demonstrate an awareness of the importance of citizen
  deliberation and come to respect panel judgments.

- As a sign of improved leadership, elected representatives should begin
  to move away from conventional public opinion in anticipation of deliberative panel judgments to the contrary. An example of this would
  be incumbents taking an unpopular stance, arguing that their position
  better represents the public interest, being vindicated by subsequent
  panel judgments, and winning reelection with favorable panel ratings.

- Panels will have succeeded in transforming the electoral environment
  if campaigns begin to focus more of their energy on deliberative
  polling (see chapter 6), argue issues raised by panels (e.g., by holding
  debates focused on panel issues), and generally incorporate panel

findings into campaign advertising (e.g., by defending positions opposed by the panels and attacking opponents for their poor ratings).

Even if the citizen panels have these impacts, the experimental approach mandates comparing panel sites with similar states or cities that have not adopted the panel process. Researchers call this the use of a control group. In a drug test, for instance, patients in the treatment group receive the experimental drug, while patients in the control group receive a placebo. Even taking a sugar pill can cure some ills, so the drug's effect is measured against the modest effect of the placebo. In social experiments, control groups are important for the same reason, but these groups also help control for other external variables. (Thus, if Alabama were to adopt citizen panels, while Mississippi did not, an increase in public trust independently brought about by a virtuous U.S. president might be misattributed to the panels in the case of Alabama if there were no Mississippi control group.)

A more interesting use of the control group would require holding deliberative random sample forums in a state or locale without full citizen panels. These forums would use the same panel techniques to determine public opinion, but they would have no connection with elections, and their judgments and those of elected officials would be likely to correspond only inconsistently (whereas areas with citizen panels would experience an improvement in the quality of their representation). So long as the control area's forums remain divorced from the electoral process, their impact should be negligible. If deliberative forums in the control area reached judgments in sync with their representatives, however, this would raise doubts about the need for citizen panels—beyond the potential restoration of public trust. In this scenario, it would be good for the public to recognize the representativeness of its elected officials, but the panels would validate—rather than improve upon—the quality of representation.

INCREMENTAL IMPLEMENTATION

Such testing would call for gradual implementation of the citizen panel process.[14] This is fortunate, because the panels are a more realistic reform when presented as an experiment. At the present time, there is tremendous public support for political reform—from campaign financing to term limits (see chapter 4). In this sense, the low level of public trust in elected officials is a boon, because it creates large majorities ready to try new electoral systems. As for the panels in particular, survey data presented earlier show that two-thirds of Americans would sooner trust the judgments of a randomly selected deliberative body of citizens than those made by Congress.[15]

With strong public support, it should be possible to pass a ballot measure instituting citizen panels. Nevertheless, it is important to consider the degree to which political and economic elites might oppose changing an electoral system that has, thus far, served their interests. In some respects, the panel proposal does not threaten powerful interests as much as do other popular reforms, such as term limits and restrictions on campaign contributions and spending. Citizen panels would give truly responsive incumbents even more job security than they had before, and panels offer prospective candidates a chance to compete with a comparable voting record in a more deliberative electoral setting. Interest groups could still have considerable influence on minor legislation and administrative rule making, and in elections, they could highlight particular panel votes and influence voters' legislative priorities. Interest groups would also provide much of the testimony before citizen panels, and these groups might devote more energy to developing their arguments to withstand the scrutiny of the citizen panels.

Proposals to use citizen panels also might prove successful because the panel concept is increasingly familiar to elites. The idea of public deliberation in citizen panels is not outrageous, and it has familiar features resembling the jury system and public opinion surveys. The unofficial random sample forums gaining popularity in the United States have made many citizens and most policy elites familiar with the concept of deliberation involving a random sample of the public. In particular, James Fishkin has had success promoting the process of deliberative polling, by which government officials can obtain more reflective public input into the policymaking process (see chapter 6).

More generally, American political elites actually have a tradition of supporting experimental adjustments to government institutions. As Richard Merelman explains, the public does not view its government as an efficient mechanism for developing public policy based on objective principles. Even if not in the midst of a true "legitimation crisis" threatening revolutionary change, U.S. political institutions are in a semipermanent state of "legitimalaise." As a result, public officials seek to maintain a tentative legitimacy by constantly pursuing structural reforms. New policies, procedures, bodies, and standards create temporary boosts in legitimacy, but the fleeting benefits of such tinkering require a near-constant state of structural change.[16] As a small-scale experiment, the adoption of citizen panels would be just such an innovation and might meet only limited political opposition.

The citizens of River Falls, Wisconsin, have had just such an experience. After participating in a forum on campaign reform, a group of residents organized a petition drive, and in October 1998, their city council voted in support of the following statement:

> We support electoral reform that provides for a public hearing in which a representative group of voters can question candidates in person about the issues that concern them the most and then share that information with the rest of the public. We therefore urge the governor, and other Wisconsin elected officials, to take the necessary steps to see that such reforms are enacted.[17]

With the support of the League of Women Voters and other nonprofit organizations, River Falls may soon implement the first publicly sponsored candidate evaluation panels.

Some groups might independently initiate candidate forums of this kind, but I recommend using the referenda panel as a first step, because of its simple design (see chapter 7). Starting in a state like California, which regularly has multiple referenda on the ballot, reformers could propose a set of citizen panels to evaluate each ballot measure. Californians would learn about and debate the basic features of the panels—the random sample, the selection of witnesses, the sequence of deliberation, and the presentation of panel judgments and rationales in voter guides. Even if this first reform did not take the bold step of putting panel recommendations on the ballot itself, the panel votes could still be used to order the ballot measures, and that would at least introduce the link between panels and ballots.[18]

Something close to this has already been tried in Minnesota. The Orono school district, west of Minneapolis, had placed a bond issue referendum on the ballot in 1995 and 1997, but voters rejected the proposal both times. In April 1998, the Jefferson Center sponsored a citizen jury on the needs of the school district. The twenty-four jurors listened to expert testimony and deliberated for five days, then presented recommendations that led the Orono Board of Education to draft of a third bond issue referendum. Although the results of the jury deliberations did not appear on voters' ballots, the small size of the school district made it possible for supporters to contact nearly every household in the dis-trict through a vigorous mail and door-to-door campaign. Mailers and brochures explained that the referendum came out of a "totally independent, community-based panel," which "validated the

severity of our [classroom] space problems." Backed by the jury's recommendations, the bond issue referendum passed in the September
1998 election.[19]

After voters become familiar with referenda panels such as this, one
could create a priority panel (see chapter 7) to identify the ten most important pieces of legislation introduced since the past election. The priority panel would identify a list of ten important bills, and voter guides
would describe the bills and present the panel's rationales for selecting
them. The panel might also have the power to write a summary of the
main purposes of each bill, and candidates would be asked to provide
unofficial votes and accompanying rationales. A concise, printed voter
guide would permit voters to compare votes and arguments on each of
the ten bills, and an Internet site would give voters even more information about the panel deliberations and the candidates' stances on the
issues.

Once voters, candidates, and all other interested parties became familiar with these two forms of citizen panels, their marriage would be
a logical next step. By combining the issue judgments of a referenda
panel with the agenda set by a priority panel, one arrives at the idea of
panels evaluating candidates through legislative, advisory, and candidate-selection panels. Cities and states with the most severe cases of
civic neglect might be the first to implement such panels, and if the panels improved local and state politics in those areas, other governments
might also embrace the process. Ultimately, citizens across the country
might want to convene congressional legislative panels, and a Congress
pressured to enact campaign reform might view the panels as the least
offensive choice on a menu of reforms its leaders disliked.

At the time of writing, there is already considerable public pressure
on Congress to reform federal elections, although there is as yet no critical mass of reformers in either the House or the Senate, notwithstanding a series of elections touching on the issue. If the public cry for reform remains constant but continues to have little impact (like most
public voices), it would be useful to transfer the public's energy from
the present set of reform proposals to another. This reform strategy
would start with a congressional priority panel and work down from
there to more local panels. The congressional panel could provide a national showcase for the panel process, and state and local publics might
adopt other panel designs after familiarizing themselves with the national panel. If Congress is where reformers direct their energy, it may
prove to be the place to start.

Notes

1. Mitchell 1996: 49, 77. The National Opinion Research Center at the University of Chicago conducts the General Social Survey.

2. The survey data are from Harris polls and a survey conducted by the *Washington Post,* the Kaiser Family Foundation, and Harvard University (Blendon et al. 1997: 206–9).

3. Kay 1998: 2. For a wide range of explanations for the recent drop in public confidence in government, see Nye, Zelikow, and King 1997. I do not argue that misrepresentation, per se, is the cause of a decline in public trust. Quite the contrary, in chapters 2, 3, and 5, I offer a critique of American politics that goes beyond the distinctive features of its present practice. There may be a greater public awareness of the inadequacy of the existing system, but the quality of representation has probably not declined so much as it has remained low. In this book, I suggest reforms that, if successful, would provide a reason for the public to place greater trust in government.

4. Herrera, Herrera, and Smith 1992. The validity of this study's findings is limited by a low response rate among members of Congress, though the sample the authors obtained did resemble the larger legislative population in some respects. Another approach would be to compare ideological ratings of elected officials with citizen voting in a high-intensity (and presumably more ideologically driven) election. Using this approach, Erikson and Wright 1993 found a significant correlation between the percentage of congressional districts' votes for Michael Dukakis in the 1988 presidential election and their House members' voting-record ratings, as calculated by the American Conservative Union and Americans for Democratic Action. To some extent, this approach simply measures partisanship twice—once as presidential vote and once as roll-call

voting. The nuances of public opinion transcend the Democratic/Republican and liberal/conservative dichotomies (as I argue more fully in chapter 3); moreover, voting in presidential elections does not necessarily reflect enlightened public interests.

5. Erikson, Wright, and McIver 1993: 247–53. As these authors write in their summary, "At the ballot box, state electorates hold a strong control over the ideological direction of policies in their states. In anticipation of this electoral monitoring, state legislatures and other policymakers take public opinion into account when enacting state policy." In the authors' view, individual voters routinely evaluate candidates and parties inaccurately, but their errors tend to cancel one another out. The net result is an aggregate voting pattern that represents the larger public. The same argument with regard to collective versus individual public opinion is made by Page and Shapiro 1992: individuals may give erratic and uninformed survey responses, but the average view shows stability, rationality, and responsiveness to changing external realities.

6. Robert Dahl considers this issue so important that he made the "Criterion of Enlightened Understanding" one of only five basic features of his democratic ideal (Dahl 1989: 127).

7. On the distinction between preference and judgment, see Fishkin 1991, 1995, Mathews 1994, and Yankelovich 1991. Daniel Yankelovich argues that the public *has* reached a solid "public judgment" on some issues, such as abortion, but remains uninformed and undecided on most issues. In chapter 3, I use John Zaller's model of public opinion to describe how the general public views issues and makes judgments. Zaller views his model as a source of optimism (Zaller 1992: 313–14), but I concur with Patricia Hurley's more pessimistic conclusion: "By the very logic of [Zaller's] model, those with limited political awareness will not be able to distinguish between" the "sublime and the ridiculous." Consequently, "the model could also be interpreted as suggesting that any observed correspondence of public opinion and policy is indirect at best and spurious at worst" (Hurley 1994: 531).

8. This is part of Robert Bernstein's critique of the "myth of constituency control." After analyzing the correspondence between congressional and constituent ideology, Bernstein concludes: "Elections serve to promote limited constituency influence, but that limited influence may not make government policy more responsive to the wishes of the people as a whole. Only to the extent that interested minorities are representative of the public as a whole does the limited influence exerted by those minorities encourage government responsiveness to the policy preferences (good or bad) of the public" (Bernstein 1989: 102). Bennett and Resnick 1990 finds just such differences between the views of voters and nonvoters; the gap between *frequent* voters and nonvoters is probably even larger. If one is concerned about enlightened preferences, then the problem is the lack of correspondence between likely voters' unreflective views and the larger public's deliberative judgments.

9. Erikson and Wright 1993: 113.

10. Dodd 1992: 425. For example, Douglas Arnold's model of legislators as "controlled agents" is designed to demonstrate how an inattentive public gets sound representation; instead, the model highlights how legislators' fears of

voter reprisal drive them toward suboptimal legislative action (Arnold 1990, 1993).

11. Dodd 1992: 426.

12. Arnold 1990: 268.

13. Dodd 1992: 426.

14. Thanks to Randy Nielsen at the Kettering Foundation for reminding me of this truism. In a survey of North Carolina residents, 61 percent directly labeled themselves "cynics" by agreeing with the statement, "I consider myself to be cynical or pessimistic about politicians." Only 22 percent disagreed with the statement, with 17 percent giving DK/NA responses. See Jim Morrill, "Politics a Turn-Off for Most Carolinians," *Charlotte Observer,* August 18, 1997, A1.

15. Hetherington 1998 finds such a causal connection between general system distrust and cynicism toward individual leaders.

16. Tolchin 1995 makes these connections in examining how distrust in elected officials grows into anger and rage toward political institutions. The Los Angeles riots that erupted after the verdict in the Rodney King case had a more immediate cause, but anger toward government may also have fueled the hostility displayed.

17. See Page 1996; Popkin 1994: 225; and Zaller 1992. "The choices of voters can be approximately rational because of, not merely despite, their shortfalls in information" (Sniderman, Brody, and Tetlock 1991: 178).

18. Crimmins 1995: xv, xvii.

19. Barber 1998b: 65. "Both government and the private sector can and should be humbled by the growth of civil society, for it absorbs some of the public aspirations of the government (its commitment to public work) without being coercive, and it maintains liberty without yielding to the jungle anarchy of commercial markets" (ibid.). Earlier, Barber 1984 had described electoral reforms as integral to transforming weak liberal democracy into a stronger, more participatory form of democracy.

20. Bell 1995 points out that most residents in these communities do not even become very active in their own residential associations.

21. For examples of prominent writings on deliberation and civil society that all but ignore elections, see Bohman and Rehg 1997; Boyte 1989; Dionne 1998; Elster 1998; Mathews 1994; and Gutmann and Thompson 1996.

22. See Putnam 1993 and Boyte 1989. I provide examples of such community-based action in chapter 6.

23. Walzer 1991: 301. The clearest exception is the work of James Fishkin (1991, 1995), who stresses the importance of elections and addresses them in depth. He connects deliberation and elections through a national debate, but I suggest making a much stronger link from the public's deliberative voice to the election of public officials. As Christiane Olivio argues, the point is not to create an autonomous civil society but to create one that "provides a rational, critical, and influential discourse influencing the state's policies and actions" (Olivio 1998: 248). Barber 1984 also tries to link deliberative democracy and electoral reform.

24. On the National Issues Convention, see Fishkin 1995; McCombs and Reynolds 1999. On the citizen juries, see Crosby 1995. For a review of a wide range of public participation programs, see Webler and Renn 1995.

25. On participant effects, see Tom W. Smith 1999. On viewer effects, see Rasinski, Bradburn, and Lauen 1999.

26. Ryfe 1998: 13.

CHAPTER 2. EXIT AND PUBLIC VOICE
IN REPRESENTATIVE DEMOCRACY

Epigraph: Hirschman 1970: 1.

1. Dahl 1989 refers to modern pluralistic states as "polyarchies" so as not to give the false impression that any nation has reached the democratic ideal.

2. There is no one-to-one correspondence between the models distinguished in Held 1987 and my own. Rather than analyzing every model in depth, I have simply tried to demonstrate the applicability of exit and voice to a wide range of models.

3. For integrations of Athenian democracy into modern participatory theories, see Barber 1984; Mansbridge 1983. The Athenenian system failed by many modern measures of democracy, but it remains a vivid illustration of some democratic institutions no longer in use.

4. For a relatively coherent and thorough description of a council system of government, see the "demarchy" outlined in Burnheim 1985.

5. See Barber 1984; Pateman 1970.

6. Influential contemporary writings on deliberation include Cohen 1989, Fishkin 1991, and Gutmann and Thompson 1996. The idea of a "general will" is often traced back to Rousseau (e.g., by Mansbridge 1983).

7. For example, the political theorist Mark Warren underscores the importance of effective collective exit: "Democratic authority can exist when an institutionalized possibility of challenge allows individuals to suspend judgment" (Warren 1996a: 57).

8. "In framing a government which is to be administered by men over men, the great difficulty lies in this: you must first enable the government to control the governed; and in the next place oblige it to control itself," *The Federalist,* No. 51, observes (Hamilton, Madison, and Jay [1788] 1947: 265). The *Federalist Papers* are available on-line at http://www.mcs.net/~knautzr/fed/fedpaper.html. Upon reviewing Madison's less well-known writings, Robert Dahl found that even Madison recognized the necessity of following the majority's will—even when it infringed upon the property rights of a minority. Madison remained worried about the tyranny of the majority, but he acknowledged that its rights to govern were fundamental (Dahl 1996: 296).

9. Held 1987: 187.

10. This capitalist model is a mix of Held 1987's "competitive elitist democracy," the "rational choice" models of politics described by Hauptmann 1996, and the elitist theory of democracy presented by Schumpeter 1976. On the nature and impact of economic assumptions, see Schwartz 1986.

11. Dahl 1989 provides a succinct description of American government as a form of "polyarchy," a term he developed to describe an actual institutional arrangement that only partially meets his criteria for the democratic process.

12. Hirschman 1970: 2.

13. Ibid.: 4.

14. Ibid.: 34, 42.

15. Ibid.: 39.

16. Ibid.: 78, 79, 90. Also see 38–39, 77.

17. Ibid.: 43; emphasis in original.

18. In a later work, Albert Hirschman writes that "exit and voice were de-fined in my book as two contrasting responses," but he points out that in some cases exit and voice have "worked in tandem and reinforced each other" (Hirschman 1993: 175–77). In this book, I use the exit, voice, and loyalty model to describe two important response modes, and I devote relatively little atten-tion to the trade-off between exit and voice.

19. The most common use of Hirschman's model is as a means of under-standing behavior in economic and nonprofit organizations (see, e.g., Bender and Sloane 1998).

20. On the expansion of economic assumptions into the social sciences and American culture, see Schwartz 1986. On the intrusion of economically inspired "public choice" theory into democratic theory, see Hauptmann 1996.

21. Hirschman 1970: 27.

22. Ibid.: 59–60.

23. Ibid.: 24, 79.

24. Ibid.: 28.

25. Ibid.: 45–46.

26. Ibid.: 83–84.

27. See Hirschman 1993 on Germany; Lehman-Wilzig 1991 on Israel; Kato 1998 on Japan; Lyons, Lowery, and DeHoog 1993 on urban politics; and Sorensen 1997 on empowerment.

28. Sorensen 1997: 558–59.

29. Throughout this book I refer to "representatives." By this I mean popu-larly elected officials in relatively democratic political systems. Using Norberto Bobbio's definition, a representative is "a person with two very specific attributes: someone who (a) enjoys the trust of the electorate by virtue of election, and so is responsible to them and cannot be dismissed; and (b) who is not directly answer-able to the electorate precisely because he is called upon to safeguard the general interests of civil society and not the particular interests of any one group" (Bob-bio 1987: 48). My model has more detail regarding individual candidate selection than would be necessary to examine proportional representation systems where officials are named after seats are allocated among victorious parties, although party evaluation is not entirely different from candidate evaluation.

30. Relating this back to the notion of public trust in chapter 1, the exit, voice, and loyalty model of representation only functions properly at moderate levels of public trust. Declining public trust would not be a problem if it was al-ready "too high" (Schudson 1998: 302). Supporting this interpretation of trust/loyalty, a study of presidential voting from 1968 to 1996 found that heightened public distrust benefited the out-party in a two-way race or the third-party in a three-way race (Hetherington 1999).

31. This definition is taken from Gastil 1993: 24. It also has much in com-mon with the critical group decision-making functions described and studied by

Gouran and Hirokawa 1996. On the historical meanings and roles of deliberation in American politics, see Fishkin 1995.

32. Mansbridge 1996: 125. On the pros and cons of emotion in argumentation, see Walton 1992.

33. I develop this definition in more detail in Gastil 1993 and Gastil and Adam 1995. It also bears some resemblance to the definition developed by Knight and Johnson 1994.

34. Cohen 1989: 22–23.

35. Habermas 1979. This idea resonates throughout the literature on political persuasion and discussion. Lupia and McCubbins 1998 make only a loose connection between their work and Habermas's interest in deliberation, but their requirement that effective deliberation include procedures for "verification" is comparable to Habermas's stress on the right to "challenge validity claims."

36. Stephen Esquith and Richard Peterson provide a useful account of how Rawls's notion of the "original position" has moved from an abstract philosophical notion to a more concrete approach to public life. In this view, "the original position describes the kind of representative citizen who would choose acceptable institutional principles for protecting and advancing freedom, equality, and reciprocity within a pluralistic world where only a limited moral consensus exists" (Esquith and Peterson 1988: 301).

37. Rawls 1971: 358–59.

38. See Burleson, Levine, and Samter 1984; Hirokawa, Erbert, and Hurst 1996. Though group discussion is more fruitful, on average, certain conditions facilitate optimal deliberation, and other factors can result in counterproductive discussion. I discuss those in detail in chapter 8.

39. Rittel and Webber 1973.

40. Dahl 1991 emphasizes this point in his criteria for the democratic process. As Mark Warren argues, "A theory of democracy should be oriented toward creating institutional environments that encourage the self-examination of preferences that brings them closer to needs" (Warren 1996b: 264–65). It is impossible to "know" objectively the enlightened interests of a person, let alone a society, but deliberation can at least aid people in arriving at more informed understandings of their interests. Warren points out that "the doctrine of revealed preferences" held by economists and rational choice theorists shows that even these theorists recognize that surface policy preferences may obscure underlying values and interests that will only "reveal" themselves after a period of reflection or deliberation.

41. See Briand 1999: ch. 8; Warren 1992.

42. Gutmann and Thompson 1996: 4. Briand 1999 argues along similar lines.

43. Walzer 1991 and Putnam 1993, 1995a, and 1995b are among the most influential modern writings on civil society.

44. The Senate recognition statistic comes from Fishkin 1995: 10. With regard to literacy, the U.S. Department of Education's National Center for Education Statistics (NCES) conducted an extensive survey of adult literacy in 1992. The NCES estimated that roughly 21 percent of Americans 16 and older

had "only rudimentary reading and writing skills." Persons in this category "could pick out key facts in a brief newspaper article, for example, but could not draft a letter explaining an error on their credit card bill." Approximately 4 percent of the total adult population could not "perform even the simplest literacy tasks." Quotations and survey available at http://www.nces.ed.gov/nad-lits/naal92.

45. The behavioral theorist Albert Bandura (1977, 1986a) turned to the concept of self-efficacy when he found himself unable to explain why people who had learned certain behaviors failed to perform them when called upon to do so. Learning theory alone could not account for the reluctance of some individuals, who were low in self-efficacy, to respond appropriately to their environment. The cognitive psychologist Icek Ajzen (1991) abandoned the widely researched and well-supported theory of reasoned action that he had helped to develop when he found that attitudes and subjective norms failed to explain adequately the actions that people took. His substitute, the theory of planned behavior, added the concept of "perceived behavioral control," which is synonymous with self-efficacy.

46. Such "internal" political efficacy (see Pollock 1983; Wolfsfeld 1986) is an important psychological resource and helps determine whether or not an individual will become an active citizen (Rosenstone and Hansen 1993: 79).

47. Bandura 1986b introduced me to the concept of group efficacy. My own research on civic participation has found inconsistent evidence in support of the group efficacy concept, partly because it has proven difficult to measure compared to people's assessments of their own abilities. See Gastil 1994b.

48. For Albert Hirschman, who claims that loyalty develops out of perceived personal influence and argues for the rational basis of loyalty versus faith, outcome expectancy almost seems to be a part of loyalty itself. On the other hand, Hirschman clearly distinguishes outcome expectancy from loyalty, which is defined as the willingness to "trade off the certainty of exit against the uncertainties of an improvement in the deteriorated product" (1970: 77–78). It appears that Hirschman is arguing that outcome expectancy influences but does not *determine* one's loyalty.

49. I discuss this at length in Gastil 1994b. For a demonstration of outcome expectancy's significance in politics, see Finkel, Muller, and Opp 1989. Ajzen and Fishbein 1980 demonstrates the variable's general significance across diverse social contexts.

50. This should be qualified somewhat. Hirschman correctly points out that it is enough for a person to believe that his or her actions or the actions of a fellow citizen with similar complaints will prove influential. "[A] customer must expect that he himself or other member-customers will be able to marshal some influence or bargaining power" (Hirschman 1970: 40–41).

51. "System responsiveness" is also called "external efficacy," but I have avoided that term to prevent confusion with self-efficacy. Despite conceptual similarities, external efficacy is only weakly associated with trust in elected incumbents per se (see Craig, Niemi, and Silver 1990).

52. On efficacy and expectancy, see Ajzen and Fishbein 1980. Gastil 1994b presents a more complete presentation of my view of the significance of these

variables in political life. On the role of duty and other altruistic motivations for political action, see Mansbridge 1990a.

53. This "psychology" phrasing is taken from Paul Weithman (1995: 317), who eloquently summarizes the definition of deliberative democracy given by Cohen 1989.

54. Lyons et al. 1993. In adapting Hirschman's model to study Japanese party politics, Junko Kato indirectly demonstrates the importance of civic neglect, noting that a critical variable is "willingness to act when one recognizes a problem with organizational performance" (Kato 1998: 859). Kato chooses to redefine loyalty as such willingness, but I prefer to use the original conceptualization of loyalty and view inaction as a third kind of response.

55. Robert Dahl's "Criterion of Enlightened Understanding" (1989: 127) addresses one of the concerns of pluralist democracy's radical critics, such as Samuel Bowles and Herbert Gintis (1987: 127), who criticize limited conceptions of democracy for "taking preferences and interests as pregiven." In a rejoinder to criticisms, Dahl acknowledges that his criterion is "vague." In general, it means that "a process for making collective decisions that incorporate reasons based on systematic research is superior to one in which reasons are based merely on conventional wisdom" (Dahl 1991: 230).

56. Deliberative democratic theorists are often concerned with the difficulty of judging what policies best meet the needs of the larger public (e.g., Briand 1999; Fishkin 1995; Mathews 1994). The idea of tacit knowledge as a common cause of behavioral choices comes from Giddens 1984.

57. An alternative is to give up on deliberative democracy and place strict limits on the scope of government (see Somin 1998). In this and the following chapters, I argue that a system using citizen panels can simulate nationwide deliberation in the short run and develop the psychosocial underpinnings of actual widespread deliberation in the long run.

58. Bessette 1994 argues for designing political institutions favorable toward official deliberation even if this means compromising other principles. For example, "sunshine laws" that expose official debate to public scrutiny may undermine officials' opportunities for honest, searching deliberation. Other advocates of deliberation, such as Joshua Cohen (1989), stress the importance of "transparent" political institutions for maintaining governmental legitimacy. My goal is to create powerful incentives for official deliberation. Whether and when such deliberation takes place is less important than the correspondence of official actions with the public's own deliberative judgment. If some officials substitute the public's reflective decisions for their own, individual deliberation, that would be only a minor loss.

59. On these and other conceptions of representation, see Pitkin 1967.

60. Bianco 1994 points out that it is not enough for representatives to deliberate and expect the public to endorse their judgments. Even if the deliberation is held in the open, it is unlikely that citizens will pay attention to its details. Those who do watch or read about the details of officials' deliberation will still remain skeptical of representatives' true motivations. "Deliberation, to have any effect at all," Bianco argues, "must be aimed at educating the public, not members of Congress. . . . Measures designed to increase congressional de-

bate and deliberation on issues of the day will certainly produce more talk. But there is considerable doubt that anyone will listen, or having listened, be swayed" (Bianco 1994: 163).

CHAPTER 3. WHY ELECTIONS FAIL TO ENSURE ACCOUNTABILITY

Epigraph: Edelman 1988: 97.
1. Barber 1984: 188.
2. Dahl 1989: 98.
3. The moral philosopher John Rawls (1971) arrives at these principles by presuming that if people did not know what lot they might draw in society, they would want a social system that protected the interests of the least-well-off. Freedom and equality, as he defines them, serve those interests.
4. "The more one knows about politics, the more effective—the more instrumentally rational—one's voice is likely to be" (Delli Carpini and Keeter 1996: 56). On how values and decision logics can go together for individuals and groups, see Macoubrie 1998.
5. Delli Carpini and Keeter 1996: 101–2, 133. Moreover, "[c]itizens generally take less interest in . . . and are less informed about their local governments than they are about their national government" (Burns et al. 1996: 11).
6. Zaller 1992: 308. For a similar view of public opinion, see Page and Shapiro 1992, which argues that measurement errors and fluctuations in individuals' opinions cancel one another out, and uninformed citizens simply follow elite cues: the result is a "rational public" with stable opinions that change only in response to changing objective conditions (as interpreted by elites).
7. Lull and Cappella 1981.
8. Andrade and Cobb 1996: 229–30.
9. Blumer and Gurevitch 1995: 214.
10. Cappella and Jamieson 1997 provides detailed evidence of the "cynical" nature of mainstream media coverage of politics. Eliasoph 1998, a more open-ended study, concludes that the media contribute to a larger process of "political evaporation" that leaves the public sphere barren. Along similar lines, Hugh Heclo argues that the quantity of political news is large but that it is misleading and superficial. "Modern media," he writes, "deluge the public with information" and "give the impression of national problems as always unresolved. . . . [They] often associate immediacy with importance, and intensity with seriousness. A dull congressional vote, agency announcement, or international agreement may represent important change in the world, but it holds little attraction for the media next to a plane crash or a public clash of personalities. . . . Even media-sponsored policy debates often merely provide, in place of a one-sided presentation of an issue, *two* one-sided presentations, albeit from opposite sides" (Heclo 1999: 66).
11. See, e.g., Ginsberg 1986 and Parenti 1995. Even those who find limited evidence of business's direct influence on policymaking still find traces of indirect influence through shaping public opinion. Mark Smith, for example, finds that when business reaches consensus on a high-profile issue, its direct influence becomes limited relative to public sentiment, yet he also finds evidence that

those sentiments depend, in part, upon the vigor of business's efforts to influence public opinion through think tanks and other means (Smith 2000). Aside from the overall bias of paid political media, these messages also have a well-deserved reputation for being deceptive (Jamieson 1992).

12. Zaller 1992: 327. Some scholars have begun to lose their optimism about the fidelity of public reception of elite cues. Kuklinski and Hurley 1996, for instance, argues that citizens routinely misinterpret elite messages.

13. Bennett 1993: 109.

14. Figures are derived from William Jacoby's (1991, 1995) analysis of 1984 and 1988 data. Using 1984 national survey data, Sniderman, Brody, and Tetlock 1991 also found that 20 percent of the population to have "intense" ideological feelings. Respondents rated liberalism and conservatism on a 100-point "feeling thermometer," and intense ideologues were defined as persons reporting a difference of 25 points or higher in their two thermometer ratings (e.g., giving liberalism a rating of 50 and conservatism as rating of 75 or greater). Only 7 percent of respondents could be categorized as intense liberals and 13 percent as intense conservatives. The most influential writing on ideology and the American public was an essay by Philip Converse (1964), which found that only a tiny fraction of the public engaged in ideological thinking but that, again, roughly one-fifth of the public has "real" attitudes. These estimates are important because they suggest what percentage of the public uncritically filters political messages.

15. Conover and Feldman 1984.

16. Benjamin Page (1996) shares John Zaller's belief in the value of learning from elites, but he raises this concern about elite versus mass interests. In chapter 6, I examine Page's view in detail. Shapiro 1998 raises similar questions about Zaller's model.

17. David Mathews (1994) has promoted the use of the phrases "public perspective" and "public voice" to remind us of the difference between aggregated self-interest and a broader public will.

18. Fiorina 1981.

19. Ibid.: 208.

20. Although the high-information voter engages in elaborate, issue- and party-based candidate evaluation, "the less well informed voter may have the information he needs provided he treats the choice before him as a choice for or against the incumbent; for poorly informed or not, he is in a position to judge if the incumbent's performance is satisfactory" (Sniderman, Brody, and Tetlock 1991: 178). I believe that evaluation of actual incumbent performance is *more* difficult than other evaluations, and if low-information voters are making their choices that way, they are likely to make haphazard candidate choices in low- and medium-intensity campaigns.

21. See Lyons, Lowery, and DeHoog 1993: ch. 6.

22. Svoboda 1995.

23. Arnold 1990: 47. For a shortened version of this argument, see Arnold 1993.

24. Ibid.: 72–73, 75, 77–78, 80–81, 272.

25. According to Sniderman, Brody, and Tetlock 1991: 178, voters with low information use this up-or-down voting approach, which the authors find to be a reasonable strategy for making voting decisions.

26. Popkin 1994: 92–94.

27. Statistics are from "A Look at Voting Patterns of 115 Demographic Groups in House Races," *New York Times,* November 9, 1998, A20. Voter News Service collected the data in this article through election day exit polling of over 10,017 respondents in 1998. It is quite possible that these surveys overestimate party loyalty, but secret ballots permit no better measure of actual voting behavior. Also see Jacobson 1997: 92–93, which finds that roughly one-quarter of voters cross party lines in congressional elections.

28. Miller and Shanks 1996. The greater predictive strength of partisanship in congressional elections is consistent with the fact that partisanship is a cognitive shortcut. When voters are exposed to tremendous amounts of information in the unique environment of a presidential election, many decide that a candidate from another party would better represent their interests. In other words, these crossover voters made a decision other than the one that the simplistic partisan cue would have suggested.

29. Miller and Shanks 1996. Though some misidentification takes place during exit surveys, partisan identity predicts voting preferences even years later.

30. Quote is from Wattenberg 1994: ix, which presents a detailed description of the decline of political parties in America. A survey by Princeton Survey Associates found that 75 percent said they vote for different parties in response to this question: "When you vote in an election for national, state or local offices, do you always vote for candidates from one particular political party, or do you vote for candidates from different parties?" A Roper Center / Institute for Social Inquiry survey found that 65 percent reported voting for different parties in response to this question: "When voting in elections do you typically vote a straight ticket—that is for candidates of the same party, or do you typically split your tick—that is vote for candidates from different parties?" See *The Public Perspective* 9, 2 (February–March 1998), 49. According to University of Michigan surveys, ticket-splitting is far more common now than it used to be: 29 percent reported splitting in 1952 compared to 63 percent in 1996 (Tarrance, De Vries, and Mosher 1998: 35).

31. Data are from Keith et al. 1992: 68, 72.

32. B. Drummond Ayres, "Political Briefing," *New York Times,* October 27, 1998, A16.

33. Dane Smith and Robert Whereatt, "Ventura Elected Governor," *Online Star Tribune,* November 4, 1998.

34. Delli Carpini and Keeter 1996: 252–54.

35. Abramowitz and Sanders 1998: 643–44.

36. Arnold 1990: 53.

37. Miller and Shanks 1996. Abramowitz and Saunders 1998 provides compelling evidence that partisanship is more ideological than it used to be. In their view, ideological debates between the two major parties made their differences

more apparent, and the newest generation of voters includes many Republicans who have severed their Democratic family roots for ideological reasons.

38. Evidence of the strength of partisanship influence on attitudes is provided by Campbell et al. 1960; Fiorina 1981; Green and Palmquist 1994; Jennings and Niemi 1981; and Miller and Shanks 1996, among others.

39. Jacobson 1997: 71.

40. George Gastil, a California Democrat and member of the Lemon Grove School Board, has discussed this possibility with me. The open primary does give minority-party voters the real chance of influencing elections, which is a real improvement over their utter powerlessness in solid majority districts. But their influence comes at the cost of closed-party primaries: a candidate's party affiliation in the general election becomes a less useful cue as to the candidate's actual stances because members of *other* parties may be responsible for the candidate's victory in the primary.

41. For the roll-call voting statistics, see King 1997: 167. On the similarities of the two parties, Michael Parenti observes: "Both the Democratic and Republican parties are committed to the preservation of the private corporate economy; huge military budgets; the use of subsidies, deficit spending, and tax allowances to bolster business profits; the funneling of public resources through private conduits, including whole new industries developed at public expense; the use of repression against opponents of the existing class structure; the defense of the multinational corporate empire and intervention against social-revolutionary elements abroad" (Parenti [1974] 1995: 181). Parenti also points out that the two major parties have jointly implemented laws across the United States to thwart efforts to form viable third parties.

42. On the increasingly ideological nature of party identity, see, e.g., Abramowitz and Saunders 1998, King 1997, and Miller and Shanks 1996. Unfortunately, this rigidification of the two major parties is further eroding public trust among those ideologically moderate Americans most distant from the two major parties (King 1997: 176).

43. The Greens have recorded electoral victories in New Mexico, California, and elsewhere. In a special 1997 congressional election in New Mexico, the Green Party gained national notice by winning 17 percent of the vote. As a result, an obscure Republican minister was able to win a seat in a safe Democratic district by a narrow margin. The Democrats took the seat back in 1998 when they ran a less objectionable candidate. On the 1997 election, see Benjamin Sheffner, "Dems See Green in Special Election Loss," *Roll Call,* May 15, 1997. On the 1998 election, see Karen Peterson, "Johnson, Udall Win," *Santa Fe New Mexican,* November 4, 1998, A1. For an optimistic assessment of the prospects for progressive third parties in the United States, see Reynolds 1997.

44. On the history of nonpartisan reforms, see Lee 1960. For criticisms of nonpartisan elections, see Sherrill 1998 and Hawley 1973.

45. Given the relatively low turnout in primary elections, most voters do not choose to exercise their right to vote, which often makes primaries unrepresentative of the views of the average party member. Since the most active voters are more ideological, primaries often result in the election of extremist candidates who do not reflect the views of the nonvoting partisans. This is

analogous to the frustration independents feel in general elections, where they also lack a partisan cue. Not surprisingly, independents have lower turnout rates than partisans, and their voting rates also have declined more rapidly from the 1960s to the 1980s (Keith et al. 1992: 58).

46. "The incumbent clearly has the upper hand in dealing with the local party," which "no longer controls renomination or reelection" (Alford and Brady 1993: 154).

47. Jacobson 1997: 13. In one such exception, officials in the Democratic Party had the opportunity to name their candidate in a special election for Congress in northern New Mexico in 1997. The chosen candidate, Eric Serna, went on to lose the general election because of unprecedented Democratic defection to a Green Party candidate. This simply illustrates that existing party organizations are not able to guarantee the nomination of a candidate whom even their own party members believe to be representative of their interests. See Benjamin Sheffner, "Dems See Green in Special Election Loss," *Roll Call,* May 15, 1997.

48. Citizens are more likely to be influenced by their immediate family and friends and known neighbors than by the perceived norms of their neighborhood or community (MacKuen and Brown 1987). On the other hand, Robert Huckfeldt and John Sprague (1995: 180–84) found that among a person's friends, the "closest" ones have less political influence.

49. Inglehart 1997: 309. Ronald Inglehart's surveys found that political discussions among friends were more common in Canada, West Germany, Norway, Sweden, Iceland, and the Netherlands, but in both the 1981 and 1990 surveys, people in the United States discussed politics with friends more often than did respondents in Britain, France, Belgium, and Ireland.

50. Yum and Kendall 1995: 135. On a more theoretical level, MacKuen 1990 provides an explanation for why people tend to avoid political conversations with others who hold different views. With some exceptions, people tend to avoid "embarrassing" conflict and use subtle cues to determine the views of conversants before launching into sustained political exchanges.

51. On influence in couples, see Huckfeldt and Sprague 1995: ch. 9. On the political influence of parents on children, a good example is Jennings and Niemi 1981.

52. This process in American politics was recognized several decades ago, though little research addressed the issue again until the 1980's. For a good example of earlier writing on this subject, see Katz and Lazarsfeld 1955.

53. For the results of the focus-group study, see Delli Carpini and Williams 1994: 793; on the Pittsburgh study, see Mondak 1995: 82.

54. Huckfeldt and Sprague 1995: ch. 9, but see Kenny 1998 for a critique of this interpretation. See also Yum and Kendall 1995; Scheufele 1999.

55. Knoke 1990. McLeod et al. 1999 also finds a link between conversation and participation in public forums.

56. Luskin 1990: 332. Also see research on political expertise (e.g., Krosnick 1990).

57. The estimate of the size of the high-sophistication population is loosely based on Jacoby 1991 and 1995. It is convenient to further subdivide the public into low- and medium-sophistication in roughly equal proportions. For

example, the League of Women Voters has found that 25 percent of the population usually have "very little or no accurate information" about elections. This is close to the 33 percent that I place in the low-sophistication category (see "Charting the Health of American Democracy," June 1997, available at http://www.lwv.org/report.html). One more parallel figure is that 21 percent of those interviewed in the 1996 National Election Study say they follow politics "most of the time," 39 percent follow politics "some of the time," and 40 percent follow politics "only now and then" or "hardly at all." Since 1960, with only minor exceptions, 20–40 percent of the public fell into each of these three categories. For complete data, see http://www.umich.edu/~nes/nesguide/nes-guide.htm.

58. Election research routinely grounds itself in studies of presidential elections such as *The American Voter* (Campbell et al. 1960) and *The New American Voter* (Miller and Shanks 1996). Perhaps tiring of such studies, election scholarship is turning increased attention to House, Senate and even gubernatorial races, but other state and local races still receive little attention.

59. See McDermott 1997; Plutzer and Zipp 1996.

60. Figures come from Burns et al. 1996: 171. These low-intensity races fall below the radar of almost all political science research on campaigns and elections. If the conventional wisdom is that a typical House race is a "low-information" race, then these elections are close to "zero-information" races. One of the few studies looking at near-zero information elections is Dubois 1984.

61. See Champagne and Thielemann 1991 for Texas information and data on judicial name recognition. They found that between elections, fewer than 5 percent of people who say they vote in judicial elections could name the elected office held by some incumbent justices.

62. For the Truman anecdote, see Brown and Giorgetti 1992. Gastil 1998 discusses how voters typically make decisions in these near-zero-information elections.

63. Fishkin 1995: 10.

64. My own mother, Janet Gastil, was one of many public officials who lost reelection bids in 1990 and subsequent local elections. She and her peers did not recognize the threat that the unknown candidates on the ballot posed until it was too late. Ralph Reed, the president of the Christian Coalition at the time, boasted of waging stealth warfare "under cover of night" where you "shimmy along on your belly." On Janet Gastil's 1990 defeat and the stealth campaign phenomenon, see Seth Mydans, "Evangelicals Gain with Covert Candidates," *New York Times,* October 27, 1992, A1. Barry Horstman of the *Los Angeles Times* also wrote two detailed stories in 1992: "Crusade for Public Office in 2nd Stage" (March 22, 1992, B1) and "Christian Activists Using 'Stealth' Campaign Tactics" (April 5, 1992, A1).

65. This figure is not meant as a formal model of voting, but rather as a means of clarifying some of the ways in which voter and campaign characteristics change how voters select candidates. Voting research has developed many detailed models, such as those advanced by Fiorina 1981 and Sniderman, Brody, and Tetlock 1991, but those tend to focus on the presidential election and other high-visibility federal races. By splitting elections and voters into

these different categories, I hope to underscore the difference between voting decisions in low-intensity and primary/nonpartisan races versus the more prominent federal general elections.

66. Incumbents concerned with reelection devote much of their time to meeting voters or even just *inviting* voters to such meetings. After shadowing congressional incumbents, Richard Fenno decided that many voters thought of "representation" in terms of access, familiarity, and trustworthiness. The average citizen appeared more concerned with officials' readiness and willingness to talk and "extra policy behavior" than with actual policy decisions (Fenno 1978: 240). In this sense, voters who select a candidate because they have met him or her during a precinct walk or a community forum might reason that the candidate will prove more accessible in public office than the opponent. Even minimal familiarity—the mere recognition of a candidate's name—might suggest to a voter that the candidate will make as much effort to stay in contact while in office as he or she did through yard signs and political mail during the campaign.

67. In a review of campaign advertising research, Ansolabehere and Iyengar 1996 found that decent ads can give a typical candidate a 7–8 percent boost.

68. Morris Fiorina (1981: 208) estimates that 40 percent of voters in congressional races can give meaningful appraisals of congressional candidate voting records.

69. Some might argue that ideology is a factor *only* in high-intensity, partisan elections. I argue that for as much as a third of the electorate, it does play a role in other races. Paul Raymond's (1992) study of the 1985 Lexington, Kentucky, city council elections provides support for the influence of perceived candidate ideology, along with name recognition and candidate personality, background, and competence as district representative.

70. On the philosophy of adversary democracy in America and its alternative, see Mansbridge 1983.

71. "Negative advertising" has been "a major feature of recent presidential elections" and "is now a factor in state and local campaigns" as well (MacGregor et al. 1996: 88). See Jamieson 1992 for a brief history of modern negative campaigning. Scher 1996 argues that name-calling and attack advertising ("mudslinging") are old American traditions.

72. On the advantages of congressional incumbency, see Jacobson and Kernell 1981; Alford and Brady 1993.

73. Jacobson 1997: 100. The power of the "personal vote" that incumbents develop through both mere exposure and actual constituent service is discussed at length in Cain, Ferejohn, and Fiorina 1987, which stresses the value of "warm, humane interventions" by elected officials but concludes: "Without constraints . . . such behavior can corrode the conduct of democratic government by undermining the ability of that government to act in ways that improve the lot of its citizens" (229). Cultivating and maintaining the "personal vote" can make elected officials servants of particularistic interests rather than true public representatives.

74. Jacobson 1993: 119. The 1997–98 figures are official numbers compiled by the Federal Election Commission, available at http://www.fec.gov. Earlier

studies raised questions about the net added value of incumbent spending, but
methodologically refined studies have since confirmed the electoral importance
of this fund-raising advantage in House races (Erikson and Palfrey 1998) and
Senate elections (Gerber 1998).

75. On incumbent intimidation tactics, see Jacobson 1997: 43–47. All
spending data are provided by the Federal Election Commission. For congressional spending totals in every Senate and House election, plus the presidential
and gubernatorial races, see Barone and Ujifusa 1998.

76. Dan Morain, "Wealth Buys Access to State Politics," *Los Angeles
Times,* April 18, 1999, A1.

77. "The cost of running for local office is much lower than running for Congress or the governorship," but "campaigns are becoming increasingly expensive
at all levels" (MacGregor et al. 1996: 88). The New Mexico race was for State
Senate District No. 39: the incumbent, Senator Liz Stefanics, the only "out" les-
bian in the legislature, raised $71,000, and her opponents spent $63,800 and
$149,000. Stefanics's sexual orientation became an issue in the race (Mark Os-
wald, "Griego Edges Stefanics," *Santa Fe New Mexican,* June 5, 1996, A1).

78. Jacobson 1993: 131. I witnessed this cost firsthand while assisting my
mother with her 1992 and 1994 congressional campaigns. In effect, she had to
campaign continuously for three years, and few citizens can afford to take off
so much time from work.

79. Rachel Zoll, "Congressional Races See Little Competition," *Chattanooga Times,* August 5, 1998. The artful drawing of district boundaries is
also a common explanation for entrenched incumbencies, but it does not explain why incumbents handily win their party primaries.

80. Jacobson 1993: 132–33.

81. Burns et al. 1996: 90.

82. Barone and Ujifusa 1998.

83. Ibid.: 906–7.

84. One might argue that high reelection rates partly reflect the "forced retirement" of members who would have been defeated had they not resigned.
On the contrary, analysis of congressional behavior suggests that resignations
have more to do with thwarted agendas and waning interest in holding office
than imminent defeat. It is the cost of campaigning weighed against the declining perceived value of holding office (rather than simply the fear of defeat) that
motivates voluntary departures (Jacobson and Kernell 1981; Moore and Hibbing 1998).

85. Alford and Brady 1993: 155.

86. Ibid.: 154. On victory margins, see Jacobson 1997, ch. 3. Although the
incumbency advantage remains strong, Jacobson argues that it has actually
waned compared to the 1980s.

87. For example, Krebs 1998 found that incumbency offers a tremendous
advantage to Chicago city council candidates.

88. See, e.g., Dionne 1991; Mathews 1994: chs. 1, 4; Tolchin 1995; Sanders
1990.

89. Mitchell 1996: 49, 77. Data are from the General Social Survey, conducted by the National Opinion Research Center.

90. Schudson 1998: 302. Later, Schudson adds that he doubts "trust" is an "intelligible indicator of anything" and focuses instead on "social capital," which also proves to be an unwieldy concept (307).

91. For 1964–88 data, see Rosenstone and Hansen 1993. Complete National Election Study data are available at http://www.umich.edu/~nes/nes-guide/toptables/tab5c_1.htm and tab5c_2.htm. Asked why they distrusted government, eight in ten members of a national sample group cited its inefficiency ("wastes money," "spends on wrong things"), roughly two-thirds cited the undue influence of special interests, and over 60 percent said that "politicians lack integrity" (Blendon et al. 1997: 250).

92. Hibbing and Theiss-Morse 1995: 45, 166. Approval ratings are the percentage of respondents who "strongly approve" or "approve" of Congress, as opposed to those who "disapprove" or "strongly disapprove." In-depth interview research by Arthur Sanders (1990) also found that a small sample of citizens in Utica, New York, distinguished between trust in leaders versus trust in the system as a whole.

93. Craig, Niemi, and Silver 1990: 296.

94. "[V]oting has declined for the last thirty years," David Mathews (1994: 29) argues, for example. The League of Women Voters also sees a "long-term downward trend in voter participation that began in the early 1960s." See "Charting the Health of American Democracy," June 1997, available at http://www.lwv.org/report.html. One reason that voting is perceived to be in decline is that comparison usually begin roughly ten years prior to the lowering of the voting age in 1972. That is why I present figures *starting* in 1972. Everett Ladd (1996: 5) has pointed out that turnouts at recent presidential elections do not seem particularly low in comparison with elections going back to 1932. The 1992 election, for example, falls right in the middle of the range.

95. It is difficult to calculate precise turnout figures, but the Federal Election Commission numbers are as reliable as any. Estimates of the overall voting-age population sometimes include resident aliens and felons, who are not eligible to vote, but they also normally make no correction for the U.S. Census's undercounting of minorities and the homeless population. For a brief discussion of these issues, see "The Not So Indifferent Voter," *Wilson Quarterly* 22 (Winter 1998). To the extent that turnout has declined, this drop may be due to a generational shift, as the steady voters of the New Deal era pass away (Miller and Shanks 1996).

96. Engstrom and Caridas 1991 found compelling evidence that black voters drop-off in New Orleans judicial races at a greater rate than white voters. National drop-off figures are from the U.S. Bureau of the Census's *Statistical Abstract of the United States, 1997,* table 464. On low turnout in state and local elections, see Burns et al. 1996.

97. Such a view can be found in early pluralist theories of democracy, which found that despite nonvoting and other alleged "problems" with American democracy, the political system was accurately incorporating the public's interests into public policy. See, e.g., Dahl 1961.

98. Ironically, nonvoting *is* a powerful form of encouragement for elected representatives who believe that they will not be held accountable for their

actions in public office so long as the general public remains inactive. The interview cited is from Mathews 1994: 29. On protest voting, see Erwin Knoll, "Making My Vote Count by Refusing to Cast It," *Peace and Democracy News,* Summer 1991, 19–20, 49.

99. It is reassuring that Sellers 1998 found that campaign ads are more effective, on average, when the candidates can actually substantiate their claims. Backed up claims, both positive and negative, appear to have more influence on voters than do unwarranted attacks. If campaigns acted on these findings, it might improve campaign discourse, but it would not make focused debate any more likely. Though accuracy has merit, one can be honest even while discussing irrelevant issues and avoiding a genuine exchange of viewpoints with an opponent.

100. As an illustration of this point, campaign handbooks devote relatively little attention to substantive policy debate with opponents (e.g., Beaudry and Schaeffer 1986; Shea 1996; Grey 1994). Simpson 1996 treats the subject briefly under the subheading "Staged Events."

101. March and Olsen 1995: 45. Along similar lines, Jackman and Miller 1996 argues that political institutions structure citizens' incentives so powerfully that they can prove more influential than culture on individuals' political behavior. I share this view, and that is why I recommend *institutional* changes in chapter 7.

102. Freie 1997 found that even direct participation in conventional American political campaigns has been shown to cause many volunteers to become more alienated from the process. In other words, participation in a flawed system fails to restore confidence in the system.

103. Quotation from John Anderson in the foreword to Barber 1995: x. In support of this view, Junn 1991 found that political participation tends to have a positive effect on political knowledge. In other words, when less sophisticated voters stop voting, their nonparticipation is likely to stunt the growth of their political knowledge.

104. There is considerable debate about whether the nonvoting population differs from the voting population in terms of average attitudes (Bennett and Resnick 1990; Verba, Schlozman, and Brady 1995). Following Zaller's (1992) public opinion model, this correspondence is not surprising because nonvoters tend to have lower levels of political sophistication and thus report attitudes mirroring the average messages conveyed in the media. What is less controversial is whether the voting public demographically matches the nonvoting public: compared to nonvoters, average voters are older, more affluent, and have more formal education (Verba et al. 1995). Polling data notwithstanding, it is reasonable to expect these demographic differences to make nonvoters more concerned about class issues—social welfare, job training, and other government programs that aid the economically disadvantaged. Consistent with this view, Parenti [1974] 1995 points out many ways in which the U.S. government overrepresents the interests of the wealthy, and Hill, Leighley, and Hinton-Andersson 1995 shows that social welfare programs fare better when lower-class voters turn out to vote in greater numbers. Thus, states with more liberal party elites tend to encourage greater voter registration and turnout because it serves their interests (Jackson, Brown, and Wright 1998).

CHAPTER 4. APPRAISING RADICAL AND
CONVENTIONAL ELECTORAL REFORMS

Epigraph: Popkin 1994: 236.

1. This observation appears in Rousseau's discussion of democracy in *The Social Contract*, bk. 3, ch. 4; see Rousseau [1762] 1967: 70. For a detailed account of Rousseau's political thought, see Shklar 1969. Cronin 1989 and Mansbridge 1983 also view Rousseau as a powerful influence on subsequent writings on direct democracy.

2. O'Leary 1996: 29.

3. Burnheim (1985).

4. Cronin 1989: 197; initiative examples are from p. 199.

5. September 1, 1994, survey by Yankelovich Partners for *Time*/CNN cited in *The Public Perspective* 9, 2 (February–March 1998): 45. The full question wording was, "Would you favor or oppose having a national referendum system in which all citizens voted on proposals that deal with major national issues—voting either for them or against them—before they become law?"

6. Cronin 1989: 230.

7. Because initiatives have the same problems as elections for public office, they might also benefit from the solutions I propose for representative government. I examine this possibility in some detail in chapter 7.

8. Guinier 1994: 14–15.

9. Ibid.: 15. Engstrom and Barrilleaux 1991 shows how the Sisseton-Wahpeton Sioux have used the system in South Dakota to win a seat on the school board. Probably because they have used it effectively, in exit polls the Sioux voters rated the system positively, whereas Anglo voters had more mixed reviews of cumulative voting. Still 1992 and Brockington et al. 1998 also provide evidence that cumulative voting can facilitate minority representation.

10. This description is adapted from Erdman and Susskind 1995: 35–36.

11. Ibid.: 4.

12. Ibid.: 45.

13. Ibid.: 47.

14. Amy 1993 makes a persuasive case for the use of proportional representation in the United States. Among other advantages, one undeniable benefit relative to the winner-take-all system is its elimination of gerrymandering, because no district lines need to be drawn. In my view, proportional representation is superior to the present system, but I believe it does not solve the problem of exit and comes at the cost of a voter's direct connection to individual public representatives. On the brief history of proportional representation in Ohio, see Barber 1995.

15. Benjamin and Malbin 1992 presents a wide range of voices on term limits, as well as the texts of term-limits ballot initiatives in Oklahoma, Colorado, California, and Washington. Kamber 1995 provides a synthetic inventory of arguments against term limits.

16. John Hibbing and Elizabeth Theiss-Morse found that most supporters of term limits are firm in their convictions. Only 13 percent changed their views after hearing the following counterarguments: "Some people opposed to term

limitations have suggested that the problems Congress deals with are so complex that it takes years for members of Congress to develop the expertise needed to address those problems. Other people opposed to term limitations have suggested that limiting terms for members of Congress would only increase the power of unelected staff members and interest group lobbyists" (Hibbing and Theiss-Morse 1995: 78–79).

17. Many elected officials leave office after a decade, anyhow. Hibbing's (1993) study of careerism in Congress found that despite the increased professionalization of that institution, on average, members serve only twelve years. On the other hand, that means that the typical representative has five successful reelections. Gerald Benjamin and Michael Malbin (1992: Appendix B) provide similar data showing the gradual turnover of most state legislators. The problem isn't turnover so much as it is accountability (and a clear public voice as guidance) while in office.

18. "Fundamental distrust of government is represented by the call for term limits for elected officials" (Miller and Shanks 1996: 508).

19. Proponents make the more modest claim that the people elected under term limits would be "average" citizens who would better represent the public by virtue of having a primarily nonpolitical identity. As of yet, there is no evidence of this difference.

20. In an experimental analysis of term limits, William Bianco (1996) makes it clear that they by no means give the public more trustworthy representatives. If citizens expect representatives to be responsive to the electorate, term limits undermine the electoral connection; yet if citizens expect representatives to be untrustworthy, term limits simply give elected officials more freedom to do as they choose. "Term limits may stiffen the backbones of elected officials," Bianco writes, "enabling them to make hard choices. The problem is that constituents often do better with a representative whose backbone is subject to their recall" (166–67). Victor Kamber (1995: 53) points out that term limits encourage potential opponents to pass up opportunities to challenge incumbents, since they can wait a few years and run in an open-seat race. Thus, a twelve-year limit on senators serving six-year terms nearly guarantees an incumbent a twelve-year tenure.

21. Jacobson 1997: 54.

22. Makinson 1994: 3.

23. A move toward "video direct mail" through cable television is anticipated by Abramson, Arterton, and Orren 1988: 113–15. This and the Internet could both facilitate "narrowcasting" to voters.

24. The Gallup survey was conducted October 29–30, 1996, with 714 registered voters. This result and similar findings have been assembled by Public Campaign at http://www.publicampaign.org/pollsumm.html.

25. Gallup poll, January 31–February 2, 1997, cited in *The Public Perspective* 9, 2 (February–March 1998): 47.

26. Thomas E. Mann and Norman J. Ornstein, "Credibility for a Collapsed System," *Washington Post,* December 16, 1996.

27. The study was conducted by the Committee for the Study of the American Electorate, and its findings are available at http://tap.epn.org/csae/

spendlim.html. Gary Jacobson (1993: 137) also takes the view that "spending limits, unless pegged at improbably high levels, are inherently detrimental to challengers, because most challengers need to spend a great deal of money to have any hope at all of overcoming the advantages incumbents enjoy before the first campaign dollar is spent." In a careful study of U.S. Senate campaigns, Alan Gerber (1998) estimates that the incumbency fund-raising/spending advantage amounts to a 6 percent edge in the vote, but he argues that equalizing spending would actually be a net benefit to challengers.

28. See League of Women Voters, "5 Ideas for Practical Campaign Reform," July 21, 1997, available at http://www.lwv.org.

29. Budesheim, Houston, and DePaola 1996 found that issue-oriented attacks on an opponent work well with an audience in the advertiser's in-group, and character-based attacks work well within an advertiser's out-group. The in-group identifies with the advertiser's ideological similarity, whereas the out-group sees no such similarity and responds best to attacks with no issue relevance.

30. Ansolabehere et al. 1997.

31. On the Buchanan ad, see Cappella and Jamieson 1997; on the gubernatorial race, see Pfau and Louden 1994.

32. Associated Press, "Judge Blocks Taft TV Ad," *Elyria Chronicle-Telegram,* October 11, 1998, C1.

33. Information on the Project is available at http://www.campaignconduct.org. This website has copies of the Maine and Washington codes of conduct.

34. This argument was offered to me by Estus Smith of the Kettering Foundation.

35. The quotation comes from an editorial written by Anne Smead, the chair of the League of Women Voters Ohio Education Fund. The League partnered with many other organizations to sponsor the Ohio Project on Campaign Conduct. See "A Proposal to Stop Negative Campaigns," *Cleveland Plain Dealer,* May 8, 1998.

36. After the election 31 percent percent of all residents surveyed reported reading the guide, and 34 percent of those who reported voting said that they had read it. See the University of New Mexico Institute for Public Policy's *Quarterly Profile of New Mexico Citizens* 9 (Winter 1997): 3.

37. Surprisingly, the national office of the the League of Women Voters knew of no formal research on the use of the voters' guides, as I learned in a November 9, 1998, telephone interview. It did, however, lead me to contact a league member in Maryland, who found that direct mail distribution of voters' guides slightly increased voter turnout in traditionally low-turnout precincts (Watkins 1998).

38. November 13, 1998, interview with Cathy Mitchell, the Initiative and Ballot Pamphlet Coordinator for the California Secretary of State. The use figure comes from Magleby 1984.

39. For a comprehensive guide to on-line voting guides and other political websites, see Browning 1996. On late contributions, see California's Late Contribution Watch at http://www.calvoter.org/cvf/96gen/aboutlcw.html.

40. Rosen 1997: 22.

41. For a correlation of .32 to .35 between "reading news in the newspaper" and political knowledge, see Delli Carpini and Keeter 1996: 182–83.

42. Dubois, Feeney, and Costantini 1991.

43. Adam Nagourney and Marjorie Connelly, "In Poll, New York Voters See Senate Race as Too Negative," *New York Times,* October 27, 1998, A1, A23.

44. Chaffee and Rimal 1996: 277–78.

CHAPTER 5. PUBLIC EXPRESSION IN AMERICAN POLITICS

Epigraph: Hamilton, Madison, and Jay 1948 [1788]: 269.

1. Fenno 1978: 55–56.

2. Dunstan McNichol, "A Sampling of Klug's Mail," *Wisconsin State Journal,* May 26, 1992, B3.

3. See James Bush, "E-Maelstrom," *Seattle Weekly,* October 22, 1998, 13.

4. Ruth Messenger (1998: 5) found that the most active, informed, and concerned citizens who write letters complain "just as fiercely about the conventional letter that comes from too many elected officials" as they do when they get no reply at all.

5. Seeking to describe an "authentic," "democratic," "strong," or "true" public voice, Barber 1984, Fishkin 1995, and Mathews 1994 use similar terms.

6. Herbst 1993.

7. Different professionals have different standards for an "adequate" response rate for a phone survey, but the most common minimum standard is 50 percent. That means that a survey's sample is adequate so long as half of the eligible households contacted agreed to participate in it. Usually, a 50 percent response rate means that some fraction refused to participate and a larger percentage simply did not participate for whatever reason (not home, call-back appointment cancelled, etc.) The oversampling of households with multiple residential numbers is sometimes corrected by dividing each respondent by the number of residential phone lines in a home. See Brehm 1993.

8. MacKuen 1990: 86–87.

9. Ibid.: 88.

10. Mitchell 1996: 58–60.

11. Kay 1998: 12.

12. Alan Kay (1998: 309) provides a list of popular policies and discusses the "80% consensus" requirement in great depth. Iconoclasm toward "pundits," "players," and "politicians" sometimes gives way to simmering frustration, such as in Kay's bitter recollection of his exchanges with Jim Fishkin and Bob Luskin regarding the National Issues Convention (284–95). To browse survey data collected by Kay's Americans Talk Issues Foundation on-line, go to http://www.publicinterestpolling.com.

13. Sniderman, Brody, and Tetlock 1991: 232–34. The full wording of the initial question was, "Some people feel that the government in Washington ought to see to it that blacks get fair treatment in jobs. Others feel that this is not the government's business and it should stay out of it. How do you feel? Should the

government see to it that blacks get fair treatment in jobs or should it stay out of it?" If the respondent said that she or he favored government intervention, the interviewer read this counterargument: "Would you still feel the same—even if it means that government will have more say in telling people how to run their lives, or do you think that might change your mind?" Those who took the opposite view heard this counterargument: "Would you still feel the same way even if it means that some racial discrimination will continue?" The problem with this approach is that the researchers cannot exhaust the range of arguments, although one could at least try selecting balanced arguments by going through the same kinds of procedures I suggest in chapter 7 for witness selection.

14. This case was so extreme that the American Association of Public Opinion Researchers publicly censured Frank Luntz, the pollster behind the "Contract with America."

15. Kay 1998: 307.

16. I first heard this idea expressed by Hank Jenkins-Smith of the University of New Mexico Institute for Public Policy.

17. Noelle-Neumann 1993.

18. Mutz 1992.

19. Herbst 1993.

20. Ginsberg 1986: 82.

21. Again, the term "enlightened understanding" is used by Dahl 1989 as a criterion for the democratic process.

22. Webler and Renn 1995: 24. As one county commissioner put it, "At a public hearing you are more or less on trial" (Kettering Foundation 1989: 11).

23. Webler and Renn 1995: 24.

24. Adams 1995: 20.

25. Checkoway 1981.

26. Fiorino 1995: 226.

27. In the view of some observers, such as Charles Mahtesian (1997), the tendency toward acrimony and name-calling at public meetings is on the rise.

28. Mark Nepper, "Lawmakers Hear War Views," *Wisconsin State Journal,* January 10, 1991, A1.

29. Paul Wellstone, "Minnesota Message: War on Iraq Would Be Terrible Mistake," *Seattle Times,* January 7, 1991, A9.

30. Kent Jenkins, "Area Lawgivers Split 8 to 6 on Vote for War," *Washington Post,* January 13, 1991, A24.

31. Kettering Foundation 1989: 11.

32. Page 1996: 5.

33. Ibid.: 14–15 n. 14; and see also p. 6.

34. For example, Herman and Chomsky 1988 demonstrates how different "news filters" can result in biased coverage, even when reporters intend to report faithfully on world affairs.

35. Page 1996: 10.

36. Ibid.: 119.

37. Quotation and observations are from Ibid.: 89, which draws upon stories in the *Boston Globe, Los Angeles Times, New York Times,* and the *Washington Post.*

38. In his invitation, which aired on the cable channel Comedy Central, Franken was gracious. "You choose the venue," he offered. "The steakhouse of your choice." See Al Franken, *Rush Limbaugh Is a Big Fat Idiot and Other Observations* (New York: Delacorte Press, 1996).

39. The national survey was conducted by *Talkers Magazine* (Longmeadow, Mass.), which updates the survey every six months on-line at http://www.talkers.com/talkaud.html. For the San Diego study, see Hofstetter et al. 1994: 474–76. The Arbitron data are available at http://www.arbitron.com/studies/NewRadioToday.pdf. The term *ditto-head* comes from Limbaugh himself, who uses it without irony to refer to his listeners, who often offer "dittos" to Limbaugh. After listening to the Rush Limbaugh radio show, this begins to sound like a devoted incantation, recited by the most loyal listeners. On the nature of the talk-radio audience, see also Pfau et al. 1998.

40. Newhagen 1994. The study did not suggest a single causal direction, and it is plausible that calling shows may heighten self-efficacy, as well as vice versa. Hofstetter et al. 1994 found the same relationship.

41. John Stuart Mill (1947 [1859]) popularized the notion of a "marketplace of ideas," and this view is shared inter alia by Page 1996; Popkin 1994; and Zaller 1992. The deliberative call for debate is made forcefully by many authors, including Barber 1984; Fishkin 1995; Gutmann and Thompson 1996; and Mathews 1994. Some evidence suggests that political talk radio may be worse than useless; it may further erode public trust in government (Pfau et al. 1998).

42. Salisbury 1986 reports the results of a survey of lobbyists in the early 1980s that shows how lobbyists develop a professional expertise that transcends particular issue domains.

43. For a critical analysis of lobbying as a means of preserving the interests of the economic elite, see Parenti [1974] 1995: ch. 12, which acknowledges the role of unions as a lobbying group but argues that their influence is weak relative to business interests. Robert Dahl summarizes the problem succinctly: "Because market capitalism inevitably creates inequalities, it limits the democratic potential of polyarchal democracy by generating inequalities in the distribution of political resource" (Dahl 1998: 177).

44. Michael A. Fletcher, "The Color of Campaign Finance," *Washington Post National Weekly Edition,* September 28, 1998, 34. Rosenstone and Hansen 1993 also found a clear relationship between income and campaign contributions based on Roper Surveys conducted in the 1970s and 1980s.

45. Edelman 1988: 21–23.

46. Mansbridge 1992: 501–2.

47. Charles Lewis (1998) also notes that Boeing's merger partner, McDonnell Douglas used the same strategy to earn a 1995 tax credit of $334 million. Lewis's book *The Buying of Congress* is replete with such examples of successful lobbying, particularly by corporate interests.

48. In the Washington State 1998 Senate race, for example, the Republican candidate, Linda Smith, refused to accept PAC funds but criticized her party for failing to give her funds until late in her campaign.

49. Bennett 1996: 218, citing the Center for Public Integrity report "Well-Healed: Inside Lobbying for Heath Care Reform" (unpublished), July 1994, 75.

50. Barone and Ujifusa 1998: 1252.

51. Bennett 1994: 297.

52. "In communicating the needs of the more affluent few more effectively than those of the rest of society, the participatory process creates a polity far from the ideal of equal consideration for all" (Verba, Schlozman, and Brady 1995: 508). Barlett and Steele 1992 shows that those with greater economic power also have more influence through lobbying.

53. Lappe and DuBois 1994: 9.

CHAPTER 6. GLIMPSES OF THE DELIBERATIVE PUBLIC

Epigraph: Morone 1990: 323.

1. Morone 1990: 9, 323. On the pattern of reform, see Ibid.: 9–15.

2. This section of this chapter is adapted from John Gastil and James P. Dillard, "The Aims, Methods, and Effects of Deliberative Civic Education through the National Issues Forums," *Communication Education* 48 (April 1999): 179–182. I thank the National Communication Association for allowing my use of this material.

3. On the Lyceum, see Bode 1956; on the Chautaqua Assembly, see Gould 1961; on Great Books, see Davis 1961; on other programs, see Mathews 1994, Mattson 1998, Oliver 1987, and Tjerandsen 1980.

4. Bormann 1996: 99–103.

5. For a more detailed discussion of study circles and the National Issues Forums, see Gastil and Dillard 1999a. Mark Burton and Kevin Mattson (1999) identify civic education as one of many goals that deliberative programs can pursue, and they provide examples of different efforts to promote deliberation.

6. Study Circles Resource Center 1991b. For the rationale behind the Study Circles Resource Center, see Leighninger and McCoy 1998.

7. Study Circles Resource Center 1991a: 1.

8. Study Circles Resource Center 1991b: 1.

9. Study Circles Resource Center 1991a, 1991b.

10. Study Circles Resource Center and ACCESS 1994.

11. Study Circles Resource Center 1991b: 1, 4.

12. Data on participation are from National Issues Forums 1993. General descriptions of the NIF include Gastil 1994b, Osborn and Osborn 1991, and Pearce and Littlejohn 1997.

13. On the NIF network, see Downing 1996; on NIF history, see Archie 1986 and NIF 1992.

14. McAfee, McKenzie, and Mathews 1990: 4–5.

15. Mathews 1994.

16. National Issues Forums 1992: 23. Useful overviews of the NIF process are also provided by *Organizing Your First Forum / Study Circle* (National Issues Forums 1990), Pearce and Littlejohn 1997: 169–80, and Gastil and Dillard 1999a.

17. National Issues Forums 1991.

18. National Issues Forums 1996.

19. National Issues Forums 1992: 31–32.

20. Perry 1990: 22.

21. National Issues Forums 1992: 32.

22. National Issues Forums 1990: 14. Also see National Issues Forums 1992.

23. Loyacano 1992: 15. See Gastil 1994b for a summary of qualitative research.

24. Farkas, Friedman, and Bers 1995.

25. Doble and Richardson 1991.

26. Gastil and Dillard 1999a.

27. Gastil 1994b. On conversational dominance, see Burgoon and Hale 1984.

28. This subject came up during conversations with Kettering Foundation staff while I was in residence during October and November 1998.

29. For examples of such programs, see Matt Leighninger, "How Have Study Circles Made an Impact?" *Focus on Study Circles* 9, 4: 2.

30. Lappe and Dubois 1994: 174.

31. Ibid.: 175–76.

32. According to an October 30, 1998, telephone interview with Consortium President Stephen Littlejohn, the consortium had understood the city lists to be inclusive, but it turned out that they were lists of relatively active Cupertino residents.

33. Pearce and Littlejohn 1997: 209–10; Pearce and Pearce in press. See also Natasha Collins, "Residents Talk Safety, Diversity at Cupertino Town Hall Meeting," *Cupertino Courier,* October 29, 1998, available at http://metroactive.com/papers/cupertino.courier/11.27.96/meeting.html.

34. Podziba 1998.

35. Higgins 1998: 9.

36. For example, see Gill 1996, a study of informal meetings in a British Columbia tourist town.

37. Briand 1999. I also had the pleasure of seeing one day of the convention in person.

38. On COPS, see Boyte 1989: 87–91, Crimmins 1996: 32–39, and Lappe and Dubois 1994: 60–61, 183–84. Ruth Messenger, a New York public official who had taken part in such "accountability sessions," described the experience this way:

> Members of the sponsoring group, which has always done research on the issues at hand, give their visitor specific, detailed, and reasonably terse presentations. The officeholder is then told he or she can have thirty seconds and must begin their response by saying yes or no to a particular question that seeks to learn if they will vote with or against the group. Not only would the "wrong" answer be met with fierce booing but also so would any effort to try to engage in a discussion of the matter without stating a yes or no position. . . . I usually only went when I knew what the focus was and generally what questions I would be asked and knew I would be comfortable giving the kind of answer that was sought. It did not seem to make any sense to go otherwise. . . . I also found it irritating that people who were informed on an issue—and knew it had many complex dimensions—had decided that it was not possible for me to discuss those.
>
> (Messenger 1998: 6–7, 9)

39. The argument that public opinion polls have set a new standard for "legitimate" forms of representative public voice is consistent with Susan Herbst's

(1993) analysis of the increasing power of public opinion polls. The point is that polls are powerful, not just because they quantify the public's voice, but also because they derive it from a random sample of the public.

40. Citizen Jury is a registered service mark of what is now called the Jefferson Center for New Democratic Processes (http://www.jefferson-center.org). As its founder, Ned Crosby, explains, the center "has no desire to 'own' democracy—only to prevent others from perverting a valid method of democracy in order to serve their own ends" (Crosby 1998: 1). Beker and Slaton 1981 describes the televote from the perspective of its creators. For more critical perspectives, see Arterton 1987; Abramson, Arterton, and Orren 1988. On the Granada 500, see MacDonald 1986; Fishkin 1995. On planning cells, see Dienel 1995.

41. Hank Jenkins-Smith and I were the principal investigators of the citizen conference project, and the text that follows is based largely upon our final report. See Gastil and Jenkins-Smith 1997. For assisting with developing the conference design, thanks go to the staff of the New Mexico State Highway and Transportation Department, as well as to Anne Landy and Carol Silva at the University of New Mexico Institute for Public Policy.

42. I was the moderator for each of the citizen conferences.

43. Telephone interview with James Kozak, November 9, 1998. On the press coverage of the conferences, see Gastil and Jenkins-Smith 1997. Some of the coverage focused on the fact that public officials would pay citizens to participate in public meetings—an admittedly ironic feature of this modern democratic process. See, e.g., the transcript of the Osgood File, "Government of New Mexico Paying Its Citizens $200 a Day to Attend Public Forums on Transportation Issues," July 4, 1997, available in Lexis-Nexis and in Gastil and Jenkins-Smith 1997.

44. For general information on citizen juries, see Crosby 1995, 1998; Smith and Wales 1999.

45. The description of the jury is taken from the final report, *Citizens Jury on Hog Farming* (January 1996), compiled by St. Olaf College and available from the Jefferson Center for New Democratic Processes, Minneapolis.

46. Pauline Schreiber, "Citizens Jury Rejects Feedlot Size Limits," *Faribault Daily News,* November 10, 1995.

47. "Citizens Jury an Important Group to at Least Listen To," *Faribault Daily News,* November 11, 1995. After a Citizens Jury on traffic congestion pricing in which jurors moved away from a proposed pricing mechanism, editorials in the *St. Paul Pioneer Press* and the *Minneapolis Star Tribune* made similar statements about the jury's effort and intelligence, yet rejected the jury's main recommendation. For more information on that jury, see the Jefferson Center's 1995 *Report on Traffic Congestion Pricing.*

48. Crosby 1998.

49. Ibid. For more information on the efforts of Crosby and others to hold public forums on elections, see the Citizens Election Forum website (http://www.citizens-forum.org) and http://www.healthydemocracy.org.

50. Fishkin 1991: 93; Fishkin 1995: 43. Deliberative Polling is a trademark used by the Center for Deliberative Polling (http://www.la.utexas.edu/research/delpol/cdpindex.html).

51. On the philosophical underpinnings of the NIC, see Fishkin 1991, 1995. On the selection of participants, see Bradburn 1996. Published criticisms of the idea and the implementation of the NIC include Mitofsky 1996; Flavin and Dougherty 1996. Some critics of American public life, however, support for the idea of deliberative polling (e.g., Eliasoph 1998).

52. For a summary of my observations, see Gastil 1996.

53. On political communication networks, see Knoke 1990.

54. Hart and Jarvis 1999: 12.

55. Mitofsky 1996.

56. In interviews with participants at the NIC, I heard stories about strong initial skepticism. One woman I interviewed said she was not convinced that the convention was real until she stepped off her airplane in Austin; she said she was prepared to turn back then and there if anything looked suspicious (Gastil 1996). Tom Smith (1999) reports that 80 percent of the final pool of participants had such reservations, so I suspect that such doubts were decisive for nonparticipants. If events like the NIC became commonplace, participating might become no more mysterious than serving on a jury.

57. Daniel Merkle's (1996) tables show only modest demographic differences between attendees and the population, except that the attendees were somewhat more politically active and involved than the general population. For an extended discussion of the representativeness of the NIC, see Fishkin and Luskin 1999.

58. Merkle 1996 views these changes as a sign that deliberation had little effect. Beyond the "half empty, half full" debate, it is fair to say that the question is not how many attitudes changed, but whether the changes revealed an important pattern.

59. The full results of the NIC poll are still available at http://www.pbs.org/nic. Also see Fishkin and Luskin 1999. Luskin, Fishkin, and Jowell 1997 found similar attitude changes and educational effects in other deliberative polls. Gastil and Jenkins-Smith 1998 also found learning effects at public meetings about radiation at Los Alamos National Laboratory. See also Gastil and Dillard 1999b; Pelletier et al. 1999.

60. Rasinski, Bradburn, and Lauen 1999.

61. Tom Smith 1999: 57–58.

62. See Merkle 1996: 614; Fishkin and Luskin 1999.

63. Fishkin and Luskin 1999 mentions NIC spin-offs in the form of statewide polls and forums in Maine, Minnesota, Pennsylvania, and Texas.

64. Leighninger and McCoy 1998: 188.

65. This reflects a more general problem with writings on deliberation. As Christiane Olivio argues, most theorists promoting civil society "also maintain that citizen participation and deliberation in civil society really advance democratic ideals when they influence the official public sphere of the state. Yet how democratic activity in civil society and the state are to be connected remains unclear in their work" (Olivio 1998: 246). For this reason, she undertook a study of "round table" forums in Germany, although she found these to have the same problem as the deliberative forums described herein. Unintegrated into existing political institutions, the round tables had very limited influence on

policymaking and failed to capture the interest of the larger public. Jack Knight and James Johnson offer a similar critique of pragmatists who advocate increased deliberation, observing that these theorists "hope to avoid the sort of 'magic' solutions to political problems about which Dewey was so skeptical," yet fail to "offer an account of pragmatist democracy *and* its problems" (Knight and Johnson 1999: 583). Some advocates of deliberation respond to this criticism by underscoring deliberation's intrinsic value, apart from any influence on policy (e.g., Burton and Matson 1999).

CHAPTER 7. THE CITIZEN PANELS PROPOSAL

Epigraph: Crosby 1998: 4.

1. The phrase comes from Crosby 1998: 3. On the same page, Crosby's argument for electoral reform implicitly addresses both exit and voice. Crosby argues that contemporary electoral forms "do little to empower the average citizen to understand . . . which candidates are most likely to steer it in the proper direction." He then adds that a weak public voice makes it impossible to bridge public and special interests in crafting policy.

2. In this view, the civic skills and responsibility developed through social movements might make electoral reform less necessary. See Evans and Boyte 1992.

3. For this view, see, e.g., Barber 1984; Crimmins 1995; Kemmis 1990; Mathews 1994. Only Barber makes a direct connection between "democratic talk" and election reform.

4. Before the Internet became popular, these ideas were put forward, inter alia, by Toffler 1980, and Barber and Watson 1988. Many an Internet site now boasts that its pages can solve our political problems.

5. In a sense, a model of representation should assume citizens are more analogous to "auditors" than active observers (Arnold 1990, 1993). "The monitorial citizen engages in environmental surveillance more than information-gathering" (Schudson 1998: 311).

6. Putnam 1995b. Note that Robert Putnam has acknowledged some overestimation of the decline of citizens' organizational memberships due to miscalculation (see Helliwell and Putnam 1996).

7. Bennett 1998.

8. The term *citizen panel* has been used elsewhere, such as in Crosby 1998. By using only a small number of random sample forums, I am answering one of the challenges put forward by Michael Bailey (1996: 14–16). As described by Bailey, liberal democratic theorists doubt that "widespread and intense participation . . . can be achieved with little or no coercion or growth in bureaucracy." To achieve full deliberation, "hundreds of thousands of public meetings must be created across the nation" and "surely abuse will occur. Rather than reducing the state's influence, . . . its arbitrary power might increase." The panels I propose require only specific and very limited "incentives to deliberate" for small subsamples of the public, so there is no need for further public intrusion into the private sphere to inspire full participation in deliberation.

9. Building on his experience with citizen juries, Ned Crosby (1998) has suggested a citizen election forum (CEF) that resembles the panels proposed later

in this chapter. One major difference in the design of the CEF and the panels I propose is that I want citizen panels to affect what appears on voters' ballots. Ongoing conversations with Crosby over the past three years have considerably influenced my own ideas about citizen deliberation and random sample forums.

10. I do not mean to imply that public financing is a bad idea per se. In fact, it might complement the citizen panels. The point is simply that reformers are proposing and enacting far more expensive reform packages for state and federal elections.

11. Robert Dahl (1989) suggests a year-long "minipopulous" of 1,000 citizens, and Jim Fishkin (1995) recommends that deliberative polls require 400 or more participants. Peter DeLeon (1997: 112–13) also appears to lean toward policy panels with over 100 participants. There is a trade-off between panel size and error margin, as well as between the duration and depth of deliberation. As panels become larger and their deliberations become more lengthy, there is also a loss of the potential for face-to-face deliberation among all participants, and there is an increased risk of attrition as participants serving on relatively uncohesive panels become tired of the process or must tend to other obligations. Especially for single-issue or candidate judgments, I believe that I have chosen a balance that makes the citizen panels manageable and affordable without making them too small or hasty in their judgments.

12. Some random sample forums use "attitudinal quotas," in which previously collected survey data provide baseline quotas for attitudes relevant to panel deliberations (e.g., "50 of the 400 panelists must oppose handgun registration"). The rationale for attitudinal quotas is that they protect against skewed attitudinal samples that can occur within demographically representative samples. These quotas would be more subject to fraud and error than demographic measures, and because of public skepticism about surveys, joining them to the citizen sampling might actually undermine the validity of the panels. Partisan quotas serve the same purpose by matching the random sample to data on party registration (e.g., "the panel should consist of 150 Democrats, 140 Republicans, 100 nonpartisans, and 10 Libertarians"). In states where voters register by party, this might be feasible, but a national sample could not do this, because many states do not register by party. When partisanship is reduced to unofficial self-reporting, it is not very different from other survey attitude measures, and potential panelists could lie about their party affiliation, as some have done in previous random sample forums. In an October interview with Dennis Foley, Ombudsman at the *Orange County Register,* I learned that the *Register* forums included a participant who lied about his party affiliation intentionally to throw off the quotas.

13. Experimentation with different sizes of honoraria could determine the appropriate level. The point is to get a very high participation rate among the individuals initially contacted, which gives one more confidence that the sample is not skewed. It may turn out that $600 is too low. Over ten years ago, $50 or even $100 payments were not uncommon for focus-group participation (see Morgan 1988: 44), and a citizen panel is far more demanding.

14. Bessette 1994: 149.

15. I recommend holding the priority panel before the primary election to ensure that voting records become an issue during even the primary election. This means that a panel would consider all bills *since the previous panel,* which would mean that some key votes at the end of a term would not be considered until the subsequent election.

16. Barone and Ujifusa 1998: 16.

17. Indirectly, this system gives some encouragement to third parties, which I believe enrich the political process by articulating alternative points of view. Were there national voter registration by party, a voter registration threshold could be used to determine which parties could introduce bills. When the legislative panel is applied to states with such registration, I would recommend using registration rather than the one-seat-in-the-legislature requirement because winner-take-all districting makes it difficult for third parties to win seats, even if they have as much as 15 percent of a state's registered voters.

18. Some reviewers of the priority panel proposal have suggested that citizen panelists themselves might each have the opportunity to introduce one bill for consideration. If the initial citizen panel includes 400 members, this would permit another 400 bills to appear before the panel. My main concern is that this would unduly complicate the citizens' deliberations by overcrowding their agenda. It would also require citizens to take action prior to meeting one another, and I prefer their first official task occurring only after they convene. If citizens *were* allowed to introduce bills, it might be prudent to require that any bill suggested by a citizen panelist *not* be authored by their own representative. The panel's purpose is to move beyond the concerns of individual districts and traditional political allegiances, and this restriction might prevent exceedingly local interests from entering the process at this stage.

19. A reviewer of an earlier draft of this book suggested a fourth criterion— controversy. In this view, it is important that panelists pick bills about which candidates will disagree. I chose to leave out that criterion for two reasons. First, panel ratings of candidates should be high when there is a broad public (and candidate) consensus on how to approach the major problems of the day. Second, because they are deliberative, panel judgments will not always reflect conventional party views and public opinion. Thus, discarding "noncontroversial" legislation may cause panels to skip important issues about which there *should be* debate, and bills chosen for their controversial value may, nonetheless, result in little conflict during deliberation.

Another suggested criterion would ask panelists to look for bills that might lead to consensus among legislative panelists (described later in this chapter). I do not include this criterion because it asks too much of the priority panels. They could not complete their main task if they were also asked to discern the deliberative judgments likely to be reached on numerous bills.

20. On these influences in relation to spatial arrangement, see Davies 1994.

21. A vote could break any ties resulting from identical average ratings.

22. In either system, I prefer rankings to ratings because they give each citizen equal weight in the final evaluation: that is, each citizen's average ranking is 5.5. If, by contrast, citizens rated each bill on a ten-point scale, some citizens

might give high average ratings and others low ratings. This would provide more information about each citizen's views, but it jeopardizes voting equality.

23. David Morgan (1988: 44) discusses the difficulty of generating truly representative samples for focus groups, which are even smaller than legislative panels. The citizen jury process uses quotas to create well-balanced small groups (Crosby 1995).

24. On the other hand, simultaneous meetings would permit all deliberation to take place closer to the election, which would reduce the likelihood of legislation "slipping past" the panel process late in the final session. Such slippage is inevitable, however, because the panels would have to come early enough to permit ballot printing, and so on. Because citizens can consider bills that have not even had committee votes, the panels might nonetheless deliberate upon bills that ultimately wound up on the floor. In any case, the next round of panels could consider legislation that came after the deadline for the previous panels.

25. Crosby 1998 discusses the citizen panel in detail. Crosby described the witness procedure to me in a November 4, 1998, telephone interview.

26. Lupia and McCubbins 1998: 225. The authors argue that this and other safeguards can provide a valuable "threat of verification."

27. In a November 3, 1998, interview, Ned Crosby made the following suggestion regarding the panelists' control over the moderator role. If a panelist wanted the moderator to become more or less active, the panelist could have one minute to explain why the change was necessary, another panelist could give a counterargument for a minute, then a quick majority vote could determine whether to adopt the change. On the problems that commonly emerge in small democratic groups, see Gastil 1993.

28. Straw polls could interfere with full deliberation by committing citizens too early to particular views. If one changed this process to include a straw poll, it should be by secret ballot, for the same reasons given earlier. If the vote were public, it should still be taken by simultaneous ballot to avoid the conformity problem posed by sequential straw polls taken in groups where the initial voice votes happen, by chance, to be the same. On the problems with straw polls, see Davis, Hubert, and Au 1996.

29. Some advocates of deliberation stop short of voting, and the public forums and community deliberation initiatives described in chapter 6 work toward consensus more than they risk dividing into majority and minority viewpoints. In informal settings, it may be appropriate to avoid voting, but the citizen panels would not be able to make strong (and straightforward) recommendations without voting. As Lisa Disch argues in presenting her model of "power-sensitive deliberation," it is necessary to create "formal mechanisms to delineate the limits of consensus" (Disch 1996: 14).

30. In a sense, the two-thirds requirement is a way of compensating for the small size of the citizen panel. With a sample of 50 people, there is an enormous margin of error (approximately 14 percent) surrounding the average view of the panel in relation to the views a full public. Requiring two-thirds agreement dramatically increases the odds that the small panel's decision will match that of the entire population (had it gone through the same deliberations). By call-

ing anything less than two-thirds agreement "undecided," the panel acknowledges that its less than two-thirds majority may not match the majority of the entire population. In statistical terms, a two-thirds majority is "significant" in that the odds of the general public holding the opposite view are less than one-in-twenty (i.e., 66 percent is significantly different from 49 percent for a sample of 50).

31. Sanders 1997: 373.

32. Past random sample forums I have observed have had some unenthusiastic participants, but most take their task very seriously. Even though participating in only a trial-run citizen conference closer to a private focus group, one participant was so conscientious that she mailed back (at her expense) the notepad she had not completely filled out during her deliberations on radioactive waste. Stories like that are common and reflect the fact that even "lazy" and "selfish" citizens can become very motivated and thoughtful for short periods of time, such as when called upon to serve on a jury or as a participant in a random sample forum. This is similar to the argument I made in *Democracy in Small Groups* (Gastil 1993: 123). A small group might manage to approach the democratic ideal, but it can probably only do so for a short period of time.

33. Moon 1990: 5.

34. Conover and Feldman 1989.

35. See Rahn 1993; Moon 1990.

36. Plutzer and Zipp 1996.

37. On the use of ballot-based cues in low-intensity elections, see Gastil 1998. I believe that cue reliance is greatest for low-awareness voters in low-intensity elections (see chapter 3). Ellen Riggle argues that voters respond to simple cues in the full spectrum of elections. In moderate- and high-intensity races, voters might use cues because of the opposite problem: a media-saturated campaign can create "an information overload such that citizens resort to the use of party or image heuristics in order to cope with the overabundance of campaign trivia" (Riggle 1992: 243).

38. Lupia 1994: 72.

39. Though he denies the accusation, I believe that Perry Deess shares responsibility for the development of this idea. I have elsewhere called it a "legislative batting average," but I have not done so here to avoid confusing those who might not understand the baseball metaphor. The use of a rating has another advantage: it puts even more pressure on candidates to take both official and unofficial votes because it would treat abstentions as a non-match with the legislative panel verdict. Thus, a candidate who ignores this unofficial voting process altogether would be guaranteed a rating of zero. In cases where legislative panels deadlock on more than five bills, it might be more appropriate to print no summary ratings on the ballot. Otherwise candidates' ratings might differ by 25 percent or more based on only one disagreement.

40. Miller and Krosnick 1998. Random ordering is better than the practice common in some areas, such as Salt Lake County, Utah. There, it is customary for a clerk to list first the candidates from the clerk's own party (see Associated Press Political Service, "Demos Object to Republicans Being Listed First," *Campaign News*, November 1, 1990).

41. There are pros and cons associated with using the jury pool. An ideal jury pool would be drawn from all residents, but courts have no such list. Registered voter lists would produce an acceptable pool, but it would be too exclusive to use a list of registered drivers, as is done in some states. The next problem is "leakage" out of the original jury pool. In New Jersey, for example, Kadane 1993 found that only 30 percent of those contacted initially became available to serve. In locales where jury pools are unrepresentative, it might be necessary to use paid random samples instead.

42. See Fred Bales, "Venerable Town Meeting Is Slowly Losing Its Voice," *USA Today*, April 14, 1998, 3A. Bales also reports that in towns with populations under 1,000, town meeting attendance is usually near 25 percent, but in towns with over 2,500 people, attendance goes as low as 5 percent.

43. David Broder has argued that cutting taxes has become a "driving passion—a good in itself" for the electorate, because voters "are more affluent than their nonvoting fellow citizens" ("Catatonic Politics," *Washington Post*, November 11, 1997). Antigovernment sentiment spans the population, however, as demonstrated by the widespread cynicism toward public officials documented in chapter 2.

44. Threlkeld 1998: 5–6.

CHAPTER 8. THE POLITICAL IMPACT OF CITIZEN PANELS

Epigraph: Delli Carpini and Keeter 1996: 289.

1. Even when citizens make flawed judgments, random chance should still make their votes "correct" half of the time on "yea" or "nay" policy issues and in two-candidate elections. The goal is to improve judgments above that 50 percent threshold.

2. A useful but expensive research project would examine the extent to which citizen panels produced varied judgments under similar information conditions. Such an experiment would be difficult because it would require several days of time from thousands of participants (e.g., 5 days × 30 panel members × 100 panels = 15,000 participant days). Moreover, the practical constraints of such research would limit group size, the depth of information exposure, the amount of deliberation, and the amount of external critique of preliminary arguments. The last of these processes would probably reduce considerably the amount of variation that would occur in citizen panels that began to diverge after the initial panel deliberation.

3. Tindale 1996: 16.

4. The establishment of a solid information base is the first function in Gouran and Hirokawa's 1996 functional theory of small group communication.

5. Hirokawa 1990 argues that when information is evenly distributed among group members, communication has little influence on decision making, and following this reasoning, one might question the need for deliberation after listening to witness testimony. The problem with that view is that the understanding, interpreting, and processing of that testimony will not be uniform across panelists, and panelists also have unique life histories that they can only share with one another through group discussion.

6. Hastie, Penrod, and Pennington 1983 found that in twelve-person mock juries, there were dramatic differences in participation rates. It was common for the most active speaker to take up as much as a quarter of the group's discussion time, whereas the quietest participant might say almost nothing. Studies commonly find that demographic and other individual-difference variables cause differences in speaking frequency and duration in small groups, and participation is, in turn, associated with group influence (Bonito and Hollingshead 1997). Baker 1988, for example, found that older and male participants spoke more often in small group discussions. It is important to have procedures in place to ensure adequate participation because the natural tendency is for extreme participation inequality to result from arbitrary social and psychological differences. See also Smith 1999: 43–44.

7. As explained in chapter 6, the ability to challenge statements is central to deliberation as envisioned by Jürgen Habermas (1979).

8. In a good summary of survey research, Krosnick 1999 identifies the three causes of superficial response ("satisficing") as issue complexity, low skill levels, and low motivation. As presented in chapter 7, the citizen panels not only give participants motivation, they also provide the information and brief training necessary to engage in political debate. In a similar sense, Petty and Cacioppo 1990 found that systematic cognitive processing of information requires a high level of "involvement."

9. Mathews 1994: 36.

10. Hare 1976: 24. To counter some readers' nightmarish memories of famous studies by Solomon Asch, a meta-analytic study by Rod Bond and Peter Smith indicates that the amount of conformity found in experiments using Asch's "line judgment task" has "steadily declined since Asch's studies in the early 1950's" (Bond and Smith 1996: 124).

11. On politics, see Barber 1984. On ambiguity and conformity, see Baron, Vandello, and Brunsman 1996; Bond and Smith 1996.

12. On the influence of a single dissension, see Hare 1976: 32. The reversals Hastie, Penrod, and Pennington 1983 observed usually resulted from a change in many jurors' interpretations of the judge's instructions or a wave of jurors changing their minds about a particular argument. Fishkin and Luskin 1999 and chapter 6 in this book give examples of such shifts in random sample forums.

13. Hastie, Penrod, and Pennington 1983: 230.

14. Janis 1982. Janis originally published *Victims of Groupthink* in 1972, but many readers are probably familiar with *Groupthink*, the expanded 1982 version of his book.

15. Janis 1982 recommends this procedure. Neck and Moorhead 1992 stresses the importance of even more methodical discussion procedures as a means of preventing groupthink, but I have decided against rigid, preset discussion procedures. If the moderator has general guidelines to promote a balanced, respectful, participatory, and on-schedule discussion, that should be sufficient to keep the discussion focused and deliberative. If the moderator's role extends too far beyond that, the potential for charges of moderator bias become too great.

16. See Park 1990; Evans and Dion 1991.

17. Sanders 1997 presents such a critique and relies primarily on evidence from juries. Peter Berkowitz also raises this concern about different skills at the "deliberative arts" ("The Debating Society," *New Republic,* November 25, 1996, 36–42).

18. The mere presence of a well-trained group facilitator can greatly improve group discussions and might even be warranted in jury trials (Anderson and Robertson 1985).

19. Eagly and Karau 1991. Though structuring discussion can reduce status effects on group behavior, it may be more difficult to create neutral *perceptions* of participants' behavior (Andrews 1992; Eagly, Makhijani, and Klonsky 1992). Mansbridge 1990b raises concerns about the interplay of gender roles and group deliberation. Will women be more attentive to men's concerns than vice versa? Will men speak more forcefully and dismiss women's speech as "emotional"? Once again, I think a well-designed discussion context can diminish the impact of gender roles in small group deliberation.

20. Mansbridge 1983 effectively contrasts the adversarial and unitary democratic traditions and suggests the need for a better balance. Barber 1984 also argues along these lines.

21. Edelman 1988 documents the "symbolic uses of politics" for both generating conflict and building consensus, but in an adversarial system, the tools of the trade are used most often in the service of oppositional politics.

22. On the media's role in obstructing deliberation and civic participation, see Entman 1989; Rosen and Taylor 1992; and Cappella and Jamieson 1997, which found that the bulk of news coverage of elections frames stories in terms of campaign strategy rather than substantive issues; readers and viewers "learned" more cynical perceptions from those strategic framings.

23. On the destructive nature of political discourse in the United States, see Barber 1984, 1998b; Gastil 1992; Mathews 1994; Pearce and Littlejohn 1997; and Tannen 1998. Ryfe 1998: 11 provides a review of the relevant literature and summarizes this concern concisely: "Social fragmentation challenges models of good public discourse in three ways. First, it suggests that isolated social groups will have fewer interests in common. . . . Second, levels of trust may be much weaker between groups that have little contact with one another. . . . Finally, social fragmentation exacerbates longstanding traditions of discrimination" and stereotyping.

24. Hart and Jarvis 1999: 81. Because it does not permit face-to-face discussion and some people maintain anonymity, conventional Internet discussions among citizens tend to be more adversarial. Nonetheless, in a study of political exchanges on computer bulletin boards, Thomas Benson found that even those "uncivil" discussions are valuable: "Amidst the name-calling, the flaming, and the ideological demonization common to both sides, there is a demonstrable faith of some sort in the power of argument and passionate advocacy" (Benson 1996: 374). In a more structured face-to-face setting, those underlying discourse norms become even more visible, and debate tends to be more productive because of the relative rarity of rudeness.

25. Writings on criminal and civil juries suggest that even divided juries normally develop some camaraderie, and jurors sometimes even become friends as

a result of their shared experience. See Hans and Vidmar 1986; Bennett and Feldman 1981. These same works also document cases of personal conflict among jurors, but the point is that juries *normally* develop a healthy level of cohesion.

26. The citizen conferences and citizen juries described in chapter 6 all reached such agreements on most critical points of discussion. See Crosby 1998 on the jury experience, and Gastil and Jenkins-Smith 1997 on the citizen conferences.

27. Hans and Vidmar 1986: 129.

28. League of Women Voters, "Charting the Health of American Democracy," June, 1997, available at http://www.lwv.org/report.html.

29. Newport 1996: 7.

30. The survey results were reported in Richard Morin, "Is Anyone Listening?" *Washington Post National Weekly Edition*, February 15, 1999, 34.

31. Hans 1993: 254–57.

32. Ibid.: 259. Valerie Hans also found that judges generally agree with jury verdicts and have great confidence in the jury process.

33. Crosby 1998.

34. Public opinion surveys, summarized by Hans 1993, have found that the public knows more about the role of juries than the court system in general. This is partly due to media coverage of juries, citizens' identification with jurors, and direct personal experience serving on juries. This suggests that the public might also readily learn about the panel process, and it might be able to extend jury-related concepts (e.g., a "hung jury") to the citizen panels.

35. In the long term, the impact of the panels would be self-reinforcing. "When citizens assume that speaking in public is a source of power, public speech magically can *become* a source of power," Nina Eliasoph (1998: 263) explains. At least with regard to the panels, this process is not magic: if voters respond to panel recommendations during elections, the panels will become a powerful political cue. The importance of favorable panel evaluations will increase in proportion to the willingness of voters' to incorporate panel judgments into their own voting decisions.

36. Hirschman 1970: 2.

37. See Lyons et al. 1993: ch. 3. These authors drew the concept of "neglect" from Farrell and Rusbult 1981 and Rusbult and Lowery 1985, which apply the exit, voice, and loyalty model to dissatisfaction among private and public employees. Rusbult 1987 has also extended this same revised model to the maintenance of close personal relationships. I do not discuss the four-response model developed by these authors because it changes the meaning of the term *loyalty*. In the original model, loyalty was a variable that influenced the selection of voice versus exit (e.g., Hirschman 1970: ch. 7, esp. fig. 1 on p. 87). For Lyons et al. and Rusbult, loyalty is one of four responses. They create a two dimensional table, with "active-passive" as the vertical axis and "constructive-destructive" as the horizontal axis: voice is active-constructive, exit is active-destructive, loyalty is passive-constructive, and neglect is passive-destructive. I find their notion of neglect useful, but I do not wish to treat loyalty as a response to decline instead of a force that promotes the use of voice versus exit.

38. University of Michigan data used by Ginsberg and Shefter 1990: 189–90 show that in the 1984 presidential election, 80 percent of eligible upper-middle-class adults reported voting, compared to only 70 percent of the lower middle class and 55 percent of the working class. As the authors acknowledge, survey data overestimate voter participation rates, but the overestimation should be rather evenly distributed across different social groups. Rosenstone and Hansen 1993 found similar results in analyzing voting trends from 1952 to 1988 broken down by income percentile. Only 39 percent of eligible voters 18–20 years old participated in the 1992 election, as compared to 70 percent of Americans 65 and older. Sixty-four percent of voting-age Anglos, 54 percent of African-Americans, and 29 percent of Hispanics participated (see League of Women Voters, "Charting the Health of American Democracy," June 1997, available at http://www.lwv.org/report.html). Differences in average external efficacy are taken from National Election Study data, available at http://www.umich.edu/~nes/nesguide/2ndtables/t5b_4_1.htm.

39. Entman 1989: 26–27. Bennett and Resnick 1990 illustrates some of the differences in the political opinions of voters and nonvoters.

40. Putnam 1995b: 664–65.

41. See, e.g., Bennett 1998 and *The Public Perspective* 7, 4 (June–July 1996).

42. Galston and Levine 1998: 36. Comparison of 1990 and 1994 surveys by Gallup and the Yankelovich Group show declines in public trust in everything from the local media to religious organizations. For a summary, see League of Women Voters, "Charting the Health of American Democracy" (June 1997), available at http://www.lwv.org/report.html.

43. On the positive effect of deliberation on public trust, see Rasinski, Bradburn, and Lauen 1999; Tom Smith 1999; Tyler, Rasinski, and Spodick 1985.

44. Levi 1996: 50 makes this point in a review of Putnam et al.1993, *Making Democracy Work: Civic Traditions in Modern Italy*. Sabetti 1996 goes even further, arguing that Putnam et al. 1993 underemphasizes the importance of government as a result of an oversimplification of Italian history.

45. Warren 1996b: 259–60. See also Warren 1996a. On an equally philosophical level, Weithman 1995 argues that deliberation can provide a strong justification for authority in a democracy.

46. The Pew Center conducted the study in association with the National Journal. "A Survey of Members of Congress, Clinton Appointees, and Senior Civil Servants" surveyed 81 members of Congress, 98 presidential appointees, and 151 members of the Senior Executive Service. Results can be found at http://www.people-press.org/leadrpt.htm.

47. Ibid. The public opinion survey mentioned was a 1998 Pew study, "Deconstructing Distrust: How Americans View Government."

48. This argument comes from David Broder, "Catatonic Politics," *Washington Post,* November 11, 1997.

49. According to the opinion ballots completed by NIF participants, typical forums have relatively few participants with low levels of formal education (Gastil 1994b).

50. Mark Warren argues that "a theory of democracy should be oriented toward creating institutional environments that encourage the self-examination of preferences that brings them closer to needs" (Warren 1992: 16). The panels may create such an environment by modeling self-criticism.

51. Warren 1992: 12. On the effects of NIF, see Gastil 1994b, Mathews 1994, and Pearce and Littlejohn 1997. On the role of mutuality in small group democracy, see Gastil 1993.

52. For example, Adam Simon (1997) does this in his study of candidate discourse during campaigns. Rational actor models are common, not only in economics, but also in political psychology and other social sciences. In reality, much behavior is "irrational," but altruistic irrationality is a rare commodity in many settings (Schwartz 1986). My purpose here is to demonstrate how the panels might compel even those "rational" candidates who seek only electoral success to behave in a way that promotes more deliberative elections.

53. This partially meets Jack Knight and James Johnson's call for deliberation to establish "common understandings of what is at stake in a given political conflict" (i.e., an election) after surviving "a process of reasoned debate sustained by fair procedures" (Knight and Johnson 1994: 289).

54. Simon 1997, a study focusing on the 1994 California gubernatorial race, suggests that most contemporary reform proposals would do little to increase clashes among candidates, noting that it is exceptional for candidates in U.S. elections even to discuss the same general issue, let alone to challenge one another directly.

55. The idea that panels invite different kinds of leaders comes from Bob Kraig, who suggests that the notion of a public process rewarding certain kinds of leaders and discouraging others resembles a notion found in the political philosophy of Woodrow Wilson (November 3, 1998, telephone interview).

56. Leah Ceccarelli first brought this concern to my attention, albeit without using such a monstrous metaphor.

57. This same argument could be applied to nonlegislative officials, and my argument against the view would be roughly the same. In the case of candidate-selection panels, there is still the chance that the particular unpopular action in question might not come up, and if it does, it might not prove decisive or the panel might even see it as a positive action.

58. Gastil 1994a.

59. Barber 1998a: 118.

CHAPTER 9. ELECTORAL EXPERIMENTATION

Epigraph: Dahl 1998: 187–88.

1. Pitkin 1967: 240.

2. Dahl 1998: 187–88. Lance Bennett observes that the most important and challenging question is: "How can communication technologies be adapted to the deliberation, interest formation, and decision-making requirements of societies that may be better positioned to experiment with direct democracy than any in modern history?" (Bennett 1998: 758).

3. Jim Dillard, my dissertation adviser, is a vocal proponent of this view.

4. For a summary of the Milgram experiments and their impact, see Miller, Collins, and Brief 1995. The participants in the original study were residents of New Haven, Connecticut. The results of Milgram's initial experiment were more dramatic than even he had expected.

5. As Kuhn 1970 points out, scientists should not be idealized. Normal scientific practice tends to resist fundamental change because scientists usually become committed to prevailing paradigms.

6. Weiser 1999: 33–35.

7. In 1971 Congress passed the Federal Election Campaign Act, which it significantly amended in 1974 and 1976. These laws set guidelines for public disclosure, public financing of campaigns, and contribution limits and prohibitions.

8. Barber 1995.

9. If willing to settle for a smaller majority, the panels could use a larger sample and a lower threshold for agreement. A larger sample would be required because the confidence interval around a panel of fifty participants is so large that only a two-thirds majority can be said to have identified a true majority (with only a one-in-twenty chance of being "wrong"). See chapter 7, note 30.

10. Priority panels should sometimes introduce new issues to the public agenda. If these panels simply select the issues that have received the most media attention, it would suggest either that the media's agenda accurately reflects the public's interests, or—more likely—that the priority panels are unable to recognize important issues not already on the media's agenda. On the importance of setting the public agenda in a strong democracy, see Barber 1984.

11. In chapter 3, I explain some of the reasons why elite views can unduly influence the opinions expressed in surveys, particularly on economic issues. Given this starting point, panelists' views be expected to move away from elite views more often than not.

12. Some panels will be able to achieve a two-thirds agreement, others will not. It is to be hoped that panels will not reach contradictory judgments. An extreme test could judge the sufficiency of the four-to-five-day panel format. Dahl 1989 recommends creating a "minipopulous"—a large, representative sample of citizens who deliberate periodically on an issue for a period of months using long-distance communication technology. If the four-to-five-day format gives participants sufficient time to discern the larger public interest, their judgments should not differ significantly from those of a minipopulous.

13. If these two effects are apparent, it should also be the case that voters understand and report using panel judgments when making voting decisions. I don't require this outcome, however, because voters may be reluctant to admit using panel ratings.

14. If panels were adopted simultaneously in all areas and at all levels of government, there could be no control group.

15. Richard Morin, "Is Anyone Listening?" *Washington Post National Weekly Edition*, February 15, 1999, 34. Morone 1990 points out that throughout the relatively brief history of the United States, the public has time and again supported political reforms, although it has not always liked the result.

16. Merelman 1998.

17. The statement is from the petition circulated in River Falls. For more on the forum that sparked the petition drive, see Crosby 1998.

18. Ned Crosby has begun just such an effort in Washington State. Crosby initially attempted to develop citizen forums focusing on candidates, but he has found support among political elites for referenda panels (personal communication, September 1999).

19. In 1995, a proposed bond of $28.9 million won 23 percent of the vote. In 1997, a proposed bond of $19 million won 47 percent of the vote. In 1998, a proposed bond of $18.8 million won 57 percent of the vote. It is impossible to know whether the jury's support was essential for the successful passage of the bond in 1998, but supporters did use the jury recommendations to bolster their campaign against a vigorous "No" effort headed by the Orono School District Citizens' Committee. Information on this case was provided by the Jefferson Center, which compiled the report "Citizens Jury on Orono Public Schools: 'Now and into the Future'" (May 1998). Doug Nethercut provided additional details in a telephone interview in September 1999.

References

Abramowitz, Alan I., and Kyle L. Saunders. 1998. "Ideological Realignment in the U.S. Electorate." *Journal of Politics* 60: 634–52.

Abramson, Jeffrey B., F. Christopher Arterton, and Gary R. Orren. 1988. *The Electronic Commonwealth: The Impact of New Media Technologies on Democratic Politics.* New York: Basic Books.

Adams, Bruce. 1995. "Building a New Political Environment." *Kettering Review,* Fall: 16–21.

Ajzen, Icek. 1991. "The Theory of Planned Behavior." *Organizational Behavior and Human Decision Processes* 50: 179–211.

Ajzen, Icek, and Fishbein, Martin. 1980. *Understanding Attitudes and Predicting Social Behavior.* Englewood Cliffs, N.J.: Prentice-Hall.

Alford, John R., and David W. Brady. 1993. "Personal and Partisan Advantage in U.S. Congressional Elections, 1846–1990." In *Congress Reconsidered,* ed. Lawrence C. Dodd and Bruce I. Oppenheimer, 5th ed., 141—57. Washington, D.C.: Congressional Quarterly Press.

Amy, Douglas J. 1993. *Real Choices / New Voices: The Case for Proportional Representation Elections in the United States.* New York: Columbia University Press.

Anderson, L. Frances, and Sharon E. Robertson. 1985. "Group Facilitation: Functions and Skills." *Small Group Behavior* 16: 139–56.

Andrews, Patricia H. 1992. "Sex and Gender Differences in Group Communication: Impact on the Facilitation Process." *Small Group Research* 23: 74–94.

Ansolabehere, Stephen, and Shanto Iyengar. 1996. "The Craft of Political Advertising: A Progress Report." In *Political Persuasion and Attitude Change,* ed. Diana C. Mutz, Paul M. Sniderman, and Richard A. Brody, 101–22. Ann Arbor: University of Michigan Press.

Ansolabehere, Stephen, Shanto Iyengar, Adam Simon, and Nicholas Valentino. 1997. "Does Attack Advertising Demobilize the Electorate?" In *Do the Media Govern? Politicians, Voters, and Reporters in America,* ed. Shanto Iyengar and Richard Reeves, 149–55. Thousand Oaks, Calif.: Sage.

Archie, Michelle L. 1986. "The Domestic Policy Association and Its National Issues Forums: A Venture in Reactivating Popular Sovereignty." MS. Kettering Foundation, Dayton, Ohio.

Arnold, R. Douglas. 1990. *The Logic of Congressional Action.* New Haven, Conn.: Yale University Press.

———. 1993. "Can Inattentive Citizens Control Their Elected Representatives?" In *Congress Reconsidered,* ed. Lawrence C. Dodd and Bruce I. Oppenheimer, 5th ed., 401–16. Washington, D.C.: Congressional Quarterly Press.

Arterton, F. Christopher. 1987. *Teledemocracy: Can Technology Protect Democracy?* Newbury Park, Calif.: Sage.

Bailey, Michael E. 1996. "Is Silence Golden?" Paper presented at the Annual Convention of the Midwest Political Science Association, Chicago.

Baker, Paul M. 1988. "Participation in Small Groups: Social, Physical, and Situational Predictors." *Small Group Behavior* 19: 3–18.

Bandura, Albert. 1977. "Self-Efficacy: Toward a Unifying Theory of Behavior Change." *Psychological Review* 84: 191–215.

———. 1986a. "The Explanatory and Predictive Scope of Self-Efficacy Theory." *Journal of Social and Clinical Psychology* 4: 359–373.

———. 1986b. *Social Foundations of Thought and Action: A Social Cognitive Theory.* New York: Prentice-Hall.

Barber, Benjamin R. 1984. *Strong Democracy: Participatory Politics for a New Age.* Berkeley and Los Angeles: University of California Press.

———. 1998a. *A Passion for Democracy: American Essays.* Princeton, N.J.: Princeton University Press.

———. 1998b. *A Place for Us: How to Make Society Civil and Democracy Strong.* New York: Hill & Wang.

Barber, Benjamin R., and Patrick Watson. 1988. *The Struggle for Democracy.* Boston: Little, Brown.

Barber, Kathleen L. 1995. *Proportional Representation and Election Reform in Ohio.* Columbus: Ohio State University Press.

Barlett, Donald L., and James B. Steele. 1992. *America: What Went Wrong?* Kansas City: Andrews & McMeel.

Baron, Robert S., Joseph A. Vandello, and Bethany Brunsman. 1996. Forgotten Variable in Conformity Research: Impact of Task Importance on Social Influence." *Journal of Personality and Social Psychology* 71: 915–27.

Barone, Michael, and Grant Ujifusa. 1998. *The Almanac of American Politics.* Washington, D.C.: National Journal.

Beaudry, Ann, and Bob Schaeffer. 1986. *Local and State Elections: The Guide to Organizing Your Campaign.* New York: Free Press.

Beker, Ted, and Christa Slaton. 1981. "Hawaii Televote: Measuring Public Opinion on Complex Policy Issues." *Political Science* 33: 52–65.

Bell, Daniel A. 1995. "Residential Community Associations: Community or Disunity?" *The Responsive Community* 5 (4): 25–36.

Bender, Keith A., and Peter J. Sloane. 1998. "Job Satisfaction, Trade Unions, and Exit Voice Revisited." *Industrial and Labor Relations Review* 51: 222–40.

Benjamin, Gerald, and Michael J. Malbin, eds. 1992. *Limiting Legislative Terms*. Washington, D.C.: Congressional Quarterly Press.

Bennett, Stephen E., and David Resnick. 1990. "The Implications of Nonvoting for Democracy in the American States." *American Journal of Political Science* 34: 771–802.

Bennett, W. Lance. 1993. "Constructing Publics and Their Opinions." *Political Communication* 10: 101–20.

———. 1994. *Inside the System: Culture, Institutions, and Power in American Politics*. Fort Worth, Texas: Harcourt Brace.

———. [1992] 1996. *The Governing Crisis: Media, Money, and Marketing in American Elections*. 2d ed. New York: St. Martin's Press.

———. 1998. "The Uncivic Culture: Communication, Identity, and the Rise of Lifestyle Politics." *PS: Political Science and Politics* 31: 741–61.

Bennett, W. Lance, and M. Feldman. 1981. *Reconstructing Reality in the Courtroom*. New Brunswick, N.J.: Rutgers University Press.

Benson, Thomas W. 1996. "Rhetoric, Civility, and Community: Political Debate on Computer Bulletin Boards." *Communication Quarterly* 44: 359–78.

Bernstein, Robert A. 1989. *Elections, Representation, and Congressional Voting Behavior: The Myth of Constituency Control*. Englewood Cliffs, N.J.: Prentice-Hall.

Bessette, Joseph M. 1994. *The Mild Voice of Reason*. Chicago: University of Chicago Press.

Bianco, William T. 1994. *Trust: Representatives and Constituents*. Ann Arbor: University of Michigan Press.

Blendon, Robert J., John M. Benson, Richard Morin, Drew E. Altman, Mollyann Brodie, Mario Brossard, and Matt James. 1997. "Changing Attitudes in America." In *Why People Don't Trust Government,* ed. Joseph S. Nye Jr., Philip D. Zelikow, and David C. King, 205–16. Cambridge, Mass.: Harvard University Press.

Blumer, Jay G., and Michael Gurevitch. 1995. *The Crisis of Public Communication*. London: Routledge.

Bobbio, Norberto. 1987. *The Future of Democracy: A Defence of the Rules of the Game*. Translated by Roger Griffin. Minneapolis: University of Minnesota Press.

Bode, Carl. 1956. *The American Lyceum: Town Meeting of the Mind*. New York: Oxford University Press.

Bohman, James, and William Rehg, eds. 1997. *Deliberative Democracy: Essays on Reason and Politics*. Cambridge, Mass.: MIT Press.

Bond, Rod, and Peter B. Smith. 1996. "Culture and Conformity: A Meta-Analysis of Studies Using Asch's (1952b, 1956) Line Judgment Task." *Psychological Bulletin* 119: 111–37.

Bonito, Joseph A., and Andrea B. Hollingshead. 1997. "Participation in Small Groups." In Brant R. Burleson, ed., *Communication Yearbook 20* (pp. 227–61). Newbury Park, Calif.: Sage.

Bormann, Ernest G. 1996. "Symbolic Convergence Theory and Communication in Group Decision Making." In *Communication and Group Decision-Making,* ed. Randy Y. Hirokawa and Marshall Scott Poole, 81–113. Thousand Oaks, Calif.: Sage.

Bowles, Samuel, and Herbert Gintis. 1987. *Democracy and Capitalism.* New York: Basic Books.

Boyte, Harry C. 1989. *Commonwealth: A Return to Citizen Politics.* New York: Free Press.

Bradburn, Norman M. 1996. "How NORC Selected the Deliberative Poll's Respondents." *Public Perspective* 7, 3: 9–11.

Brehm, John. 1993. *The Phantom Respondents: Opinion Surveys and Political Representation.* Ann Arbor: University of Michigan Press.

Briand, Michael K. 1999. *Practical Politics: Five Principles for a Community That Works.*Urbana: University of Illinois Press.

Brockington, David, Todd Donovan, Shaun Bowler, and Robert Brischetto. 1988. "Minority Representation under Cumulative and Limited Voting." *Journal of Politics* 60: 1108–1125.

Brown, Ron, and Nello Giorgetti. 1992. "Downballot Doldrums: It's Hard to Run for an Office That Voters Don't Know Exists." *Campaigns and Elections* 13 (1): 50–51.

Browning, Graeme. 1996. *Electronic Democracy: Using the Internet to Influence American Politics.* Wilton, Conn.: Pemberton Press.

Bryan, Frank, and John McClaughry. 1989. *The Vermont Papers: Recreating Democracy on a Human Scale.* Chelsea, Vt.: Chelsea Green.

Budesheim, Thomas Lee, David A. Houston, and Stephen J. DePaola. 1996. "Persuasiveness of In-Group and Out-Group Political Messages: The Case of Negative Political Campaigning." *Journal of Personality and Social Psychology* 70: 523–34.

Burgoon, Judee K., and Jerold L. Hale. 1984. "The Fundamental Topoi of Relational Communication." *Communication Monographs* 51: 193–214.

Burleson, Brant R., Barbara J. Levine, and Wendy Samter. 1984. "Decision-Making Procedure and Decision Quality." *Human Communication Research* 10: 557–74.

Burnheim, John. 1985. *Is Democracy Possible? The Alternative to Electoral Politics.* Berkeley and Los Angeles: University of California Press.

Burns, James M., J. W. Peltason, Thomas E. Cronin, and David B. Magleby. 1996. *State and Local Politics: Government by the People.* Upper Saddle River, N.J.: Prentice-Hall.

Burton, Mark, and Kevin Mattson. 1999. "Deliberative Democracy in Practice: Challenges and Prospects for Civic Deliberation." *Polity* 31: 609–37.

Cain, Bruce, John Ferejohn, and Morris Fiorina. 1987. *The Personal Vote: Constituency Service and Electoral Independence.* Cambridge, Mass.: Harvard University Press.

Campbell, Angus, Philip E. Converse, Warren E. Miller, and Donald E. Stokes. 1960. *The American Voter.* New York: John Wiley & Sons.

Cappella, Joseph N., and Kathleen Hall Jamieson. 1997. *Spiral of Cynicism: The Press and the Public Good.* Oxford: Oxford University Press.

Chaffee, Steven H., and Rajiv Nath Rimal. 1996. "Time of Vote Decision and Openness to Persuasion." In *Political Persuasion and Attitude Change,* ed. Diana C. Mutz, Paul M. Sniderman, and Richard A. Brody, 267–91. Ann Arbor: University of Michigan Press.

Champagne, Anthony, and Greg Thielemann. 1991. "Awareness of Trial Court Judges." *Judicature* 74: 271–76.

Checkoway, B. 1981. "The Politics of Public Hearings." *Journal of Applied Behavioral Science* 17: 566–82.

Cohen, Joshua. 1989. "Deliberation and Democratic Legitimacy." In *The Good Polity,* ed. Alan Hamlin and Philip Pettit, 17–34. New York: Basil Blackwell.

Conover, Pamela Johnston, and Stanley Feldman. 1984. "How People Organize the Political World: A Schematic Model." *American Journal of Political Science* 28: 95–127.

Converse, Philip E. 1964. "The Nature of Belief Systems in Mass Publics." In *Ideology and Discontent,* ed. David E. Apter, 206–61. New York: Free Press.

Craig, Stephen C., Richard G. Niemi, and Glenn E. Silver. 1990. "Political Efficacy and Trust: A Report on the NES Pilot Study Items." *Political Behavior* 12: 289–314.

Crimmins, James. 1995. *The American Promise: Adventures in Grass-Roots Democracy.* San Francisco: KQED Books.

Cronin, Thomas E. 1989. *Direct Democracy: The Politics of Initiative, Referendum, and Recall.* Cambridge, Mass.: Harvard University Press.

Crosby, Ned. 1995. "Citizen Juries: One Solution for Difficult Environmental Questions." In *Fairness and Competence in Citizen Participation: Evaluating Models for Environmental Discourse,* ed. Ortwin Renn, Thomas Webler, and Peter Wiedemann, 157–74. Boston: Kluwer Academic.

———. 1998. "Citizens Election Forum: A Proposal for Electoral Reform." MS.

Dahl, Robert A. 1961. *Who Governs?* New Haven, Conn.: Yale University Press.

———. 1989. *Democracy and Its Critics.* New Haven, Conn.: Yale University Press.

———. 1991. "A Rejoinder." *Journal of Politics* 53: 226–31.

———. 1996. "Reflections on *A Preface to Democratic Theory.*" *Government and Opposition* 31: 292–301.

———. 1998. *On Democracy.* New Haven, Conn.: Yale University Press.

Davies, Martin F. 1994. "Physical Situation." In *Small Group Research: A Handbook,* ed. A. Paul Hare, Herbert H. Blumberg, Martin F. Davies, and M. Valerie Kent, 11–40. Norwood, N.J.: Ablex.

Davis, James A. 1961. *Great Books and Small Groups.* New York: Free Press of Glencoe.

Davis, James H., Lorne Hulbert, and Wing Tung Au. 1996. "Procedural Influence on Group Decision Making: The Case of Straw Polls—Observation and Simulation." In *Communication and Group Decision-Making,* ed. Randy Y. Hirokawa and Marshall Scott Poole, 55–80. Thousand Oaks, Calif.: Sage.

DeLeon, Peter. 1997. *Democracy and the Policy Sciences.* Albany, N.Y.: SUNY Press.

Delli Carpini, Michael, and Scott Keeter. 1996. *What Americans Know about Politics and Why It Matters.* New Haven, Conn.: Yale University Press.

Delli Carpini, Michael X., and Bruce A. Williams. 1994. "Methods, Metaphors, and Media Research: The Uses of Television in Political Conversation." *Communication Research* 21: 782–812.

Diamond, Gregory A., and Michael D. Cobb. 1996. "The Candidates as Catastrophe: Latitude Theory and the Problems of Political Persuasion." In *Political Persuasion and Attitude Change,* ed. Diana C. Mutz, Paul M. Sniderman, and Richard A. Brody, 225–47. Ann Arbor: University of Michigan Press.

Dienel, Peter. 1995. "Planning Cells: A Gate to 'Fractal' Mediation." In *Fairness and Competence in Citizen Participation,* ed. Ortwin Renn, Thomas Webler, and Peter Wiedmann, 117–40. Boston: Kluwer Academic.

Dionne, E. J. 1991. *Why Americans Hate Politics.* New York: Simon & Schuster.

———, ed. 1998. *Community Works: The Revival of Civil Society in America.* Washington, D.C.: Brookings Institution.

Disch, Lisa. 1996. "Publicity-Stunt Participation and Sound Bite Polemics: The Health Care Debate, 1993–94." *Journal of Health Politics, Policy, and Law* 21: 3–33.

Doble, John, and A. Richardson. 1991. *A Report on the 1990–1991 NIF Research Forums Results.* New York: Public Agenda Foundation.

Dodd, Lawrence C., and Bruce I. Oppenheimer, eds. 1993. *Congress Reconsidered.* 5th ed. Washington, D.C. : Congressional Quarterly Press. See also 6th ed., 1997.

Downing, Kim. 1996. *National Issues Forums Network Study.* Dayton, Ohio: National Issues Forums Institute.

Dubois, Philip L. 1984. "Voting Cues in Nonpartisan Trial Court Elections: A Multivariate Assessment." *Law and Society Review* 18: 395–436.

Dubois, Philip L., Floyd Feeney, and Edmond Costantini. 1991. "The California Ballot Pamphlet: A Survey of Voters." Preliminary report prepared for the Office of the Secretary of State, California. University of California, Davis.

Eagly, Alice H., Mona G. Makhijani, Bruce G. Klonsky. 1992. "Gender and the Evaluation of Leaders: A Meta-Analysis." *Psychological Bulletin* 111: 3–22.

Eagly, Alice H., and Steven J. Karau. 1991. "Gender and the Emergence of Leaders: A Meta-Analysis." *Journal of Personality and Social Psychology* 60: 685–710.

Edelman, Murray. 1988. *Constructing the Political Spectacle.* Chicago: University of Chicago Press.

Eliasoph, Nina. 1998. *Avoiding Politics: How Americans Produce Apathy in Everyday Life.* Cambridge: Cambridge University Press.

Elster, Jon, ed. 1998. *Deliberative Democracy.* Cambridge: Cambridge University Press.

Emigh, Phyllis, ed. 1991. *Focus on Study Circles.* Pomfret, Conn.: Study Circles Resource Center.

Engstrom, Richard L. and Charles J. Barrilleaux. 1991. "Native Americans and Cumulative Voting: The Sisseton-Wahpeton Sioux." *Social Science Quarterly* 72: 388–93.

Engstrom, Richard L., and Victoria M. Caridas. 1991. "Voting for Judges: Race and Roll-Off in Judicial Elections." In *Political Participation and American Democracy,* ed. William Croty, 171–91. New York: Greenwood Press.

Entman, Robert M. 1989. *Democracy without Citizens: Media and the Decay of American Politics.* New York: Oxford University Press.

Erdman, Sol, and Susskind, Lawrence. 1995. *Reinventing Congress for the Twenty-First Century: Beyond Local Representation and the Politics of Exclusion.* New York: Frontier Press.

———. 1996. *Reinventing Congress for the Twenty-First Century: Toward a Politics of Accountability, Participation and Consensus.* Cambridge, Mass.: MIT–Harvard Public Disputes Program.

Erikson, Robert S., and Gerald C. Wright. 1993. "Voters, Candidates, and Issues in Congressional Elections." In *Congress Reconsidered,* ed. Lawrence C. and Bruce I. Oppenheimer, 5th ed., 91–114. Washington, D.C.: Congressional Quarterly Press.

Erikson, Robert S., Gerald C. Wright, and John P. McIver. 1993. *Statehouse Democracy: Public Opinion and Policy in the American States.* New York: Cambridge University Press.

Erikson, Robert S., and Thomas R. Palfrey. 1998. "Campaign Spending and Incumbency: An Alternative Simultaneous Equations Approach." *Journal of Politics* 60: 355–73.

Esquith, Stephen L. and Richard T. Peterson. 1988. "The Original Position as Social Practice." *Political Theory* 16: 300–334.

Evans, Charles R., and Kenneth L. Dion. 1991. "Group Cohesion and Performance: A Meta-Analysis." *Small Group Research* 22: 175–86.

Evans, Sara M., and Harry C. Boyte. 1992. *Free Spaces: The Sources of Democratic Change in America.* Chicago: University of Chicago Press.

Farkas, Steve, Will Friedman, and Ali Bers. 1995. *The Public's Capacity for Deliberation.* New York: Public Agenda.

Farrell, Daniel L., and Rusbult, Caryl E. 1981. "Exchange Variables as Predictors of Job Satisfaction, Job Commitment, and Turnover: The Impact of Rewards, Costs, Alternatives, and Investments." *Organizational Behavior and Human Performance* 27: 78–95.

Fenno, Richard F. 1978. *Home Style: House Members in Their Districts.* Boston: Little, Brown.

Finkel, S. E., Muller, E. N., and Opp, K.-D. (1989). "Personal Influence, Collective Rationality, and Mass Political Action." *American Political Science Review* 83: 885–903.

Fiorina, Morris P. 1981. *Retrospective Voting in American National Elections.* New Haven, Conn.: Yale University Press.

Fiorino, Daniel. 1995. "Regulatory Negotiation as a Form of Public Participation." In *Fairness and Competence in Citizen Participation,* ed. Ortwin Renn, Thomas Webler, and Peter Wiedmann, 17–33. Boston: Kluwer Academic.

Fishkin, James S. 1991. *Democracy and Deliberation: New Directions for Democratic Reform.* New Haven, Conn.: Yale University Press.

———. 1995. *The Voice of the People.* New Haven, Conn.: Yale University Press.

Fishkin, James S., and Luskin, Robert C. 1999. "Bringing Deliberation to the Democratic Dialogue: The NIC and Beyond." In *A Poll with a Human Face: The National Issues Convention Experiment in Political Communication,* ed. Maxwell McCombs and Amy Reynolds, 3–38. New York: Erlbaum.

Flavin, Catherine, and Regina Dougherty. 1996. "Science and Citizenship at the NIC." *Public Perspective* 7, 3: 46–49.

Franken, Al. 1996. *Rush Limbaugh Is a Big Fat Idiot and Other Observations.* New York: Delacorte Press.

Freie, John F. 1997. "The Effects of Campaign Participation on Political Attitudes." *Political Behavior* 19: 133–56.

Galston, William A., and Peter Levine. 1998. "America's Civic Condition: A Glance at the Evidence." In *Community Works: The Revival of Civil Society in America,* ed. E. J. Dionne, 30–36. Washington, D.C.: Brookings Institution.

Gastil, John. 1992. "Undemocratic Discourse: A Review of Theory and Research on Political Discourse." *Discourse and Society* 4: 469–500.

———. 1993. *Democracy in Small Groups: Participation, Decision Making, and Communication.* Philadelphia: New Society Publishers.

———. 1994a. "A Definition and Illustration of Democratic Leadership." *Human Relations* 47: 953–75.

———. 1994b. "Democratic Citizenship and the National Issues Forums." Ph.D. diss., University of Wisconsin, Madison.

———. 1996. *Deliberation at the National Issues Convention.* Albuquerque, N.M.: Institute for Public Policy.

———. 1998. "Clueless but Not Cueless: The Influence of Candidate Ethnicity and Sex on Low-Information Voting Choices in Partisan Elections." MS. University of Washington, Seattle.

Gastil, John, and Gina Adam. 1995. *Understanding Public Deliberation.* Albuquerque, N.M.: Institute for Public Policy.

Gastil, John, and Hank Jenkins-Smith. 1997. *Public Views on Transportation: The Results of the Six New Mexico Citizen Conferences on Transportation.* Albuquerque, N.M.: Institute for Public Policy.

———. 1998. *The Attitudes and Beliefs of Los Alamos National Laboratory Employees and Northern New Mexicans: A Study of the Interplay of Culture, Ideology, Political Awareness, and Public Deliberation.* Albuquerque, N.M.: Institute for Public Policy.

Gastil, John, and James P. Dillard. 1999a. "The Aims, Methods, and Effects of Deliberative Civic Education through the National Issues Forums." *Communication Education* 48: 179–82.

———. 1999b. "Increasing Political Sophistication through Public Deliberation." *Political Communication* 16: 3–23.

Gerber, Alan. 1998. "Estimating the Effect of Campaign Spending on Senate Election Outcomes Using Instrumental Variables." *American Political Science Review* 92: 401–411.

Giddens, Anthony. 1984. *The Constitution of Society: Outline of the Theory of Structuration.* Berkeley and Los Angeles: University of California Press.

Gill, Alison M. 1996. "Rooms with a View: Informal Settings for Public Dialogue." *Society and Natural Resources* 9: 633–43.

Ginsberg, Benjamin, and Martin Shefter. 1990. *Politics by Other Means: The Declining Importance of Elections in America.* New York: Basic Books.

Ginsberg, Benjamin. 1986. *The Captive Public: How Mass Opinion Promotes State Power.* New York: Basic Books.

Gould, J. E. 1961. *The Chautauqua Movement.* New York: State University of New York.

Gouran, Dennis S., and Randy Y. Hirokawa. 1996. "Functional Theory and Communication in Decision-Making and Problem-Solving Groups: An Expanded View." In *Communication and Group Decision-Making,* ed. Randy Y. Hirokawa and Marshall Scott Poole, 55–80. Thousand Oaks, Calif.: Sage.

Green, Donald P., and Bradley Palmquist. 1994. "How Stable Is Party Identification?" *Political Behavior* 16: 437–466.

Grey, Lawrence. 1994. *How to Win a Local Election: A Complete Step-by-Step Guide.* New York: M. Evans.

Guinier, Lani. 1994. *The Tyranny of the Majority: Fundamental Fairness in Representative Democracy.* New York: Free Press.

Gutmann, Amy, and Dennis Thompson. 1996. *Democracy and Disagreement.* Cambridge, Mass.: Harvard University Press, Belknap Press.

Habermas, Jürgen. 1979. *Communication and the Evolution of Society.* Translated by T. A. McCarthy. Boston: Beacon Press.

Hamilton, Alexander, James Madison, and John Jay. [1788] 1948. *The Federalist.* Baltimore: Johns Hopkins Press.

Hans, Valerie P. 1993. "Attitudes toward the Civil Jury: A Crisis of Confidence?" In *Verdict: Assessing the Civil Jury System,* ed. Robert E. Litan, 248–81. Washington, D.C.: Brookings Institution.

Hans, Valerie P., and Neil Vidmar. 1986. *Judging the Jury.* New York: Plenum Press.

Hare, A. Paul. 1976. *Handbook of Small Group Research.* New York: Free Press.

Hart, Roderick P., and Sharon E. Jarvis. 1999. "We the People: The Contours of Lay Political Discourse." In *A Poll with a Human Face: The National Issues Convention Experiment in Political Communication,* ed. Maxwell McCombs and Amy Reynolds, 59–84. New York: Erlbaum.

Hastie, Reid, Steven D. Penrod, and Nancy Pennington. 1983. *Inside the Jury.* Cambridge, Mass.: Harvard University Press.

Hauptmann, Emily A. 1996. *Putting Choice before Democracy: A Critique of Rational Choice Theory.* Albany, N.Y.: SUNY Press.

Hawley, Willis D. 1973. *Nonpartisan Elections and the Case for Party Politics.* New York: John Wiley & Sons.

Heclo, Hugh. 1999. "Hyperdemocracy." *Wilson Quarterly* 23 (Winter): 62–71.

Held, David. 1987. *Models of Democracy.* Stanford, Calif.: Stanford University Press.

Helliwell, John F., and Robert D. Putnam. 1996. "Correction." *PS: Political Science and Politics* 29: 138.

Herbst, Susan. 1993. *How Opinion Polling Has Shaped American Politics.* Chicago: University of Chicago Press.

Herman, Edward S., and Noam Chomsky. 1988. *Manufacturing Consent: The Political Economy of the Mass Media.* New York: Pantheon Books.

Herrera, Cheryl Lyn, Richard Herrera, and Eric R. A. N. Smith. 1992. "Public Opinion and Congressional Representation." *Public Opinion Quarterly* 56: 185–205.

Hetherington, Marc J. 1998. "The Political Relevance of Political Trust." *American Political Science Review* 92: 791–808.

———. 1999. "The Effect of Political Trust on the Presidential Vote, 1968–1996." *American Political Science Review* 93: 311–26.

Hibbing, John R. 1993. "Careerism in Congress: For Better or for Worse?" In *Congress Reconsidered,* ed. Lawrence C. Dodd and Bruce I. Oppenheimer, 5th ed., 67–88. Washington, D.C.: Congressional Quarterly Press.

Hibbing, John R., and Elizabeth Theiss-Morse. 1995. *Congress as Public Enemy: Public Attitudes toward American Political Institutions.* Cambridge: Cambridge University Press.

Higgins, Damon. 1998. "Revised Birmingham Story." Memorandum, Doble Research Associates, September 15.

Hill, Kim Q., Jan E. Leighley, and Angela Hinton-Andersson. 1995. "Lower-Class Mobilization and Policy Linkage in the U.S. States." *American Journal of Political Science* 39: 75–86.

Hirokawa, Randy Y. 1990. "The Role of Communication in Group Decision-Making Efficacy: A Task-Contingency Perspective." *Small Group Research* 21: 190–204.

Hirokawa, Randy Y., Larry Erbert, and Anthony Hurst. 1996. "Communication and Group Decision-Making Effectiveness." In *Communication and Group Decision-Making,* ed. Randy Y. Hirokawa and Marshall Scott Poole, 55–80. Thousand Oaks, Calif.: Sage.

Hirschman, Albert O. 1970. *Exit, Voice, and Loyalty.* Cambridge, Mass.: Harvard University Press.

———. 1993. "Exit, Voice, and the Fate of the German Democratic Republic: An Essay in Conceptual History." *World Politics* 45: 173–202.

Hofstetter, C. Richard, Mark C. Donovan, Melville R. Klauber, Alexandra Cole, Carolyn J. Huie, and Toshiyuki Yuasa. 1994. "Political Talk Radio: A Stereotype Reconsidered." *Political Research Quarterly* 47: 467–79.

Huckfeldt, Robert, and John Sprague. 1995. *Citizens, Politics, and Social Communication: Information and Influence in an Election Campaign.* Cambridge: Cambridge University Press.

Hurley, Patricia A. 1994. Review of *The Nature and Origins of Mass Opinion,* by John R. Zaller. *Journal of Politics* 56: 528–31.

Inglehart, Ronald. 1997. *Modernization and Postmodernization: Cultural, Economic, and Political Change in Forty-three Societies.* Princeton, N.J.: Princeton University Press.

Jackman, Robert W., and Ross A. Miller. 1996. "A Renaissance of Political Culture?" *American Journal of Political Science* 40: 632–59.

Jackson, Robert A., Robert D. Brown, and Gerald C. Wright. 1998. "Registration, Turnout, and the Electoral Representativeness of U.S. State Elections." *American Politics Quarterly* 26: 259–87.

Jacobson, Gary C. 1993. "The Misallocation of Resources in House Cam-
paigns." In *Congress Reconsidered,* ed. Lawrence C. Dodd and Bruce I.
Openheimer, 5th ed., 115–39. Washington, D.C.: Congressional Quarterly
Press.

———. [1983] 1997. *The Politics of Congressional Elections.* 4th ed. New
York: Longman.

Jacobson, Gary C., and Samuel Kernell. 1981. *Strategy and Choice in Congressional Elections.* New Haven, Conn.: Yale University Press.

Jacoby, William G. 1991. "Ideological Identification and Issue Attitudes."
American Journal of Political Science 35: 178–205.

———. 1995. "The Structure of Ideological Thinking in the American Electorate." *American Journal of Political Science* 39: 314–35.

Jamieson, Kathleen Hall. 1992. *Dirty Politics: Deception, Distraction, and Democracy.* New York: Oxford University Press.

Janis, Irving L. [1972] 1982. *Groupthink: Psychological Studies of Policy Decision and Fiascoes.* 2d ed. Boston: Houghton Mifflin.

Jennings, M. Kent, and Richard G. Niemi. 1981. *Generations and Politics: A
Panel Study of Young Adults and Their Parents.* Princeton, N.J.: Princeton
University Press.

Junn, Jane. 1991. "Participation and Political Knowledge." In *Political Participation and American Democracy,* ed. William Croty, 193–212. New York:
Greenwood Press.

Kadane, Joseph B. 1993. "Sausages and the Law: Juror Decisions in the Much
Larger Justice System." In *Inside the Juror: The Psychology of Juror Decision
Making,* ed. Reid Hastie, 229–34. Cambridge: Cambridge University Press.

Kamber, Victor. 1995. *Giving Up on Democracy: Why Term Limits Are Bad for
America.* Washington, D.C.: Regnery.

Kato, Junko. 1998. "When the Party Breaks Up: Exit and Voice among Japanese Legislators." *American Political Science Review* 92: 857–70.

Katz, Elihu, and Paul F. Lazarsfeld. 1955. *Personal Influence: The Part Played
by People in the Flow of Mass Communications.* Glencoe, Ill.: Free Press.

Kay, Alan F. 1998. *Locating Consensus for Democracy: A Ten-Year U.S. Experiment.* Saint Augustine, Fla.: Americans Talk Issues Foundation.

Keith, Bruce E., David B. Magleby, Candice J. Nelson, Elizabeth Orr, Mark C.
Westlye, and Raymond E. Wolfinger. 1992. *The Myth of the Independent
Voter.* Berkeley and Los Angeles: University of California Press.

Kemmis, Daniel. 1990. *Community and the Politics of Place.* Norman: University of Oklahoma Press.

Kenny, Christopher. 1998. "The Behavioral Consequences of Political Discussion: Another Look at Discussant Effects on Vote Choice." *Journal of Politics* 60: 231–44.

Kettering Foundation. 1989. *The Public's Role in the Policy Process: A View
from State and Local Policymakers.* Dayton, Ohio: Kettering Foundation.

King, David C. 1997. "Fall from Grace: The Public's Loss of Faith in Government." In *Why People Don't Trust Government,* ed. Joseph S. Nye Jr., Philip
D. Zelikow, and David C. King, 155–78. Cambridge, Mass.: Harvard University Press.

Knight, Jack, and James Johnson. 1994. "Aggregation and Deliberation: On the Possiblity of Democratic Legitimacy." *Political Theory* 22: 277–96.

———. 1999. "Inquiry into Democracy: What Might a Pragmatist Make of Rational Choice Theories?" *American Journal of Political Science* 43: 566–89.

Knoke, David. 1990. "Networks of Political Action: Toward Theory Construction." *Social Forces* 68: 1041–63.

Krebs, Timothy B. 1998. "The Determinants of Candidates' Vote Share and the Advantages of Incumbency in City Council Elections." *American Journal of Political Science* 42: 921–35.

Krosnick, Jon A. 1990. "Lessons Learned: A Review and Integration of Our Findings." *Social Cognition* 8: 154–58.

———. 1999. "Survey Research." *Annual Review of Psychology* 50: 537–67.

Kuhn, Thomas. 1970. *The Structure of Scientific Revolutions*. Chicago: University of Chicago Press.

Kuklinski, James H., and Norman L. Hurley. 1996. "It's a Matter of Interpretation." In *Political Persuasion and Attitude Change,* ed. Diana C. Mutz, Paul M. Sniderman, and Richard A. Brody, 125–44. Ann Arbor: University of Michigan Press.

Ladd, C. Everett. 1996. "The Data Just Don't Show Erosion of America's 'Social Capital.' " *Public Perspective* 7, 4: 1, 5–6.

Lappe, Frances Moore, and Paul Martin DuBois. 1994. *The Quickening of America: Rebuilding Our Nation, Remaking Our Lives*. San Francisco: Jossey-Bass.

Lee, Eugene C. 1960. *The Politics of Nonpartisanship: A Study of California City Elections*. Berkeley and Los Angeles: University of California Press.

Lehman-Wilzig, Sam N. 1991. "Loyalty, Voice, and Quasi-Exit: Israel as a Case Study of Proliferating Alternative Politics." *Comparative Politics* 24: 97–109.

Leighninger, Matt, and Martha McCoy. 1998. "Mobilizing Citizens: Study Circles Offer a New Approach to Citizenship." *National Civic Review* 87, 2: 183–89.

Lewis, Charles, and the Center for Public Integrity. 1998. *The Buying of Congress: How Special Interests Have Stolen Your Right to Life, Liberty, and the Pursuit of Happiness*. New York: Avon Books.

Levi, Margaret. 1996. "Social and Unsocial Capital: A Review Essay of Robert Putnam's *Making Democracy Work*." *Politics and Society* 24: 45–55.

Loyacano, Marjorie E., ed. (1992). *National Issues Forums Literacy Program: Linking Literacy and Citizenship, 1988–1991*. Dayton, Ohio: Kettering Foundation.

Lull, James, and Joseph Cappella. 1981. "Slicing the Attitude Pie: A New Approach to Attitude Measurement." *Communication Quarterly* 29: 67–80.

Lupia, Arthur. 1994. "Shortcuts versus Encyclopedias: Information and Voting Behavior in California Insurance Reform Elections." *American Political Science Review* 88: 63–76.

Lupia, Arthur, and Mathew D. McCubbins. 1998. *The Democratic Dilemma: Can Citizens Learn What They Need to Know?* Cambridge: Cambridge University Press.

Luskin, Robert C. 1990. "Explaining Political Sophistication." *Political Behavior* 12: 331–61.

Luskin, Robert C., James S. Fishkin, and Roger Jowell. 1997. "Considered Opinions: Deliberative Polling in the U.K." MS. University of Texas at Austin.

Lyons, W. E., David Lowery, and Ruth DeHoog. 1993. *The Politics of Dissatisfaction: Citizens, Services, and Urban Institutions.* Armonk, N.Y.: M. E. Sharpe.

MacDonald, Gus. 1986. "Election 500." In *Political Communications: The General Election Campaign of 1983,* ed. Ivor Crewe and Martin Harrop, 125–34. Cambridge: Cambridge University Press.

MacKuen, Michael. 1990. "Speaking of Politics: Individual Conversational Choice, Public Opinion, and the Prospects for Deliberative Democracy." In *Information and Democratic Processes,* ed. John A. Ferejohn and James H. Kuklinski, 59–99. Urbana: University of Illinois Press.

MacKuen, Michael, and Courtney Brown. 1987. "Political Context and Attitude Change." *American Political Science Review* 81: 471–90.

Macoubrie, Jane. 1998. "Decision Logics in Juries." Ph.D. diss, University of Washington, Seattle.

Magleby, David B. 1984. *Direct Legislation: Voting on Ballot Propositions in the United States.* Baltimore: Johns Hopkins University Press.

Mahtesian, Charles. 1997. "The Politics of Incivility." *Governing Magazine* 10, 9 (June): 18–22.

Makinson, Larry. 1994. *Follow the Money Handbook.* Washington, D.C.: Center for Responsive Politics.

Mansbridge, Jane J. 1983. *Beyond Adversary Democracy.* Chicago: University of Chicago Press.

———, ed. 1990. *Beyond Self-Interest.* Chicago: University of Chicago Press.

———. 1990. "Feminism and Democracy." *American Prospect* 1, 2: 126–39.

———. 1992. "A Deliberative Perspective on Neocorporatism." *Politics and Society* 20: 493–505.

———. 1996. "Reconstructing Democracy." In *Revisioning the Political: Feminist Reconstructions of Traditional Concepts in Western Political Theory,* ed. Nancy J. Hirschmann and Christine Di Stefano, 117–38. Boulder, Colo.: Westview Press.

March, James G., and Johan P. Olsen. 1995. *Democratic Governance.* New York: Free Press.

Mathews, David. 1994. *Politics for People: Finding a Responsible Public Voice.* Urbana: University of Illinois Press. 2d ed. 1999.

Mattson, Kevin. 1998. *Creating a Democratic Public: The Struggle for Urban Participatory Democracy During the Progressive Era.* University Park: Pennsylvania State University Press.

McAfee, Noelle, Robert McKenzie, and David Mathews. 1990. *Hard Choices.* Dayton, Ohio: Kettering Foundation.

McCombs, Maxwell, and Amy Reynolds, eds. 1999. *A Poll with a Human Face: The National Issues Convention Experiment in Political Communication.* New York: Erlbaum.

McDermott, Monika L. 1997. "Voting Cues in Low-Information Elections: Candidate Gender as a Social Information Variable in Contemporary United States Elections." *American Journal of Political Science* 41: 270–83.

McLeod, Jack M., Dietram A. Scheufele, and Patricia Moy. 1999. "Community, Communication, and Participation: The Role of Mass Media and Interpersonal Discussion in Local Political Participation." *Political Communication* 16: 315–36.

Merelman, Richard M. 1998. "On Legitimalaise in the United States: A Weberian Analysis." *Sociological Quarterly* 39: 351–68.

Merkle, Daniel M. 1996. "The National Issues Convention Deliberative Poll." *Public Opinion Quarterly* 60: 588–619.

Messenger, Ruth. 1998. *Relationships: Officeholders and Citizens*. Dayton, Ohio: Kettering Foundation.

Mill, John Stuart. [1859] 1947. *On Liberty*. New York: Appleton-Century-Crofts.

Miller, Arthur G., Barry E. Collins, and Diana E. Brief. 1995. "Perspectives on Obedience to Authority: The Legacy of the Milgram Experiments." *Journal of Social Issues* 51: 1–19.

Miller, Joanne M., and Jon A. Krosnick. 1998. "The Impact of Candidate Name Order on Election Outcomes." *Public Opinion Quarterly* 62: 291–94.

Miller, Warren E., and J. Merrill Shanks. 1996. *The New American Voter*. Cambridge, Mass.: Harvard University Press.

Mitchell, Susan. 1996. *The Official Guide to American Attitudes: Who Think What about the Issues That Shape Our Lives*. Ithaca, N.Y.: New Strategist.

Mitofsky, Warren J. 1996. "The Emperor Has No Clothes." *Public Perspective* 7, 3: 17–19.

Mondak, Jeffery J. 1995. "Media Exposure and Political Discussion in U.S. Elections." *Journal of Politics* 57: 62–85.

Moon, David. 1990. "What You Use Depends on What You Have: Information Effects on the Determinants of Electoral Choice." *American Politics Quarterly* 18: 3–24.

Moore, Michael K., and John R. Hibbing. 1998. "Situational Dissatisfaction in Congress: Explaining Voluntary Departures." *Journal of Politics* 60: 1088–1107.

Morgan, David L. 1988. *Focus Groups as Qualitative Research*. Newbury Park, Calif.: Sage.

Morone, James. 1990. *The Democratic Wish: Popular Participation and the Limits of American Government*. New York: Basic Books.

Mutz, Diana C. 1992. "Impersonal Influence: Effects of Representations of Public Opinion on Political Attitudes." *Political Behavior* 14: 89–122.

National Issues Forums. 1990. *For Convenors and Moderators: Organizing Your First Forum / Study Circle*. Dayton, Ohio: National Issues Forum Institute.

———. 1991. *The Boundaries of Free Speech: How Free Is Too Free?* Dubuque, Iowa: Kendall/Hunt.

———. 1992. *National Issues Forums Leadership Handbook, 1991–1992.* Dayton, Ohio: National Issues Forums Institute.

———. 1996. *Mission Uncertain: Reassessing America's Global Role.* Dayton, Ohio: National Issues Forums Institute.

Neck, Chris P., and Gregory Moorhead. 1993. "Jury Deliberations in the Trial of *U.S. v. John DeLorean:* A Case Analysis of Groupthink Avoidance and an Enhanced Framework." *Human Relations* 45: 1077–91.

Newhagen, John E. 1994. "Self-Efficacy and Call-in Political Television Show Use." *Communication Research* 21: 366–79.

Newport, Frank. 1996. "Why Do We Need a Deliberative Poll?" *Public Perspective* 7, 1: 7–9.

Noelle-Neumann, Elisabeth. [1984] 1993. *The Spiral of Silence: Public Opinion, Our Social Skin.* 2d ed. Chicago: University of Chicago Press.

Nye, Joseph S., Jr., Philip D. Zelikow, and David C. King, eds. 1997. *Why People Don't Trust Government.* Cambridge, Mass.: Harvard University Press.

O'Leary, Kevin. 1996. "Twenty-First-Century Democracy: Local Legislative Assemblies." *Good Society* 6, 3: 28–34.

Oliver, Leonard P. 1987. *Study Circles: Coming Together for Personal Growth and Social Change.* Cabin John, Md.: Seven Locks Press.

Olivio, Christiane. 1998. "The Practical Problems of Bridging Civil Society and the State: A Study of Round Tables in Eastern Germany." *Polity* 31: 245–68.

Osborn, Michael, and Suzanne Osborn. 1991. *Alliance for a Better Public Voice.* Dayton, Ohio: National Issues Forums Institute.

Page, Benjamin I. 1996. *Who Deliberates? Mass Media in Modern Democracy.* Chicago: University of Chicago Press.

Page, Benjamin I., and Robert Shapiro. 1992. *The Rational Public: Fifty Years of Trends in Americans' Policy Preferences.* Chicago: University of Chicago Press.

Parenti, Michael. [1974] 1995. *Democracy for the Few.* 6th ed. New York: St. Martin's Press.

Park, Won-Woo. 1990. "A Review of Research on Groupthink." *Journal of Behavioral Decision Making* 3: 229–45.

Pateman, Carole. 1970. *Participation and Democratic Theory.* Cambridge: Cambridge University Press.

Pearce, W. Barnett, and Kimberly A. Pearce. In press. "Listening for the Wisdom in the Public's Whining." In *Managing on the Edge of Uncertainty,* ed. Peter Lang and Carolyn Whalley.

Pearce, W. Barnett, and Stephen W. Littlejohn. 1997. *Moral Conflict: When Social Worlds Collide.* Thousand Oaks, Calif.: Sage.

Pelletier, David, Vivica Kraak, Christine McCullum, Ulla Uusitalo, and Robert Rich. 1999. "The Shaping of Collective Values through Deliberative Democracy: An Empirical Study from New York's North County." *Policy Sciences* 32: 103–31.

Petty, Richard E., and John T. Cacioppo. 1990. "Involvement and Persuasion: Tradition versus Integration." *Psychological Bulletin* 107: 367–74.

Pfau, Michael, and Allan Louden. 1994. "Effectiveness of Adwatch Formats in Deflecting Political Attack Ads." *Communication Research* 21: 325–41.

Pfau, Michael, Patricia Moy, R. Lance Holbert, Erin A. Szabo, Wei-Kuo Lin, and Weiwu Zhang. 1998. "The Influence of Political Talk Radio on Confidence in Democratic Institutions." *Journalism and Mass Communication Quarterly* 75: 730–45.

Pitkin, Hanna Fenichel. 1967. *The Concept of Representation.* Berkeley and Los Angeles: University of California Press.

Plutzer, Eric, and John F. Zipp. 1996. "Identity Politics, Partisanship, and Voting for Women Candidates." *Public Opinion Quarterly* 60: 30–57.

Podziba, Susan L. 1998. *Social Capital Formation, Public-Building and Public Mediation: The Chelsea Charter Consensus Process.* Dayton, Ohio: Kettering Foundation.

Pollock, P. H. (1983). "The Participatory Consequences of Internal and External Political Efficacy: A Research Note." *Western Political Quarterly* 36: 400–409.

Popkin, Samuel L. [1991] 1994. *The Reasoning Voter: Communication and Persuasion in Presidential Campaigns.* 2d ed. Chicago: University of Chicago Press.

Putnam, Robert D. 1995a. "Bowling Alone: America's Declining Social Capital." *Journal of Democracy* 6, 1: 65–78.

———. 1995b. "Tuning In, Tuning Out: The Strange Disappearance of Social Capital in America." *PS: Political Science and Politics* 28: 664–83.

Putnam, Robert D., with Robert Leonardi and Raffaella Y. Nanetti. 1993. *Making Democracy Work: Civic Traditions in Modern Italy.* Princeton, N.J.: Princeton University Press.

Rahn, Wendy M. 1993. "The Role of Partisan Stereotypes in Information Processing about Political Candidates." *American Journal of Political Science* 37: 472–96.

Rasinski, Kenneth A., Norman M. Bradburn, and Douglas Lauen. 1999. "Effects of NIC Media Coverage among the Public." In *A Poll with a Human Face: The National Issues Convention Experiment in Political Communication,* ed. Maxwell McCombs and Amy Reynolds, 145–65. New York: Erlbaum.

Rawls, John. 1971. *A Theory of Justice.* Cambridge, Mass.: Harvard University Press.

Raymond, Paul. 1992. "The American Voter in a Nonpartisan, Urban Election." *American Politics Quarterly* 20: 247–60.

Reynolds, David. 1997. *Democracy Unbound: Progressive Challenges to the Two Party System.* Boston: South End Press.

Riggle, Ellen D. 1992. "Cognitive Strategies and Candidate Evaluations." *American Politics Quarterly* 20: 227–46.

Rittel, Horst W. J., and Melvin M. Webber. 1973. "Dilemmas in a General Theory of Planning." *Policy Sciences* 4: 155–69.

Rosen, Jay. 1997. "Public Journalism as a Democratic Art." In *Theory and Practice: Lessons from Experience,*ed. Davis Merritt and Lisa Austin, 3–24. Dayton, Ohio: Kettering Foundation.

Rosen, Jay, and Paul Taylor. 1992. *The New News v. The Old News: The Press and Politics in the 1990s.* New York: Twentieth Century Fund Press.

Rosenstone, Steven J., and John M. Hansen. 1993. *Mobilization, Participation, and Democracy in America.* New York: Macmillan.

Rousseau, Jean-Jacques. [1762] 1967. *The Social Contract.* New York: Pocket Books.

Rusbult, Caryl E. 1987. "Responses to Dissatisfaction in Close Relationships: The Exit-Voice-Loyalty-Neglect Model." In *Intimate Relationships: Development, Dynamics, and Deterioration,* ed. Daniel Perlman and Steve Duck, 209–37. Newbury Park, Calif.: Sage.

Rusbult, Caryl E., and David Lowery. 1985. "When Bureaucrats Get the Blues: Responses to Dissatisfaction among Federal Public Employees." *Journal of Applied Social Psychology* 15: 80–103.

Sabetti, Filippo. 1996. "Path Dependency and Civic Culture: Some Lessons from Italy about Interpreting Social Experiments." *Politics and Society* 24: 19–44.

Salisbury, Robert H. 1986. "Washington Lobbyists: A Collective Portrait." In *Interest Group Politics,* ed. Allan J. Cigler and Burdett A. Loomis, 146–61. Washington, D.C.: Congressional Quarterly.

Sanders, Arthur. 1990. *Making Sense of Politics.* Ames: Iowa State University Press.

Sanders, Lynn M. 1997. "Against Deliberation." *Political Theory* 25: 347–76.

Scher, Richard K. 1997. *The Modern Political Campaign: Mudslinging, Bombast, and the Vitality of American Politics.* Armonk, N.Y.: M. E. Sharpe.

Scheufele, Dietram A. 1999. "Deliberation or Dispute? An Exploratory Study Examining Dimensions of Public Opinion Expression." *International Journal of Public Opinion Research* 11: 25–58.

Shklar, Judith N. 1969. *Men and Citizens: A Study of Rousseau's Social Theory.* Cambridge: Cambridge University Press.

Schudson, Michael. 1998. *The Good Citizen: A History of American Civic Life.* New York: Free Press.

Schumpeter, Joseph. 1976. *Capitalism, Socialism, and Democracy.* New York: Harper & Row.

Schwartz, Barry A. 1986. *The Battle for Human Nature.* New York: W. W. Norton.

Sellers, Patrick J. 1998. "Strategy and Background in Congressional Campaigns." *American Political Science Review* 92: 159–71.

Shapiro, Robert Y. 1998. "Public Opinion, Elites, and Democracy." *Critical Review* 12: 501–28.

Sherrill, Kenneth. 1998. "The Dangers of Non-Partisan Elections to Democracy." *Social Policy* 28, 4: 15–22.

Shea, Daniel M. 1996. *Campaign Craft: The Strategies, Tactics, and Art of Political Campaign Management.* Westport, Conn.: Praeger.

Simon, Adam. 1997. "The Winning Message? Candidate Behavior, Campaign Discourse, and Democracy." Ph.D. diss., University of California, Los Angeles.

Simpson, Dick. 1996. *Winning Elections: A Handbook of Modern Participatory Politics.* New York: HarperCollins.

Smith, Graham, and Corinne Wales. 1999. "The Theory and Practice of Citizen Juries." *Policy and Politics* 27: 295–308.

Smith, Mark A. 2000. *American Business and Political Power: Public Opinion, Elections, and Democracy.* Chicago: University of Chicago Press.

Smith, Tom W. 1999. "The Delegates' Experience in Austin." In *A Poll with a Human Face: The National Issues Convention Experiment in Political Communication,* ed. Maxwell McCombs and Amy Reynolds, 39–58. New York: Erlbaum.

Sniderman, Paul M., Richard A. Brody, and Philip E. Tetlock. 1991. *Reasoning and Choice: Explorations in Political Psychology.* Cambridge: Cambridge University Press.

Somin, Ilya. 1998. "Voter Ignorance and Democracy." *Critical Review* 12: 413–58.

Sorensen, Eva. 1997. "Democracy and Empowerment." *Public Administration* 75: 553–67.

Still, Edward. 1992. "Cumulative Voting and Limited Voting in Alabama." In *United States Electoral Systems: Their Impact on Women and Minorities,*ed. Wilma Rule and Joseph F. Zimmerman, 183–96. New York: Greenwood Press.

Study Circles Resource Center. 1991a. *An Introduction to Study Circles.* Pomfret, Conn.: Study Circles Resource Center.

———. 1991b. *Guidelines for Organizing and Leading a Study Circle.* Pomfret, Conn.: Study Circles Resource Center.

Study Circles Resource Center and ACCESS. 1994. *In Harm's Way: When Should We Risk American Lives in World Conflicts?* Pomfret, Conn.: Study Circles Resource Center.

Svoboda, Craig J. 1995. "Retrospective Voting in Gubenatorial Elections: 1982 and 1986." *Political Research Quarterly* 48: 135–50.

Tannen, Deborah. 1998. *The Argument Culture: Moving from Debate to Dialogue.* New York: Random House.

Tarrance, V. Lance, and Walter De Vries, with Donna L. Mosher. 1998. *Checked and Balanced: How Ticket-Splitters Are Shaping the New Balance of Power in American Politics.* Grand Rapids, Mich.: William B. Eerdmans.

Threlkeld, Simon. 1998. "A Blueprint for Democratic Law-Making: Give Citizen Juries the Final Say." *Social Policy* 28, 4: 5–9.

Tindale, R. Scott. 1996. "Groups Are Unpredictably Transformed by Their Internal Dynamics." *Public Perspective* 7, 1: 16–18.

Tjerandsen, C. 1980. *Education for Citizenship: A Foundation's Experience.* Santa Cruz, Calif.: Emil Schwarzhaupt Foundation.

Toffler, Alvin. 1980. *The Third Wave.* New York: William Morrow.

Tolchin, Susan J. 1996. *The Angry American: How Voter Rage Is Changing the Nation.* Boulder, Colo.: Westview Press.

Tyler, T. R., Rasinski, K. A., and Spodick, N. 1985. "The Influence of Voice upon Satisfaction with Leaders: Exploring the Meaning of Process Control." *Journal of Personality and Social Psychology* 48: 72–81.

Verba, Sidney, Kay L. Schlozman, and Henry E. Brady. 1995. *Voice and Equality: Civic Voluntarism in American Politics.* Cambridge, Mass.: Harvard University Press.

Walton, Douglas. 1992. *The Place of Emotion in Argument*. University Park: Pennsylvania State University Press.

Walzer, Michael. 1991. "The Idea of Civil Society." *Dissent* 38: 293–304.

Warren, Mark E. 1992. "Democratic Theory and Self-Transformation." *American Political Science Review* 86: 8–23.

———. 1996a. "Deliberative Democracy and Authority." *American Political Science Review* 90: 46–60.

———. 1996b. "What Should We Expect from More Democracy? Radically Democratic Responses to Politics." *Political Theory* 24: 241–70.

Watkins, Ralph. 1998. "Report on an Experiment in Direct-Mail Distribution of the Voters Guide." MS. Prepared for the League of Women Voters of Montgomery County, Maryland.

Wattenberg, Martin P. 1994. *The Decline of American Political Parties, 1952–1992*. Cambridge, Mass.: Harvard University Press.

Webler, Thomas, and Ortwin Renn. 1995. "A Brief Primer on Participation: An Evaluative Yardstick." In *Fairness and Competence in Citizen Participation*, ed. id. and Peter Wiedmann, 17–33. Boston: Kluwer Academic.

Weiser, Philip J. 1999. "Chevron, Cooperative Federalism, and Telecommunications Reform." *Vanderbilt Law Review* 52: 1–54.

Weithman, Paul J. 1995. "Contractualist Liberalism and Deliberative Democracy." *Philosophy and Public Affairs* 24: 314–43.

Wolfsfeld, G. 1986. "Political Action Repertoires: The Role of Efficacy." *Comparative Political Studies* 19: 104–29.

Yankelovich, Daniel. 1991. *Coming to Public Judgment: Making Democracy Work in a Complex World*. Syracuse, N.Y.: Syracuse University Press.

Yum, June O., and Kathleen E. Kendall. 1995. "Sex Differences in Political Communication during Presidential Campaigns." *Communication Quarterly* 43: 131–41.

Zaller, John R. 1992. *The Nature and Origins of Mass Opinion*. Cambridge: Cambridge University Press.

Index

Text: 10/13 Sabon
Display: Sabon
Composition: Binghamton Valley Composition
Printing and binding: Maple-Vail Book Manufacturing Group